*For Cosis
and Mary Lynne*

CONTENTS

Acknowledgements

We would like to thank Cosis Brown for her thoughtful commitment to the aims of this book and her unstinting facilitation of writing time; Mary Lynne Ellis for her conceptual clarity, her challenge to our ideas, and painstaking help at every stage of the book. Their generosity and sensitivity have been crucial in bringing this book to fruition. We are grateful to our children for their forebearance, and especially to Niamh O'Connor for her unique contribution.

We would also like to thank our various friends, relatives, colleagues, supervisors and students for their interest and their patience and their many helpful comments. We would particularly like to thank Stephanie Dowrick, Keith Ellis, Marie Maguire, Suzanne Raitt, and Marion Rickett for their help and interest in this book. We acknowledge the privilege it is to engage in clinical practice. We are grateful to Ruthie Petrie, our editor, for her help throughout; and also to Maggie Wilkinson for typing part of the manuscript.

— Introduction —

HOMOSEXUALITY, BOTH MALE and female, is one of the most problematic areas of psychoanalysis. Countless lesbians and gay men have not turned to psychoanalysis for help when this might well have been the most fruitful form of therapy for them, from an often realistic fear of how their sexuality would be seen and dealt with. Psychoanalysis, as a body of theory and practice, has not been able to integrate homosexuality into itself. Instead, homosexuality remains largely split off, inadequately discussed and understood, subject to rigid and sometimes attacking theorising, and to excluding practices. Psychoanalytic theory, in many different ways that will be examined in this book, has seen all homosexuality as various forms of pathology, perversity, or immaturity. It provides no articulated conception within its own terms of an integrated, non-perverse, mature and manifest homosexuality, or of what is required to achieve this.

In this Introduction we lay out the scope of this book, our frames of reference, and the various theoretical and other issues we think are posed by a consideration of psychoanalysis in relation to lesbianism. Our concern is with both practice and theory, most particularly with understanding psychoanalysis as a whole discourse that leads to certain constructions of lesbianism and not others, creates certain forms of practice and not others. Such a concern leads us towards the unquestioned presuppositions of these various theories, their ethical and metapsychological underpinnings, which determine what can and cannot be said or thought about, and in what form.

Even to refer to psychoanalysis as a 'discourse' is to invoke a particular way of understanding whole systems of thought and practice associated with the name of Michel Foucault, albeit extensively developed by various feminist theoreticians. Here we attempt to show how the issues that are raised by the different psychoanalytic approaches to lesbianism require such an analysis as a starting point, in conjunction with various other considerations more specific to psychoanalysis.

– *Psychoanalysis and homosexuality* –

In raising the possibility, as we do in this book, of different psychoanalytic conceptions of homosexuality, we are not thereby assuming that homosexuality is never associated with various forms of pathology, however these are rendered. We are arguing, rather, that it should not be seen as always and necessarily so, and that there should be theoretical and conceptual space in psychoanalytic theory for non-pathological possibilities in relation to homosexuality. This, of course, raises the difficult question of what is meant by 'pathological'. Psychoanalysis is centrally and importantly concerned with the pathological in several senses. There is the diluted sense in which everything is grist to the analytic mill, and all adult behaviour and patterns of feeling are seen to be the result of a process of conflict and compromise. There is the stronger sense in which some forms of behaviour, structures of feeling, or personality characteristics are seen according to various criteria to be more pathological than others, especially when these manifest themselves in well-specified symptoms or forms of individual suffering. There are historically, and also in the present, tensions within psycho-

10

analysis about the adoption of more or less psychiatric approaches to the question of what is seen as pathological, how indeed this term is used, and frequent arguments to the effect that the unique contribution of psychoanalysis, in understanding the individual and subjective meanings of various phenomena, gets lost in an overly psychiatric approach. Homosexuality is at one of the many points of this contestation, perhaps sharpened by the scope it provides for the unacknowledged incorporation of moral and social criteria into what is deemed pathological. Psychoanalysis, and Freud most especially, has richly described the many forms of pathology to which heterosexuality is prone, the many psychic tasks faced in the process of evolving an adult heterosexuality, and the attempted resolutions of conflicts which result in symptoms of various kinds, or in unsatisfactory relationships. This diverse pathology associated with heterosexuality is not taken as meaning that heterosexuality itself is a sign of pathology. Despite its interest in understanding the variety of ways in which heterosexual development is vulnerable to difficulties, psychoanalysis also holds open the possibility of a relatively unpathological state of affairs, in the strong sense of pathology. An equivalent conception of the possibilities for homosexuality would greatly advance psychoanalytic understanding of homosexuality in its many forms.

Lesbians and gay men have also been largely absent from the psychoanalytic training organisations, an issue we discuss in Chapter 10. Homosexuality has been widely seen as a disqualifying factor in a training candidate, so that until recently there have been few lesbian or gay psychoanalysts or psychoanalytic psychotherapists, and certainly none who could be open about their sexuality. Although this situation is beginning to change in some organisations, there are still some which, as far as can be ascertained, refuse to train lesbians or gay men. There are also – and probably always have been – lesbian and gay psychoanalysts, psychotherapists and trainees in various organisations who feel obliged to remain in the closet, to remain silent about their sexuality; we discuss this further in Chapter 11. There have thus been few voices to challenge prevailing views, and indeed the absence of dialogue or reflection is a striking feature of this whole topic in relation to theory, clinical practice and training.

Our aim in writing this book, therefore, is to initiate a dialogue about psychoanalytic theories of female homosexuality, and to identify the fundamental issues that have to be addressed by anyone who wishes to work or think within a psychoanalytic framework, but does not subscribe to the or universal pathology of homosexuality. The various psychoanalytic case histories and writings on female homosexuality have never been reviewed or discussed as a whole body of thought and practice; so one of our main aims is the exposition of psychoanalytic thought on this subject, bearing in mind the huge developments that have taken place since Freud. Looking critically at these texts throws up many questions – not just about the substantive claims made on the basis of clinical observations about lesbian patients, but also about the nature of the theories and philosophical positions that lead to such statements.

Our overall questions, therefore, are: what is it about psychoanalytic theory that leads to its specific views about female homosexuality, and what has to change in its theoretical stances for this to be different? Does a more diverse, less inevitably pathologising view imply a fundamental revision of basic concepts, or can the category of perverse just be dropped as it applies to homosexuality, and nothing else be changed, as some have suggested? Do some psychoanalytic theories offer more possibilities than others? In order to address and answer these questions, we look at the way homosexuality is constructed and understood by various authors. We identify recurring issues: the alignment of gender and sexuality in the notions of identification and desire; the reliance on concepts such as oral sadism and unconscious identification with the father as developmental explanations; the consignment of homosexuality to the pre-oedipal and the narcissistic; the appeal to biological phenomena as constitutive of psychic reality; the *a priori* theorising based on normative notions of innate heterosexuality; the obliviousness to countertransference problems stemming from the personal and theoretical position of the practitioner.

We are aware that there are many psychoanalysts and psychoanalytic psychotherapists who do not see homosexuality necessarily as a symptom of underlying disturbance, who would not so totally privilege heterosexuality, and who could conceive of lesbians and gay men as practitioners in this field. Important as the existence of such individuals is, especially in providing effective therapy for those lesbians and gay men who happen to find them, it is a practice that is at present largely unreported. There are almost no case histories of lesbians or gay men presenting other points of view, so that such practice, although it exists, does not contribute as it could to the development of psychoanalytic thought. There is also very little theorising which challenges the dominant positions from within psychoanalysis, with some exceptions that we discuss in Chapter 10. We hope that this book will address these silences and absences, and provide those psychoanalysts and psychotherapists who do in fact take a different view from that of their trainings with a basis from which to speak out and discuss their work. We do not underestimate how the power and influence of the prevailing hierarchies, the nature of many psychoanalytic organisations, and the complex emotions surrounding this subject make this a difficult task for many individuals.

A consideration such as ours of how psychoanalysis has thought about and dealt with homosexuality also offers many insights into perennial questions about psychoanalysis, such as the split-off nature of the social, the regressive use of the biological and the causal, the unreflective incorporation of social norms into notions of maturity, the difficulty of really letting the patient speak, and engaging with this, and finally, the complexities of rendering social forms of oppression psychoanalytically. Homosexuality provides an interesting case study of the perversion of psychoanalytic methods and values. Rather than benefiting from a psychoanalytic dedication to individual difference and uniqueness, from an eschewal of educative aims of treatment, and from an appreciation of the powerful complexities of transference and countertransference, it has been the site of some of the worst excesses of psychoanalysis – gross and inaccurate generalisations, explicitly manipulative goals of therapy, and a striking failure to consider vital countertransference issues. These perversions of psychoanalytic values suggest that we are at the nexus of some unthinkable anxieties, as we illustrate in relation to particular authors, and – especially in Chapter 9 – in relation to sexuality.

In pursuing our aims we have examined a fairly wide range of psychoanalytic positions and theories, and this forms the main part of the book. We have inevitably been selective in our inclusion and exclusion of specific texts and authors; however, we do cover the main schools of thought, and some lesser-known writings. In Chapter 1 we address Freud's general position, and also his specific case history on the subject. In Chapter 2 we consider some of his immediate followers and critics, including Karen Horney, Ernest Jones and Joan Riviere. Helene Deutsch's understanding of female homosexuality is the focus of Chapter 3, and Melanie Klein's of Chapter 4. Chapter 5 considers the writings of object-relations theorists such as Masud Khan, Adam Limentani, Hanna Segal and Donald Meltzer. Joyce McDougall's extensive work on female homosexuality and her views on gender identity are the focus of Chapter 6. In Chapter 7 we consider Lacanian formulations and also the ideas of Luce Irigaray and Julia Kristeva, and in Chapter 8 Jungian ideas. Our major omission as regards English-language thought is any detailed consideration of object-relations theory associated with the names of Fairbairn and Winnicott, although we do briefly consider statements of some other writers in this tradition. This is because the work of such authors is largely devoid of any detailed mention of homosexuality, and does not contain a specific theory of sexuality in the way that Kleinian theory, for example, does. In Chapter 9 we discuss specific psychoanalytic approaches to questions of lesbian sexuality and eroticism, and also some important issues of transference and countertransference. In Chapter 10 we consider more oppositional views, such as those of Robert Stoller and other critics, issues relating to training, and also feminist psychoanalytic writings. In Chapter 11 and in the Postscript, we attempt to draw together the implications of our various expositions and criticisms, as regards clinical, institutional and theoretical issues.

——————— *Questions of theory* ———————

Our own critical efforts necessarily start from a particular position and express certain interests; the very engagement in such an enterprise implies a belief in different or better ways of approaching these matters. This is something that we attempt to formulate throughout the book, but especially in the final chapters. It involves a commitment to seeing lesbian issues in a less heterosexually normative perspective, with a real acknowledgement of the diversity of lesbian sexualities and histories, and an understanding of the vicissitudes and complexities of lesbian identities. It also involves an understanding of the social forces that make homosexual love so difficult to live out, such that desire and oppression are entwined and constitutive of each other in a multiplicity of ways. It further involves an interest in theory which does not rely on over-arching and universal metapsychological concepts, but takes a phenomenological (more accurately, post-phenomenological) approach to the diversity of human experience, with a specific understanding of language.[1] Many psychoanalytic theories, whilst they provide useful guidelines and pointers to significant processes, and complex phenomenological descriptions, are none the less inappropriate if they are used as causal theories which claim universal truth across individuals and cultures. As Chris Oakley (1989) says:

> It is true that the practice of psychoanalysis involves allowing
> one's attention to float, and being satisfied with a partial
> understanding; nevertheless at the core of psychoanalytic
> thinking a tendency towards privileging systematic

> explanations can be discerned. Anything that cannot be
> woven into a universalizable system – any irreducible
> otherness – will tend to be discarded in order to preserve a
> manifest consistency.[2]

To which we might add: or incorporated in a distorting form.

Although we hope to lay the ground for more fruitful future psychoanalytic explorations of lesbianism, we do not aim to provide an alternative developmental theory of lesbianism within the parameters of existing theories. The reasons for our eschewal of an alternative or reformed developmental theory of lesbianism lie not only in what seems to us the somewhat grandiose level of universalisation involved, but also in the whole enterprise of finding causal explanations in assumed developmental origins, which often have an extremely narrow focus. The inevitably normative nature of mechanistic developmental explanations means that there is little scope for difference and diversity to be seen as other than lack, deviation or deficit. In relation to lesbianism, the invariable developmental question is 'What went wrong?'. Developmental concerns, imperialistically universalised, have dominated the psychoanalytic literature on homosexuality to the virtual exclusion of all others, and despite their relative lack of success within their own terms. It is not fanciful to suggest that some of this preoccupation has as a subtext the possibility of the prevention of homosexuality. This, as Kenneth Lewes (1989) shows for male homosexuality,[3] was an explicit interest on the part of psychoanalysts who carried out the major developmental studies of the 1950s and 1960s, just as they saw 'cure' of homosexuality as an appropriate aim of treatment. Whilst other investigators may be less concerned to do away with or remedy homosexuality, none the less the emphasis of all developmental concerns has been on deviations from the supposed normal pattern of development, with little reflection on the status of this norm. Within such a framework, the question 'What went right?' is never asked of the process of becoming gay or lesbian; yet psychoanalytically there is much to consider in what enables someone to have the resources to achieve a viable lesbian sexuality in a predominantly heterosexual and homophobic world. This does not enter the psychoanalytic discourse as a relevant question.

Although we do not see ourselves as putting forward an alternative developmental theory of lesbianism, we do think that there are very often important questions of personal history involved in understanding someone's lesbian desires, their process of becoming and experiencing themselves as attracted to women, and their ability to express this in ways which are enabling rather than restrictive or destructive. Whilst we use aspects of existing psychoanalytic theories where we feel these are productive and illuminating, we do this in the spirit that they provide phenomenological descriptions both of the patient's experience in the world and of the interaction between therapist and patient, always open to revision, rather than imposing a rigid schema on the patient's communications, or claiming to know the truth about the patient. Our own clinical work relies on many basic aspects of psychoanalytic method, in the creation of an analytic framework and in the use of transference and countertransference to further the understandings of unconscious communications. Such an approach offers a critical understanding of theory, combined with a sensitivity to the texture and language of experience and relatedness, and is therefore particularly useful in an area such as homosexuality, which has suffered from the worst excesses of rigid, universalising and unreflective theorising, and other anxious attempts to impose order on a threatening and disruptive topic.

Our concern with – and criticism of – the generalising nature of much of psychoanalytic theory, the positing of universal psychic structures, owes much to post-modernist thinking. The understanding of lesbianism in relation to psychoanalysis that we put forward illustrates one aspect of this position: that the dismantling of fixed universal certainties can establish new contexts which express and point to significant gaps, omissions and denials of human experience; such expressions having been previously impossible or unintelligible. Jacques Derrida's[4] elaboration of 'deconstructive strategies' is useful for our purposes, as it has been in cultural critiques regarding racism, sexism and class. He provides us with an important analysis of knowledge and power that focuses on issues of identity and difference. He argues that much modern Western theorising, including psychoanalytic theory, is characterised by a 'logic of identity', in which the establishment of a unity excludes other attributes. The unity designates what is held to be the true, the good or the healthy, and what is excluded is defined as false, bad or pathological, resulting in the establishment of a hierarchical opposition, or dualism. Derrida introduced the method of deconstruction to show that a category of identity includes that which it claims to exclude, yet which defines it. This deconstructive strategy involves detailed analyses of what are assumed or claimed to be 'fixed entities' in order to uncover hitherto denied differences. As Gayatri Spivak describes it:

> Deconstruction points out that in constructing any kind of an
> argument we must move from implied premises, that must
> necessarily obliterate or finesse certain possibilities that
> question the availability of these premises in an absolutely
> justifiable way. Deconstruction teaches us to look at these
> limits and questions. It is a corrective and critical movement.[5]

Within psychoanalysis certain implied premises determine heterosexuality as the healthy desire and homosexuality as the pathological one; it is these premises that we attempt to discern in our deconstructive efforts.

—— *Language and identity* ——

Derrida[6] also criticises notions of language which posit a universal, ever-present meaning, where 'truth' is seen as outside time and change, as extra-linguistic. Such a notion of language is found in many psychoanalytic formulations, most particularly the Kleinian and post-Kleinian ones, with their very strong claims to 'know' the truth about lesbians, as we describe in Chapters 4, 5 and 6. Against such essentialist notions Derrida stresses the variety of meanings, interpretations, ranges of reference that are associated with any utterance. He analyses difference primarily in terms of language functioning.

Issues of language and identity are central to any consideration of homosexuality; this has a context that it is important to acknowledge for our ensuing discussions. Questions of sexual identity – whether and how people identify themselves as heterosexual, bisexual, lesbian, homosexual or celibate – have a historical relativity that has been described by many authors.[7] The fact that such questions are even articulated reflects contemporary Western concerns about the relationships between persons, identification and sexuality, which Michel Foucault[8] has described in terms of the regulative production of sexual categorisations.

Psychoanalysis's problematising of the notion of identity has been extremely important; it has shown it to be far from a seamless or simple matter. However, this has taken place in a context where the claiming or ascribing of identities, especially sexual identities, has assumed certain meanings. We have so far assumed that it is obvious what we mean by the various terms we have used to describe our subject matter, but in fact significant ambiguities surround the various usages, which relate to important issues of language and identity.

'Lesbians' do not appear in psychoanalytic texts, whereas 'female homosexuals' do. The significance of this is more than the difference a between a colloquial and a professional usage, though it is also this. It rather betokens the difference between a self-ascribed and an attributed or imposed identity, with concomitant differentiations of meaning and value. Few lesbians would describe themselves as female homosexuals (except as an ironic joke), mainly because of its medico/psychiatric/pathological connotations. Many would feel happy with 'lesbian'; others would not, but would nonetheless use it; still others would avoid this usage altogether. Some would accept the notion of being 'a' lesbian; others would dislike the reifying implications of this kind of ascription. Underlying these differences are important issues of self-definition and self-perception in relation to sexuality, which in turn may relate to important unconscious conflicts. However, the female homosexuals of psychoanalytic texts, the patients, are never asked about their self-definitions, they are just named as such; thus, many vital issues of self-perception and identity are sidestepped. This omission reflects the way in which some considerations are excluded from the start and do not figure within the psychoanalytic discourse. It is in this way that the sexual subject becomes the discursive object, and female homosexual patients are seen as having 'deviant' identities.

This double and not-neutral nomenclature leaves us with a difficulty in referring to our subject matter. We would most commonly use 'lesbian' in many contexts, although we are mindful of the kinds of complexities we have outlined, but it jars to impose it on psychoanalytic texts both because of expository accuracy and also because of the significance of the different terms. Therefore, we use the two terms interchangeably as the context warrants.

A similar difficulty exists with the terms 'lesbianism' and 'female homosexuality', with a further difficulty about what the two suffixes '-ism' and '-ity' convey. 'Lesbianism' can convey something unduly concrete, almost a substance, and makes it seem specific to and inherent in lesbians. With this come overtones of essentialist attributions. 'Female homosexuality' is a wider-ranging term which is not specified as a property of particular individuals but, rather, denotes a structuring of sexuality in the individual and social domains. For these reasons we would prefer it, although we do not, in view of the other considerations relating to self-ascription and identity, always use it.

We use the term 'homosexuality' to refer to the infinite variety of feelings, fantasies and acts, conscious or unconscious, that pertain to same-sex desire, in whomever and however they occur. However, it does not have a meaning that can be described just in this way, as entirely separate from heterosexuality. Rather, they are each not-the-other, but with very different significances attached to this, the way in which they are not-the-other. Nor is their meaning exhausted by reference just to intra- or interpsychic events; they both denote significant aspects of the 'deployment' of sexuality – to use Foucault's term – within the social order. Psychoanalytically, both in relation to individuals and in theory, the construal of the relationship between them is of immense importance.

These considerations reflect the significance of language in areas that are subject to discrimination and stigma, where political struggle, the claiming of social rights and more positive identities, is often accompanied by contestations over naming. The sense of breaking uncharted ground is indicated by the absence of appropriate terms to refer to significant others in lesbian relationships or families, most especially to the non-biological lesbian parent.

Other issues concerning language also occur frequently in relation to lesbians. The lack of what is felt to be an appropriate language to express important aspects of lesbian experience has often been remarked upon – we discuss this further in relation to questions of sexuality and gender identity, in Chapters 9 and 10. This sense of straining at the boundaries of language is similar to the experience many women have remarked upon, especially in the early days of contemporary feminism, of lacking a language in which to articulate their perceptions or desires, of having to 'break a silence'. The centrality of language to the process of psychoanalysis means that it is vital to be aware of these confusing silences where lesbian experiences are concerned. 'The love that dare not speak its name' is one of the most enduring epithets about homosexuality, as much for the 'speak' as the 'dare not'. What every speaker requires in such a case is not just courage (though he/she certainly needs that), but also a language in which to speak and a listener who can hear and understand what is said or not said. It is this task that psychoanalysis, with its rich appreciation of the complexity of subjectivity, is in principle uniquely suited to carry out, but it is also one where it has been at its most deaf and uncomprehending.

Further issues of identity are raised by the recurrent question we have been asked: 'Who or what are you talking about anyhow?' The charge has been that it is misleading to talk of 'lesbians' or 'homosexuals' as a whole category, because psychoanalysis concerns itself primarily with individuals, or because to do so is to attribute a fixity to sexual identity that is misleading, or because we should really be talking about homosexuality, and the homosexuality in all of us. As will become apparent, we agree with many aspects of these charges (although perhaps not with all of the motivation behind them). In most instances we would avoid referring to 'lesbians' as a general category; indeed, part of our argument (see especially Chapter 6) is that psychoanalysis has departed from its own basic principles in making unwarranted generalisations about such patients, in support of a general theory of homosexuality. We argue in Chapter 11 that a way of understanding lesbian diversity and difference is needed rather than trying to homogenise the category, and also that if generalisation is appropriate it is in the area of the structuring of lesbian oppression, rather than in anything supposedly inherent in lesbians.

We would agree that naming and identifying oneself as belonging to a specific sexual category can run the risk of seeming to be an inappropriately labelling or reifying process which ignores the fragmented, precarious and changeable nature of sexuality and sexual identity. This, however, is far from being the only consideration, because what is ignored are the historical, social and personal contexts in which such identities present themselves and are claimed (or disowned). Sexual identity permeates, mediates and is mediated by all our social and cultural interactions. Sexual identity is not simply a question of isolated individuals repressing or discovering their 'true' desires, or of a logical definition, but is variously inscribed in cultural, religious, legal and political systems and practices. These differ greatly in different societies and subcultures, but produce various personal exigencies, as we discuss in Chapter 11. Judith Butler (1990),[9] in her analysis of the generation of notions of identity, points out how, in philosophical discourses about personhood or personal identity, the social context which the person is 'in' remains external to the definitional structure of personhood, however that may be seen. She argues, rather, that identity should be seen as a regulatory ideal, as well as a descriptive feature of experience. Identity is not just a matter of logical or definitional features, but rather an aspect of socially instituted and maintained notions of intelligibility by which persons are defined, and which produce some people who fail to conform to these notions of cultural intelligibility. The institution of psychoanalysis is particularly influential in interpretations of sexual desire and identity as normal or abnormal, healthy or pathological, but itself has its own historical and social location in Western discourses about sexuality and sexual identity.

The issues of identity surrounding lesbianism or homosexuality are not simply the mirror of those for heterosexuality, because of their differing social locations. Identifying oneself as heterosexual is a very different kind of act from identifying oneself as lesbian or gay. As the dominant form of sexuality, such an identification is, on the whole, not required and does not commonly occur, except in special circumstances. To identify thus may be seen as a recognition of the possibility of different identifications, of diverse sexualities, that what is taken for granted is not a necessary and absolute truth about human sexuality.

—— *Textual and clinical matters* ——

Since texts can be read and interpreted in many ways, it is appropriate to make clear how we have approached the writings we consider. On first reading Freud's (1920) case history 'The Psychogenesis of a Case of Female Homosexuality',[10] and then subsequent texts, it can seem that very little historical or conceptual development is discernible in the ideas expressed, and very little sustained argument or interchange of ideas between authors. The articulation of any debate about these ideas is relatively undeveloped. There are several main texts entirely devoted to female homosexuality (e.g. Ernest Jones, 1927; Helene Deutsch, 1933; Masud Khan, 1962; Joyce McDougall, 1979, 1989a);[11] there are also many other writings where female homosexuality or lesbian patients are referred to as part of wider ideas – for example, on female sexuality generally, or bisexuality. We have therefore had to comb an extensive literature to glean what is often a rather sparse and seemingly fragmented picture. This is especially the case with Melanie Klein, whose writings have had an immense impact in certain quarters on how female homosexuality is seen, but who never actually presented any case material on lesbian patients, or wrote about the subject in an extended way. The overall trend, if there is one, has been towards 'discovering' more and more diverse forms of pathology held to characterise lesbians, rather than trying to review and evaluate thought on this subject. We are therefore concerned to look at the various ideas that have been put forward, to trace their development or disappearance, bearing in mind the theoretical perspectives from which they are advanced.

It is usual to survey a field such as this in historical sequence, starting with Freud and proceeding through time to the present, and indeed we do partly do this. We are concerned with exposition, but we also allow ourselves considerable engagement with the various ideas, both as they stand and with a view to what has preceded them and what follows. This means our discussions of various texts are quite discursive, following up implications of new ideas and arguments as they arise.

There has recently been much historical and sociological work on changing conceptions of lesbianism (e.g. Lilian Faderman, 1992).[12] Defining the precise nature of the relationships between the psychoanalytic ideas about lesbians and contemporaneous social practices and values is a highly important and complex problem, but we can only glance at it. The 1920s, when many psychoanalytic ideas about female homosexuality were first formulated, was a particularly important period in lesbian history, with the visibility of certain upper-class expressions of lesbianism, literary and artistic circles of women, and the publication and banning of Radclyffe Hall's *The Well of Loneliness*, but we can only acknowledge this, and subsequent historical contexts, as important backdrops to the ideas we present. An understanding of the inter-connections between what is expressed psychoanalytically and what is expressed socially, in legislation and in other practices or attitudes, would require an extensive study in its own right. Lewes[13] suggests some connections between the post-Second World War political atmosphere and the rapidly growing conservatism and homophobia of the psychoanalytic world.

Our main concerns in looking at these texts, therefore, are with the use of ideas as explanatory or synthesising devices, with implicit presuppositions and narrative strategies. We are also concerned with evidential issues, with the way in which clinical observation and argument are intertwined. We are not thereby assuming that there is any privileged or neutral status to be given to clinical material, important as this may be. Clinical observation when it reaches the written page is not 'pure' observation, nor could it ever be so. Rather, it is the product of the relationship between patient and psychoanalyst, and the latter's view of this. This is a relationship formed in the context of the psychoanalyst's theoretical position and style of practice, and subject to all the complex transference and countertransference dynamics of any analytic relationship. Because this is such a basic issue in reading psychoanalytic reports, it is appropriate to explore this question further, and make our own position clear.

It is well known that Jungian patients produce Jungian dreams, Freudian ones Freudian symptoms, and so on. In a sense this does not matter; it is all part of the crucial engagement that is psychoanalysis, the lifeblood of a therapeutic relationship. It comes as no surprise to learn that research suggests that the theoretical adherence of the analyst has no bearing on the outcome of the therapy,[14] whereas other factors such as the personality and 'warmth' of the psychoanalyst, and his/her experience, do. Such a state of affairs matters only if claims of truth are made concerning what is observed clinically, if an uncomplicated factual status is given to what the analyst claims to perceive in his/her patients. We are not advancing the philistine criticism that psychoanalysis is not 'scientific' enough – far from it, although there are times when we may feel that respect for basic principles of inductive reasoning might benefit psychoanalytic thought. The psychoanalytic relationship does not even approach the ideal fiction of the disinterested observer and the observed world 'out there'. Rather, the psychoanalytic practice from which psychoanalytic theories have grown is an engagement of an intense kind between two human beings. Although one, the psychoanalyst, is there in a special position, this is not the position of the scientist or the disinterested observer; indeed, psychoanalysis would not work, would not be psychoanalysis, if it were.

One of the concerns of the psychoanalyst is with the split-off, denied or otherwise unconscious aspects of the patient's being. This concern takes its form through the changing therapeutic relationship, the transference and countertransference, and the psychoanalyst's skill at enabling, containing and understanding all this. Part of analytic competence lies in both sustaining this engagement and retaining the ability to think. The analytic ideas and theories that emerge from such encounters are formed in and by this therapeutic relationship, as well as all the other factors influencing the writer.

What these considerations add up to is a certain caution in approaching claims of knowledge based on clinical work, a respect for the complexity of issues involved in appearing to make statements of truth or fact – something that is missing from the work of many of the authors we consider. Thus part of our concern is with the way in which clinical material is used to make certain statements about female homosexuality, and the extent to which the writer/psychoanalyst reflects on him/herself as part of the total analytic situation, with respect to both theoretical and countertransference considerations. In many instances with lesbian patients these dimensions have been ignored or denied, with, we argue, limiting and distorting effects.

To refer to analysands as 'patients' is to use a language that is often associated with pathology, illness and cure, with a medical model. In many contexts and circles 'client' is the preferred term, because it expresses an eschewal of the pathological, and a desire for a more egalitarian professional relationship. The drawbacks to the use of 'client' are its consumerist overtones, and the way in which it can seem to reduce the complexities of the therapeutic relationship to a service provided. It also fails to acknowledge the centrality of suffering and the search for help of some kind that the term 'patient', despite its other drawbacks, does convey. For the purposes of this book, because most of the writings we consider do themselves use 'patient', we have largely followed this usage. As is often acknowledged, neither term is fully satisfactory.

In considering how we could best make use of our own clinical experience, we have been mindful not only of these various issues, but also of the crucial issue of confidentiality. Confidentiality is at the basis of any psychoanalytic or psychotherapeutic process, but it is usually understood that discussion in supervision, clinical seminars, professional journals or conferences does not break this essential confidentiality, when possibly identifying features are altered. Books such as this, which exist in a more public domain, present a more complex and potentially compromising situation, because the audience is a much wider one than the usual professional readership, with much greater scope for misunderstanding. Furthermore, the patients whose clinical material is involved may themselves read such books (as indeed they may read professional journals, although circumstances may make this less likely). Some psychoanalysts negotiate this issue by directly asking the patients in question for permission to use their material in a suitably disguised form, and then presumably – though this is seldom recorded – work with the impact of this on the therapeutic relationship, whatever it may be. One psychoanalyst, Joyce McDougall, who has written extensively about her clinical work, even appears to involve her patients in the process of choosing their fictional names (McDougall, 1989b).[15] Others, such as Patrick Casement (1985),[16] consider that the intrusiveness into the therapeutic relationship of directly asking permission is too great, and would do more harm than patients possibly recognising themselves in his descriptions. He alters information about his patients to an extent which ensures that they would not be recognised by anyone except themselves, whilst remaining true to the clinical issues involved. This appears to us to be a strategy many writers adopt, although this is hardly an extensively or publicly discussed issue. There are infinite possibilities as to what patients may feel about being asked within the therapy, and at either withholding or giving permission, or at finding themselves written about without being directly asked, or, equally, not included in their therapist's public writing; and there are also possibilities of misrecognition. None of this, however, alters the basic premise of confidentiality on which therapeutic work is based.

It would appear that every psychoanalytic writer takes an essentially individual and perhaps rather private decision on this issue. We have felt that our first allegiance is to our patients and the trust they invest in us, and only secondarily to the purpose of this book and the benefit we hope it could bring to other patients. We have not considered it appropriate to ask directly for permission, because it does on the whole seem to us to be disruptive and disturbing to the therapeutic relationship, and to serve an aim which is the therapist's, not the patient's. This has meant that we have used clinical material only where we have felt that no possibility of other-recognition exists, and where the possibilities for self-recognition are very limited and partial, or material is presented in a sufficiently abstract way for this to be a rather general form of self-recognition, in which many individuals might share. At times this has limited our range of clinical illustrations. It has also meant that some of our clinical descriptions are circumscribed in ways which are not optimal from the point of view of clinical or descriptive richness, but represent our judgement of what we feel adheres to adequate confidentiality in a context such as this. We have also used clinical information from a considerable diversity of sources. Furthermore, some of our clinical material concerns therapists and their handling of transference and countertransference issues, and here we have felt at liberty to be rather more detailed, since possible breaches of confidentiality concerning patients are remote.

This Introduction has served to situate what follows within a framework of the moral, political, theoretical and philosophical issues which are raised by any discussion of psychoanalytic approaches to lesbianism. All these issues have implications for the kinds of clinical practices and theoretical writings to which psychoanalysis gives rise, as we attempt to show in our more detailed consideration of psychoanalytic texts.

1

Freud:
Disappointment and Repudiation

F REUD'S MAIN ACCOUNT of female homosexuality is
to be found in his one explicit case history on the subject,
'The Psychogenesis of a Case of Female Homosexuality',
written in 1920,[1] where the framework he set out in the *Three
Essays on the Theory of Sexuality* (1905)[2] for understanding
homosexuality is developed and modified. Subsequent
remarks on the subject occur in his later writings on female
sexuality and femininity. Compared to his writing on male
homosexuality, the extent of Freud's concern with female
homosexuality is not great, and Freud himself, at the beginning of 'Psychogenesis', notes this relative neglect by psychoanalysts. He maintains, however, that it is no less common as
a phenomenon. Such neglect is also evident in how relatively
little 'Psychogenesis' has been discussed compared to Freud's
other case histories, of which it is the sixth and last. The
secondary literature is sparse.[3] This marginalisation is further
reflected in the fact that Freud did not give the patient concerned a name, unlike the patients in his other histories, who
are all given pseudonyms. Instead he refers to her as 'the girl';
later writers call her 'the female homosexual'. This omission is
striking: not to name someone is to refuse them full subjecthood. It has the effect of creating distance, impersonality and

reification, and is perhaps the first indication of the widespread difficulty psychoanalysts have had in approaching this subject.

'Psychogenesis' however, is a key text in which Freud discusses many issues that were to dominate subsequent analytic work on the subject: the acquired or congenital nature of homosexuality; its status as pathology; its link to masculinity; the role of disappointment by and rejection of men; early mother fixation; the possibilities of cure; and the difficulties for the analyst of the patient's transference. Freud's writing in this case history necessarily reflects many wider aspects of his theories, in particular his notions of drives, of libido, and of sexual repression, as elaborated in the *Three Essays*. Although he makes reference to oedipal conflicts, it is written before his full elaboration of the Oedipus complex and his subsequent discussions of female sexuality; it also predates his writings on identification. In this chapter we will set 'Psychogenesis' within the context of Freud's thought on homosexuality in general, then elaborate on certain themes within the case history, in particular those of masculinity, repudiation and countertransference.

— *The diversity of homosexuality* —

In the *Three Essays* Freud begins his discussion of homosexuality, both male and female, by noting how 'inverts' varied in their behaviour, their type of inversion, and their life histories. In 'Psychogenesis' he refers to the 'manifold' forms of homosexuality. In both works he emphasises the multiplicity of factors that determine inversion, and warns against forming too simple a conception of its nature and genesis, thus problematising any notion of homosexuality as a clinical entity. Throughout his lifetime he elaborated at least four different theories of male homosexuality (Lewes, 1989),[4] which concerned the various routes he discerned of becoming homosexual, in relation to different clinical material. In his monograph on Leonardo da Vinci (1910)[5] he reiterates his warning against seeing homosexuality as a unitary phenomenon, commenting on the incomplete state of knowledge regarding causation, and on the small number of people on which his conclusions are based. Freud's acknowledgement of constraints on theory construction are striking: such circumspection and respect for difference are largely missing from more modern works, where postulations of 'the homosexual' take over from his emphasis on diversity.

Freud also emphasised the continuity between homosexuality and heterosexuality. In a footnote to *Three Essays* he says:

> Psychoanalytic research is most decidedly opposed to any attempt at separating off homosexuals from the rest of mankind as a group of special character . . . [It] has found that all human beings are capable of making a homosexual object choice and in fact have made one in their unconscious . . . Thus from the point of view of psychoanalysis the exclusive sexual interest felt by men for women is also a problem that needs elucidating and is not a self-evident fact based upon an attraction that is ultimately of a chemical nature.[6]

This is one of the clearest psychoanalytic statements putting homosexuality on a footing with heterosexuality, and questioning the seeming naturalness or givenness of the latter. The importance of these remarks lies in bringing homosexuality out of the realm of the abnormal and different into that of the normal and familiar, part of everybody. It also lies in the statement that homosexuality is not a diagnostic category: the implication is that it would be just as implausible to make heterosexuality one, and indeed, that as much needs explaining about the latter as the former. He also considers, in *Three Essays*, that many more people would show homosexual preferences if it were not for its 'authoritative prohibition by society', an acknowledgement of powerful social forces. This rare acknowledgement, however, coexists with his simultaneous assertion that one of the 'tasks' of object choice is to find the way to the opposite sex, with the attraction of the opposing sexes facilitating this.

In 'Psychogenesis' Freud also maintains that the young woman is not 'ill', and that her sexual proclivities do not constitute a neurotic conflict. She herself did not suffer from her sexuality. It was her parents, particularly her father, who could not tolerate it, and sent her to Freud for treatment, a state of affairs which was to become very common in this area, but one which Freud notes as inauspicious for analysis. He also expresses his scepticism about the possibilities of 'cure', maintaining that it would be equally difficult to convert someone from heterosexuality to homosexuality. In other parts of his work Freud variously describes homosexuality – by which he means mainly male homosexuality – as narcissistic (Freud, 1914),[7] or as an 'arrest in sexual development' (Freud, 1935).[8] In 'Psychogenesis' he explains his patient's homosexuality as involving, in part, an infantile fixation on the mother. Thus, although Freud was emphatic about the huge diversity encompassed by the term 'homosexual', he was more ambiguous about its status as pathology.

In *Three Essays* Freud also distinguished between inversion and perversion, and classified homosexuality as an inversion. Inversions involved variations in the sexual object, whereas perversions consisted of variations of the sexual aim, such that regions of the body other than the genitals, or other objects or activities, replaced genital union. Perversions, of which fetishism was one predominant example, also had the quality of exclusiveness and fixation. This clear differentiation of homosexuality from the category of perversion has not been continued in psychoanalytic writing, except by Stoller (1975).[9] Instead it has been largely assimilated to perversion, especially by modern writers in the Kleinian tradition, and by McDougall (see Chapters 4, 5 and 6 below), with elaborations and changes in what perversion is taken to mean.[10]

Freud was also emphatic that homosexuality, like the other 'aberrations' he described, did not necessarily betoken any wider disorder in the person concerned. That is, although he saw neurosis as a sign of underlying sexual disturbance and repression, inversion and perversion were themselves seen as discrete sexual phenomena. Indeed, Freud emphasised how some of the greatest contributions to civilisation have been made by homosexuals (men). This is strikingly different to the subsequent psychoanalytic assimilation of homosexuality and perversion to a character disorder, and the many accusations of inauthenticity and antisocial impulses against 'perverts' of all kinds.[11]

— *Male and female homosexuality* —

There are many occasions when Freud talks of homosexuality in general without always specifying whether male or female, or both, are meant. At other times he explicitly compares them, but general statements are most often illustrated by male examples. His various statements imply that male and female homosexuality could be subsumed under the same general theory – a position which stems from his overall theory of libido, his conceptualisation of bisexuality, and his contention that female sexuality developed in a similar way to that of males in the early years. Indeed, Judith Roof (1991)[12] argues that Freud's writings about lesbian sexuality fail to establish it as a phenomenon between women, but always reduce it in some way to a form of male homosexuality; and that this, not female homosexuality, was Freud's primary preoccupation. It is certainly striking how he uses the case history of a woman, in 'Psychogenesis', to make many remarks about male homosexuality or homosexuality in general, but never does the reverse. For the most part subsequent writers, apart from Otto Rank (1923),[13] have tended to treat male and female homosexuality separately, with no comparisons made and no general theory of both. This raises the question not just of their possible similarities and differences, but also of whether it is a comparison we might be interested in at all. Any pursuit of this question does also raise the issue of gender construction in psychoanalysis – how male and female genders are seen in relation to heterosexuality.

Lewes (1989)[14] claims that female homosexuality is not so well understood psychoanalytically as male homosexuality, and also that the dynamics that psychoanalysts have uncovered are quite distinct in the two cases. However, the much greater amount of writing on male homosexuality is no guarantee of superior understanding, as Lewes himself makes only too clear. It is rather, perhaps, an indication of the greater degree of social anxiety aroused by male homosexuality compared to female, and its greater prominence generally. The second part of Lewes's claim is also open to doubt. There is a surprising similarity in some of the accounts put forward separately for male and female homosexuality: for example, mother fixation, inability to deal with or denial of castration anxiety, lack of a suitably effective father, inappropriate gender identity, have all been proposed for both men and women. This suggests that alongside the apparently quite separate clinical writing and theorising, there is an unacknowledged overlap in conceptualisation. This may be due not so much to any psychodynamic similarities between male and female forms of homosexuality as to the generally heterosexual vantage point from which homosexuality of all kinds is viewed, and some underlying assumptions about the construction of heterosexuality.

Lewes also maintains that female homosexuality has not suffered from the same degree of psychoanalytic hostility as male homosexuality, a hostility he amply documents. However, he cites only one article as evidence for this allegedly more benign attitude – Clara Thompson's, published in 1947.[15] This article, as we argue in Chapter 10 below, is neither as benign in its totality nor as central a text as he claims. The extraordinary depths and extremes of analytic hostility towards male homosexuality that Lewes describes may not obtain in full for women, but they certainly have their parallels in writers of the same period; and overall, a similarly negative and pejorative attitude prevails, with an equivalent failure even to entertain the possibility of a positive or healthy homosexuality.

Disappointment and early
—————— mother-love ——————

Freud sees the crucial event that precipitated his 'Psycho-genesis' patient into homosexual love as the oedipal disappointment she experienced in relation to her father when, during her adolescence, her mother became pregnant by him. She felt, Freud says, that it should have been her; 'furiously resentful and embittered', she sought another goal for her libido, and fell in love with a disreputable older woman. Freud notes that not every girl falls 'victim' to homosexuality as a result of such common oedipal disappointments, and asks what special factors were operative here that did not enable her to find a different solution. Resorting to innatist explanations, he describes the young woman's pre-existing homosexual 'tendencies', present in everyone, as especially strong. He also adds her 'masculinity complex' – her determination, as a child, not to be inferior to boys. He thus opts for an account that combines both acquired and congenital characteristics. Freud also emphasises how her adolescent disappointment allowed a revival of her original love for her mother, a love that was very ambivalent, owing to the mother's harsh and discriminatory attitude. This revival allowed her to overcome her hostility towards her mother and was, Freud says, a continuation of her unresolved infantile fixation on her mother. This, in fact, suited the real mother, who was relatively permissive towards her daughter's homosexuality, since it removed any competition between them for the attentions of men, and was also a secondary gain for the daughter.

Whilst he identifies this revival of pre-oedipal love, Freud devotes no further attention to it; instead he explores much more fully the repudiation of men that he feels constitutes the patient's homosexuality. Later analysts such as Deutsch and McDougall, in different ways, placed much greater emphasis on pre-oedipal factors.

── *Masculinity and femininity* ──

The use of these problematic concepts has dominated the psychoanalytic discussion of female homosexuality, putting it in a straitjacket from which it has not as yet escaped. The founding moment of this appears to be Freud's description, in 'Psychogenesis' of the young woman's love for another woman as the taking up of a masculine position – despite the fact that he is emphatic, in both *Three Essays* and 'Psychogenesis', that object choice, and the sexual characteristics and attitudes of the subject making this choice, are not necessarily linked. Thus he argues against the prevailing view that an inverted man 'feels he is a woman in search of a man' (Freud, 1905).[16] Instead, he says, many male inverts 'retain the mental quality of masculinity' and possess 'relatively few of the secondary characters of the opposite sex'. In 'Psychogenesis' he argues that just as 'masculine' men may love only men and 'feminine' men may be heterosexual, so also with women, 'mental sexual character and object choice do not necessarily coincide'. The mystery of homosexuality is not, therefore, so simple as is popularly supposed: that of a feminine mind in a masculine body or a masculine mind in a feminine body. Freud claims that 'tendentious literature' has exaggerated the supposed association between object choice and sexual characteristics; here he is arguing against the contemporaneous notion of homosexuals as a 'third sex'. It is also striking that in these passages Freud is clearly arguing against any presupposed alignment of what has become known as gender identity and object choice, an alignment that was to become common in subsequent writings.

However – and this was to be decisive – Freud also claims that this much-vaunted view of the independence of object choice and secondary sexual characteristics did not hold so completely for women as for men. Rather, he says:

> The position in the case of women is more ambiguous; for among them the active inverts exhibit masculine characteristics, both physical and mental, with peculiar frequency

and look for femininity in their sexual objects – though here again a close knowledge of the facts might reveal greater variety.[17]

Whilst Freud keeps open here the possibility of greater diversity in relation to these supposed characteristics, in his subsequent writings he effectively forecloses upon this. In 'Psychogenesis', having given an outline of the patient's history and how she came for treatment, he proceeds to ask whether she shows any physical characteristics 'plainly belonging to the opposite sex'. He puts this question in the mouths of readers 'unversed in psychoanalysis' who, he says, 'will long have been awaiting an answer' – a striking use of popular prejudice to displace his own interest. He then dismisses the question as unimportant because of the independence between object choice and other characteristics, but next he proclaims again that this independence does not hold for women, 'where bodily and mental traits belonging to the opposite sex are apt to coincide'. He does not comment on this complete change of view; instead he sets about trying to answer the original question about the patient's masculinity. Although, as he says, he has to forgo a physical examination (would this issue even have arisen with any other patient?), he observes 'no obvious deviation from the feminine physical type'. He finds her 'beautiful and well-made'; he notes that she had 'her father's tall figure, and her facial features were sharp rather than soft and girlish, traits which might be regarded as indicating a physical masculinity'. He then comments that some of her intellectual qualities could be 'connected with masculinity: for instance, her acuteness of comprehension and her lucid objectivity . . .'. Whilst Freud then says that these distinctions are 'conventional' rather than 'scientific', he none the less lets them stand; indeed, he has attached enough importance to them to mention them at all.

It seems that Freud is having to strain very hard to find signs of what he regards as masculinity in this patient. The impression he leaves us with is not just of someone who might have masculine characteristics but that, were this the case,

these would include physical attributes. Freud's careful quali-
fications and disclaimers about these attributes do nothing to
diminish the sense that he is very interested in the patient's
possible masculinity, and in the evocation of her in this way.

Freud's evident unease with this whole passage could also
have another source. His pronouncements on the patient's
appearance run the risk of being not just conventional but
also highly subjective and superficial. He attempts to draw
quite far-reaching implications from the patient's looks and
behaviour, as described by him. There is something very
unpsychoanalytic about the way in which these observations
are given such importance: the patient's own experience of
herself in these matters is not considered, and the question
of what relationship these aspects of her appearance bear to
anything unconscious is not discussed. This passage in
'Psychogenesis' is in fact relatively restrained and qualified
in the weight he gives to these superficial observations: later
writers were to produce highly evaluative descriptions of their
patients' looks and appearances, and to pass them off as disinterested observation with profound psychoanalytic significance (see Chapter 6 below).

Freud's masculinisation of his patient, however, brooks no
qualification in the succeeding passage:

> What is certainly of greater importance is that in her behav-
> iour towards her love-object she has throughout assumed the
> masculine part: that is to say, she has displayed the humility
> and the sublime overvaluation of the sexual object so charac-
> teristic of the male lover, the renunciation of all narcissistic
> satisfaction, and the preference for being the lover rather than
> the beloved. She had thus not only chosen a feminine love-
> object, but had also developed a masculine attitude towards
> that object.[18]

Thus he characterises the patient as masculine on the basis of
her style of loving. The terms of this characterisation derive
from Freud's metapsychology concerning love and gender, in
particular his claims that women love narcissistically while

men love 'anaclitically', with 'complete' object-love of the attachment type (Freud, 1914).[19] Furthermore (although Freud does not spell this out), his patient's love-object, a woman of loose reputation, corresponds to one very special type of object choice which Freud earlier described as being made by some men, that of unavailable and disreputable women.[20]

Freud notes the young woman's 'bliss' when she was allowed to accompany the lady a little way and kiss her hand on leaving; and also how all 'more sensual wishes' were silenced by her passionate preoccupation. He likens this love to the 'first passionate adoration of a youth for a celebrated actress whom he regards as far above him, to whom he scarcely dares lift his bashful eyes'. Lacan (1982),[21] as we shall see in Chapter 7, was later to redescribe this as 'courtly' love, making it, as Freud had made it, a defining feature of female homosexuality.

It appears that for Freud there is no possibility of a girl or a woman loving in this way without it being assimilated to a masculine style of loving. As love between women, it appears to have no specificity of its own. Here we are also right up against the confines of the wider Freudian theory, where masculinity and femininity are cast in terms of activity and passivity; Freud's whole theory of female homosexuality rests on these dualisms. It is also notable that his theory is based on one instance of a highly specific form of love – an adolescent, unconsummated and highly idealising passion, a choice which is never discussed, but facilitates his comparison with a kind of male courtly love.

Subsequently, summing up his understanding of how and why the patient came to love a woman, Freud extends his masculinisation of his patient in a somewhat sensational way:

> This girl had entirely repudiated her wish for a child, her love of men, and the feminine role in general. It is evident that at this point a number of very different things might have happened. What actually happened was the most extreme case. *She changed into a man* and took her mother in place of her father as the object of her love.[22] [emphasis added]

40

With this description Freud conjures up notions of sex change and unstable gender identity, and in so doing implicitly links homosexuality to transsexualism, as more modern writers have done.

At the end of this case history he introduces the notion of the masculinity complex. He finds evidence for this in the fact that in childhood the patient was 'a spirited girl, always ready for romping and fighting, [she was] not at all prepared to be second to her slightly older brother . . . she was in fact a feminist' – a passage that became decisive for the way feminism and the link between feminism and homosexuality were seen by later psychoanalysts. We are thus, as Mandy Merck (1986) points out,[23] left with no possibility of reconciling the patient's love for a woman with her femininity. Instead of Freud's initial clarity about the independence of object choice from other gender-related characteristics, we have the muddied waters of the masculinity complex as part and parcel of both female homosexuality and feminism.

Repudiation

The notion of repudiation is central to 'Psychogenesis', as indeed it is elsewhere in Freud. Masculinity in men is based on a repudiation of femininity, and 'normal' femininity on a repudiation of the mother, the clitoris and the wish to have a penis. Rachel Bowlby (1989)[24] describes how Freud sees many aspects of sexual life as based on repudiation, but argues that the exact sense and original German words for this are significantly different in different instances. In 'Psychogenesis' the sense of repudiation is equivalent to expel, exile or banish, and Freud uses it as part of his explanation of how the young woman came to love another woman – she repudiated men. In other places, Bowlby argues, repudiation is given a somewhat milder sense, equivalent to decline, refuse or remove. In 'Psychogenesis' the repudiation of men and the love of women are made virtually constitutive of each other – Freud does not advance any other grounds, such as dreams or fantasies, for saying that his patient repudiated men, apart from the fact that she fell in love with a woman.

We are thus presented with some startling forced choices, where choosing something of one kind (women) means repudiating another (men). The possibility of a woman choosing another woman as a love-object without repudiating men, or femininity, or motherhood, is foreclosed upon, and we are left with female homosexuality as inevitably a negative and reactive choice, based on the exclusion of men. A crucial question here is whether a choice between two alternatives always amounts to repudiation or rejection of the one not chosen.

An example, put in the first person for expository purposes, may help to clarify what is involved in this question. If I am offered tea or coffee (as often happens) and I choose tea, does this mean I have repudiated coffee or my desire for it? The answer may depend on all the surrounding considerations, events and feelings contributing to my choice. If I were to say, 'I'd love some tea, the sort you have smells delicious', it is hardly appropriate then to describe me as having repudiated coffee. I haven't accepted coffee, but neither have I repudiated or rejected it. Nor have I given any indication of not liking coffee, or having any feeling about it that would lead me to reject it for itself. If, on the other hand, on being presented with this choice, I say, 'Yuk, coffee, how revolting', then it would be reasonable to say that I had repudiated coffee, and that my choice of tea was based, at least to some extent, on this rejection. I could be described as having a negative attitude to coffee and choosing tea as an alternative. Even here, however, it might not be entirely accurate to say that I opted for tea just because of my revulsion for coffee, to explain one preference entirely in terms of negativity towards the other. I might well have some independently positive feelings for tea, and though my *choice* of tea versus coffee when presented with these two options may have been partly determined by my negative feelings for coffee, my *positive taste* for tea may not have anything to do with my dislike of coffee; indeed, it was probably formed independently. That is, my taste for tea and coffee may not be constitutive of each other. It is a fact of modern social life that these drinks are frequently offered as alternatives, and may thus seem inextricably linked as choices, but this may be irrelevant to what determines my taste for each.

Women and men are not, of course, tea and coffee, and there are plausibly more grounds for supposing that feelings about either gender affect or construct feelings about the other. But this example brings out the restrictiveness of the assumption that if a woman chooses a woman as a love-object, it means or is explained by her having repudiated men. This may well be true in some instances, but it is not necessarily generally so. To suppose this is to confuse an apparently necessary choice between two exclusive binary terms with the formation of feelings towards either. Just as with tea and coffee, there are many other possibilities, surrounding circumstances and emotions underlying such choices that might lead to a different formulation of what is involved. Seeing the choice of a woman entirely in terms of repudiation of men denies or minimises the operation of any positive desire *for* a woman, and sidesteps any detailed exploration of the nature of this desire in its own right. It is as if the dualism of male/female so constructs our thoughts that we cannot think around or outside what appear to be necessarily linked alternatives.

There is a further aspect of repudiation, tied to Freud's notions of bisexuality. As Bowlby says:

> It [repudiation] is strong language, and it seems to imply not just rejection or refusal, but also that what is rejected is somehow a part of the repudiator: that it is illegitimately cast off . . . There is the implication that what you repudiate really belongs to you, stays behind to haunt you, however hard you try to get rid of it.[25]

In 'Psychogenesis', however, Freud does not convey the sense that the patient's love for her father lingers. Indeed, Lacan (1979)[26] criticises Freud for not sufficiently seeing how she 'sustains the desire of the father' through her defiance of him and her collapse into suicide when this does not work.

Furthermore – and despite Freud's claim in *Three Essays* that everyone makes both homo- and heterosexual object choices unconsciously – there is a crucial asymmetry in the way these respective homo- and heterosexual repudiations are seen, which subverts the much-vaunted liberalism of this statement. In Freudian theory, for a young girl to become heterosexual she has to give up her love for her mother and take her father as a love-object. In his later 'Female Sexuality', Freud (1931)[27] describes this repudiation of the mother as a 'turning-away'. This is notably different from expel or banish. The girl's attachment to her mother is described as increasingly ambivalent, full of disappointments, frustrations and reproaches, but this turning-away from and detachment from the mother is seldom total. Freud and many subsequent writers describe how adult female heterosexuality coexists with a strong attachment to the mother, and how the male partner may be invested with many of the emotions associated with the mother. For heterosexuality, an adult love based on disappointment and repudiation, is normal, albeit difficult – a turning-away from and a turning towards, in which the attractions of the new male object are given an important role. No such leeway, however, is granted to adult homosexual love: here the repudiation involved is seen as more total, an expulsion rather than a turning-away from, absolute and apparently unambivalent. No lingering or sublimated attachment to the repudiated object is described, as it is for heterosexuality; instead its rejection is emphasised, as we have already seen. Homosexual love is construed almost entirely in terms of what is repudiated, and the attractiveness of the woman love-object is minimised, or given only a problematic rather than a desirable status. In this way the potential that exists in the *Three Essays* for putting homosexuality on an equivalent basis with heterosexuality is subverted by the subsequent developments in Freud's thought.

The characterisation of homosexual love so entirely in terms of repudiation gives it a rigid and defensive nature that leaves very little analytic space for considerations of ambivalence or love for the object in any other terms, a feature that has continued to the present day. That this characterisation had something to do with the difficulties Freud found in the analytic relationship with his patient is suggested by the following considerations.

—— *Countertransference issues* ——

Freud abruptly terminated his treatment of his 'Psycho-genesis' patient after three months. Significantly, he did this because of the trouble the young woman's alleged repudiation of men caused him. Discussing her 'unconquerable' resistance to the analysis beyond a certain point, he wrote:

> In reality she transferred to me the sweeping repudiation of
> men which had dominated her ever since the disappointment
> she had suffered with her father. Bitterness against men is as
> a rule easy to gratify upon the physician; . . . it simply
> expresses itself by rendering futile all his endeavours . . .[28]

As soon as he recognised this, Freud broke off the treatment. Lacan[29] sees Freud as being 'overwhelmed' by the patient, as with Dora, whose homosexual feelings Freud acknowledged he did not recognise, and who broke off the treatment herself. Merck[30] describes Freud's identification with the father as 'paranoic'. What is apparent from Freud's description of these difficulties, and from his peevish tone, is that he cannot tolerate the patient's apparent repudiation of men, and of him. He gives up at this point; he reacts rather than analyses. The extent of the patient's repudiation of men is exaggerated. One of the least plausible parts of the case history is Freud's inter-pretation of the patient's dreams of passionate love for men and desire for marriage as lying dreams designed to deceive him. This is another instance where no lingering attachment or ambivalence on the patient's part is allowed. This failure to recognise the young woman's ambivalence also means that Freud takes at face value her defiance and cool revenge towards her father. He does not see how this defiance is also a way of trying to remain engaged with the father – or, as

Lacan says, trying to sustain the desire of the father – as is the patient's apparent non-engagement with him, about which he feels so strongly.

What we are left with is the singular potency and difficulty of this homosexual material for Freud. He feels rejected by the young woman's love for a woman, and he rejects in kind, with a mirroring response: he recommends that the patient should go to a female analyst.

This is the first of what were to be many subsequent unsatisfactory analyses and failures to consider the impact of homosexual material on the analyst. Freud, because of the unrivalled detail and honesty of his writing, allows us some insight into this impact, and the difficulties that ensue where it is unrecognised or misunderstood. Later commentators (e.g. Lewes, 1989; Kwawer, 1980)[31] have suggested that in other places Freud did recognise the degree of anxiety and sadism provoked in others by homosexuality, but it appears that this recognition was not extended to the analytic context. Later analytic accounts are full of descriptions of broken-off analyses, negative therapeutic reactions, or sticky transferences with lesbian patients, but there is no attempt to understand the analyst's difficulties which may contribute to this. There is virtually no mention of countertransference issues in the whole literature on lesbian patients, despite the modern interest in this subject, something we discuss further in Chapter 9, in relation to lesbian eroticism.

We have seen how Freud's writings about female homosexuality, especially in 'Psychogenesis', initiated many themes that were subsequently to be developed in various directions, especially those of sexual object choice and masculinity/ femininity, and heterosexual disappointment leading to a repudiation of men. The gendered split between identification and desire, which was to become such a prominent feature of subsequent psychoanalytic accounts, is implicit in 'Psychogenesis', but not theorised as such. This had to await the development of Freud's ideas about identification and the Oedipus complex. Despite the limitations we have indicated, we can only be struck by the relative openness of much of Freud's thought on homosexuality, the multifaceted approach that he maintains, and the – to him – relative normality of a homosexual object choice. Even though this perspective was less evident in his later writings, and the seeds of this subsequent subversion are to be found in the bases of his theories, nonetheless Freud maintains a much less pathologising and pejorative attitude to female homosexuality than almost any other psychoanalytic writer.

Freud's writings on female homosexuality, and 'Psychogenesis' in particular, were developed and extended in many different directions by, on the one hand, Karen Horney and Ernest Jones, and, on the other, Helene Deutsch. Their accounts of female homosexuality reflect their different positions in relation to Freud's ideas about female sexuality in general.

2

The Masculine Woman:

Identification and Rivalry with the Father

THE 1920s AND 1930s were notable for vigorously conducted debates about female sexuality. It was during this period that important elaborations of and departures from Freud's ideas about homosexuality occurred, developments which have continued to the present and which, in different ways, signify the limitations of psychoanalytic thought on the subject. Ernest Jones (1927)[1] and Helene Deutsch (1933)[2] were the two analysts to consider homosexuality in any detail, but many others referred to it as part of their thoughts about women's sexuality in general. It is striking that one of the subtexts of the debates about female sexuality was how to reconcile femininity with women's participation in professional life, an issue that was of great autobiographical relevance to many of the women analysts. The link to homosexuality was through the assimilation of professional ambitions to masculinity.

Jones, although he was a faithful and indefatigable proponent of psychoanalysis, disagreed with Freud's ideas about female sexuality, especially with the notion that female sexuality develops from a masculine libido. This led him, along with Karen Horney and, later, Melanie Klein, to propose that female sexuality was essentially different from male sexuality, that there was not one originally common libido, and that female development depended on, amongst other things, the apprehension of sensations arising from the female genital organs, particularly the vagina. He also abandoned Freud's notion of bisexuality. Jones adopted some aspects of Freud's theory about female homosexuality and discarded others, but he does not make his agreements and disagreements explicit – indeed, Freud is scarcely referred to. The analyst whom he mainly cites is Karen Horney, whose article on the castration complex in women contains some important comments on homosexuality.[3] Jones's position depends on some theoretical assumptions made by Horney, so it is to her argument that we turn first.

—— *Playing the father's part* ——

Horney, in the period we are concerned with, adopted many of Freud's basic principles, and used his language of drives and libido. She is well known for her feminist critique of Freud's ideas about female sexuality, in particular for her argument that penis envy should be seen as a secondary rather than a primary phenomenon. She also emphasised and criticised Freud's male-centred stance, and in this she appears to have been influenced by Georg Simmel, a social philosopher (see page 210). Horney argues that the castration complex in women, by which she means the fantasy of having suffered castration, is to be seen not in terms of primary penis envy but instead as an effect of the love relation with the father, and the disappointment of incestuous wishes. She describes a woman whose apparent penis envy – manifested in an attitude of revenge against men, repudiation of feminine tasks and functions, and a strong unconscious homosexual tendency – is explained as her envy on account of her mother, and not herself, receiving a child (her younger brother) from her father. Horney argues that the father as love-object was given up, and the object relation to him was regressively replaced by an identification with him. This process of identification is shown by the woman's 'pretensions' to manhood, by her adoption of the same profession as her father and behaving like a husband towards her mother after his death. Horney sees this identification with the father as displacing an earlier phase of identification with the mother, and as one important root of the castration complex. She then claims that such a process underlies homosexuality:

> We know that in every case in which the castration complex
> predominates there is without exception a more or less
> marked tendency to homosexuality. *To play the father's part,*
> *always amounts also to desiring the mother in some sense.* There
> may be every possible degree of closeness in the relation
> between narcissistic regression and homosexual object
> cathexis, so that we have an unbroken series culminating in
> manifest homosexuality.[4] [emphasis added]

Horney maintains that it was Freud's 'Psychogenesis' that enabled her to understand the castration complex in women. She considers that Freud had shown that 'identification with the father is one of the bases of manifest homosexuality'. As we have already noted, Freud does not explicitly use the notion of identification with the father in 'Psychogenesis'. However, Horney does, at the very end of her article, cite Freud as having shown how generally important the process of identification is in human mental life, and she refers to other writings by Freud (*Mourning and Melancholia* and *Group Psychology and the Analysis of the Ego*, written after 'Psychogenesis'), as illustrations of this. She sums up the – for her – pivotal role of identification with the parent of the opposite sex as the point of evolution of both homosexuality and the castration complex.

Whilst the far-reaching nature of Freud's ideas on identification is indisputable, Horney's 'explanation' of female homosexuality as identification with the father is questionable, although it was to become quite widely adopted. There is an ineffable circularity to her argument. The girl's difficulties in becoming a woman and being suitably feminine, though they are viewed sympathetically in the light of the cultural disparagement of women that Horney describes, and are not seen as necessarily neurotic, are conceptualised only in terms of being, or wanting to be, more like a man. Once again there is no other alternative, no other way in which difficulties with femininity can be seen, except as a recourse to masculinity. Furthermore, to be like a man in these respects means that desire will inevitably be for a woman, if only unconsciously; there is no possibility of desiring a man from this position, or of desiring a woman from a 'feminine' identification. The homosexual position is cast as an inevitably masculine one, involving a repudiation of femininity.

Horney's account of homosexuality, further aspects of which we consider in Chapter 10, bears many resemblances to Freud's. Indeed, the case history on which she mainly bases her argument, albeit very brief by comparison and not involving manifest homosexuality, has some striking points of similarity to his. In both cases the birth of a younger brother produces a degree of disappointment in relation to the father that is apparently dealt with by abandoning him as a love-object. However, there are also some important differences. The crucial event in Freud's case happened at puberty, before which the patient had shown many signs of heterosexual wishes. Furthermore, the patient had an unresolved longing for her mother that was activated by her disappointment with her father. In Horney's case not only did the disturbing birth occur when the patient was much younger (two), but there is no mention of any particular longing for the mother. Horney casts homosexual love in terms of the felt rejection of heterosexual desire for the father, whereas Freud's account, though it incorporates this element, also bases it on original homosexual desire for the mother. Early love of the mother was to become a central theme in Deutsch's account, but it is missing from Horney's.

Identification

Jones (1927)[5] develops in an even starker way the notions of repressed desire for and identification with the father. Although at the beginning of his article he notes the 'phallocentric' bias of Freud's theory of female sexuality, this does not prevent him from conceptualising female homosexuality almost entirely in terms of the penis or its absence, the father and men in general. (Socarides, with no conscious irony, describes Jones's account as 'penetrating'.[6]) Jones begins by asking what in women corresponds to the fear of castration in men, and what differentiates homosexual from heterosexual development in women; he then says that what links these two questions is the word 'penis'.

Jones puts forward his theory of female homosexuality with matter-of-fact certainty. He uses very little clinical material or case description, despite basing his ideas on what he says were 'deep' analyses of five women, lasting from three to five years. The basis of his description is their attitude to men: 'only two had an entirely negative attitude' – as if this were self-evidently of central importance in addressing the subject. The individual women do not come alive in the text at all, and the relationship between Jones's clinical work and theorising is completely obscure; we simply have no idea what kind of analyses these were, or how observation, interpretation and theory mesh together.

Jones's theory is one of the simpler accounts of homosexuality, but he does propose a categorisation into two different groups, based on his sample of five, later altered in a footnote to three groups. One group retains an interest in men, and in being accepted as one of them, but they have surrendered their sex – that is, their femininity – and become masculine. These are the 'familiar type of women who ceaselessly complain of the unfairness of women's lot'. So much for Jones's much-vaunted support for feminists. The second group shows no such interest, and their libido centres on women. Analysis, however, shows that 'this interest in women is a vicarious way of enjoying femininity; they merely employ another woman to exhibit it for them'. Such women have surrendered the object (the father), and replaced him by themselves through identification.

Jones bases his theory on what he sees happening developmentally for all girls, who, he maintains, must choose between sacrificing their erotic attachment to their father and sacrificing their femininity. In the first instance a substitute for the father will be found, and 'feminine wishes' will develop, so that the incestuous object, but not the aim, is given up. In the second the vagina has to be renounced, the bond with the father is retained, but he is changed from an object of incestuous love to one of identification. The motive in this instance is the avoidance of incest. For the homosexual woman, to have the sexual organ of her own sex is out of the question, from fear of incest. Sexual integrity becomes equated with possessing the penis, and such girls 'become pathologically dependent on possessing the penis themselves in their imagination'. The alternative is aphanisis, or extinction of their sexuality, and they alternate between this and potency based on 'inverted gratification'. Jones sums up: 'Identification with the father is thus common to all forms of homosexuality . . . There is little doubt that this identification serves the function of keeping feminine wishes in repression.'

The logic of this account is that identification with the father allows the retention of some kind of bond with him, but in a way which eschews all notions of incestuous desire, or indeed any kind of object-love for the father or father substitutes. The presumption is that identification really will protect the girl from these unwanted desires, but we might well ask: why should this be so? Do identification and object-love concerning the same person or same kind of person never coexist? Why this stark either/or? Jones does indeed say that a homosexual woman cannot desire a man's penis for gratification because she already has one of her own, as though it was self-evident that a certain kind of similarity rules out desire, that a woman who does identify with her father cannot also desire him. However, we are left not really knowing why this is so, except in terms of the reason that was given for her identification in the first place: she had to get rid of her love for him, and she did this by identifying with him.

Subsequent psychoanalysts, such as McDougall (see Chapter 6), who rely heavily on the notion of identification with the father, do relate it more to their clinical material. With Jones it is simply a construction, presented as part of his overall theory. What we are left with, as with Horney, is a sense of homosexual love being based on a failure or repression of heterosexual love, a way of preserving some sexuality in the face of the desire for and prohibition of (heterosexual) incest. Desire for a woman is seen negatively, as *instead of* desire for a man, with no sense of any positive or original desire for a woman. What has been dropped in these accounts, compared to Freud's, is any notion of original bisexuality, so that incestuous desires are conceived of only in heterosexual terms, and as having an innate or natural status – Horney's 'biological principle of heterosexual attraction', for example. Freud's adherence to the principles of bisexuality allowed him to conceive of his homosexual patient's love as having something to do with original love for a woman, rather than only as a failure of her heterosexual desires. Her disappointment with her father was not, as he said, sufficient to explain why the woman fell in love with a woman. Furthermore, Freud's account of his patient's difficulties with heterosexuality involve not so much a terror of incestuous desires, as does Jones's, but rather their disappointment – and in this way Freud keeps more of his patient's sexuality alive, compared to Jones's complete extinction.

A similar position to that of Jones, regarding homosexuality as a defence against heterosexual incest, is found in Otto Rank's (1923)[7] article on perversion and neurosis. Here incest is seen as unquestionably heterosexual, and the flight from it leads to alienation from the opposite sex and to an attachment to objects of the same sex, but no notion of identification is invoked.

We have seen how central the notion of identification with the father is to Horney's and Jones's conceptualisation of female homosexuality. Lacan (1982),[8] in his brief comments

54

on these writings, criticises Jones for relying so heavily on what he calls the 'prop of identification'. What we have here, as with Horney, is a gendered split between desire and identification, between having and being, such that identification with one gender appears to require desire of the other, and desire correspondingly seems to imply opposite-gender identification (we discuss this further in Chapter 11). Although homosexuality, on this model, is taken to indicate a repression and failure of heterosexuality, nonetheless heterosexuality is retained or reinstituted in the very conception of homosexual desire. This is just one illustration of how desire in psychoanalytic terms is thought of only heterosexually.

Oral-sadism

Jones seems to have been aware that his theory of identification with the father may not have been sufficient as a total explanation, because at the end of his article he returns to the question of what differentiates homosexual from heterosexual women, given that all girls pass through a phase of penis envy and father identification. He finds this question impossible to answer without resorting to 'fundamental or inborn factors' which, he feels, despite the extensive elaboration of his foregoing theory, are decisive. These are an unusual intensity of oral eroticism, converging in an intensification of the oral-sadistic phase, which he regards as the 'central characteristic' of homosexuality in women. What the grounds are for this, and how this intensification leads to homosexuality, is left unexplained, although earlier in his article Jones claims that homosexual women show an especial development of oral eroticism as manifested by the importance of the tongue in lovemaking. Freud (1905) had also commented how there appeared to be a special preference for 'contact with the mucous membrane of the mouth' amongst women homosexuals.[9]

Jones proceeds to equate the tongue with the penis, claiming that this identity reaches an 'extraordinary degree of completeness' in homosexual women, and that in some cases the tongue is an 'almost entirely satisfactory substitute for the penis'. No details or reasons are given for this ascription. What it represents, however, is the complete assimilation of homosexual lovemaking to the assumed heterosexual mode, so that it has no specificity of its own, but is seen only from the perspective of the (missing) penis and the vagina – the tongue as substitute or surrogate, implicitly as second best, not the real thing.

The domination of Jones's thought by organs is also evident in his comments on the sadism supposedly manifested by homosexual women, which shows itself in the 'specially active thrusting quality of clitoral impulses which heightens the value of any penis that may be acquired in fantasy'. Here the clitoris is made equivalent to the penis, and again there is no space for homosexual activity to be viewed in its own right, except as a derivation of heterosexual activity. It is striking that Jones resorts to these special factors. In doing so he relegates homosexuality to a distinct category, rather than seeing it on a continuum with and as a variation of normal development, as Freud did.

Jones's remarks on oral-sadism were to be developed to a much greater extent, and on a rather different basis, by Joan Riviere and Melanie Klein. In his case the attribution of oral-sadism to female homosexuals seems to be based on the questionable assimilation of the tongue to the penis, and the supposition that parts of the body used by adults in sexual intercourse have a similar significance to the stage of childhood development where such zones allegedly predominate.

—— *Masculinity and masquerade* ——

The attribution of necessary masculinity to homosexual women was reiterated in several subsequent writings whose main focus was female development in general rather than homosexuality alone. Jeanne Lampl de Groot (1928)[10] reaffirms the basic Freudian postulate concerning masculinity/

femininity and love, claiming that a woman who is wholly feminine does not know object-love in the true sense – she can only let herself be loved. This is seen as the result of giving up the mother as love-object and, with it, the masculine position. We are once again presented with some stark either/ors: masculine/lover/mother-as-object versus feminine/loved/father-as-object. A patient (not manifestly homosexual) who tried 'to woo' the analyst's love is described as behaving 'just like a young man in love', displaying violent jealousy of an assumed rival (a supposedly exclusive masculine attribute?). Lampl de Groot conveys the impression that she finds this transference difficult to handle, and it comes as no surprise to find that the patient broke off the analysis, allegedly because of the disappointment of her love for the analyst. This is another instance of the particular difficulty analysts appear to have with homosexual transferences, perhaps increased by Lampl de Groot's insistence that the patient was behaving like a man. She also describes her second patient as wooing her 'in a thoroughly masculine manner'; she sums up this woman as someone who 'could not derive satisfaction from her husband because she herself really wanted to be a man in order to be able to possess the mother'.

Lampl de Groot also introduces the idea that a denial of difference between the sexes is involved in homosexuality, something that was to be emphasised by later analysts. She arrives at this conclusion by a discussion of Freud's 'Psychogenesis', claiming that his patient was a pronounced feminist, 'denying the difference between men and women'. What is striking about this is not just the common assimilation of feminism to denial of sexual difference, but also the fact that she, like Horney, is reading into Freud something he did not say. In the passage in question Freud describes the girl's rebellion against the inferior and unequal status of women, but nowhere does he imply a disavowal of sexual difference.

A much more sophisticated understanding of the constraints surrounding female identity is to be found in Joan Riviere's (1929) article 'Womanliness as a Masquerade'.[11] This highly significant work was ignored by most contemporary analysts, apart from Klein, and also by later commentators on this period, despite its foreshadow-ing of many subsequent feminist insights into the conflicts of femininity. Its main thesis, that femininity is always a mask or masquerade, has been developed by Lacan (1985), Heath (1986) and Butler (1990),[12] but her ideas about homosexu-ality have not received the same attention from any of these writers. Her arguments open up, and then tantalisingly foreclose upon, the interplay of social norms, male–female relationships and infantile identifications in the construction of femininity.

Riviere's main concern is how to characterise psychologically women who are both highly active and successful professionally yet also 'feminine' in their domestic and personal lives. She provides a partial context for this question by saying that 'not long ago' intellectual pursuits for women were associated with 'overtly masculine' types, but that this has now changed. She is thereby both asserting a historical specificity to the construction of femininity, and withdrawing it as it applies to her time. She describes a woman, the main subject of the article (whom Heath maintains, has strong autobiographical links to Riviere herself),[13] who was extremely successful professionally, had excellent relations with her husband with full and frequent sexual enjoyment, and prided herself on her domestic skills. However, after every public performance she felt assailed by fears of having done something inappropriate, and compelled to seek reassurance and sexual attention from men.

Riviere analyses this compulsive flirting as an attempt to ward off anxiety about the reprisals she anticipated from these father figures for her possession of the penis, as symbolised by her public achievements. Her dread of this retribution was very great, and she attempted to placate by offering herself sexually, by 'masquerading' as guiltless and innocent, compulsively reversing her public performance. Such defusing and self-abnegating behaviour will be familiar to many women even now, as are the further examples Riviere gives of women who hide their competence in deference to men, or are inappropriately flippant on occasions of public success.

Riviere does not consider the contribution that men and the construction of masculinity make to this, the actual reprisals women might suffer for outshining men, or the sustaining of male identity by the exclusion of women from certain spheres. She does, however, put forward a view of femininity – or 'womanliness' as she terms it – as something constructed, 'assumed and worn as a mask, both to hide the possession of masculinity and to avert the reprisals expected . . .' Even more radically, she suggests that there is no difference between genuine womanliness and the masquerade, they are the same thing; femininity *is* the mask.

This argument inevitably raises questions not just about femininity in the sense of typically feminine behaviour, but also about female heterosexuality. Riviere goes on to describe how the gratification her patient obtained in her sexual relations, despite their full and frequent nature, was not that of pure sexual enjoyment, but rather that of reassurance and restitution of her lost self-esteem. Womanliness, as manifested in this kind of sexual engagement, did not 'represent her main development' – a description that appears to question the woman's heterosexuality. Indeed, Riviere then considers, at the same time as she underplays, the woman's possible homosexuality by saying that it is striking that she had no homosexual experiences, except with her sister before puberty. She mentions, but does not comment on, the woman's frequent homosexual dreams with intense orgasm, occurrences which, one might suppose, would have been worthy of further exploration and analysis. It appears that Riviere is as unable to countenance her patient's possible homosexuality as is the patient herself, whilst she puts forward an argument that demonstrates the constructed and often tenuous nature of heterosexuality, and clinical material that suggests strong but ignored homosexual desires.

Riviere returns to the relationship between homosexuality and heterosexuality when she later asks what the difference is between her type of professional heterosexual woman and Jones's first type of homosexual woman, whose apparent aim was to obtain recognition of her masculinity from men. In the case of her patient, she says, 'recognition of possession of the penis' was not claimed openly – indeed, it was avoided, but none the less claimed indirectly. 'With less anxiety' her patient would have claimed such recognition, which suggests that one of the differences between homosexual and heterosexual women lies in the latter's greater anxiety about claiming a place in public discourse, and thus seeming to occupy the position of men. But how, she asks, is the anxiety averted by these homosexual women? Part of her answer is that the homosexual woman obtains more gratification from her sadism in relation to the father: not only has he been defeated, but he also recognises it and absolves her. This, however maintains men in a position of importance to her, a feature, Jones maintains, of such women. The lesser anxiety of homosexual women that Riviere perceives might also lie in the lesser psychological importance that men and male approval have for them, thus leaving them freer to pursue their professional lives without the same conflicts as heterosexual women, a view that Charlotte Wolff (1971)[14] was to advocate in a different era.

Riviere's account of heterosexuality is as a reaction-formation to the frustrations of the oral-sadistic phase, and in this she closely follows Klein's[15] account of young girls' development. The acceptance of castration, the humility, the admiration of men, come chiefly from the renunciation of sadistic castration wishes, as she puts it: 'I must not take, I must not even ask; it must be given me.' Here Riviere appears to be describing many well-known features of female psychology, which have so often been debilitating for women, but from which – she seems to imply – homosexual women are relatively free. For her, both the 'normal' and the homosexual woman desire the father's penis and rebel against frustration, but one of the important differences lies in the degree of sadism, and the ability to deal both with it and with the anxiety to which it gives rise. The depiction of homosexuality as arising from a greater degree of sadism reflects Klein's views (see Chapter 4). What is different is Riviere's understanding that the repression of sadism that heterosexuality demands may create a conflictful or debilitating outcome, and the sadism that homosexuality allegedly involves (taking, demanding, getting) may well contain advantages, particularly in the enhancement of a woman's professional life.

Riviere's understanding of homosexuality is thus entirely in terms of access to conventionally male domains, and she does not make reference to object-love of any kind. Sexuality is not analysed except in relation to the heterosexual woman, who dares not be seen to be in possession of the penis and uses her sexuality to hide this, rather than as an expression of desire for an object. As Butler comments, the lesbian is here signified as an asexual position, the patient as a homosexual without homosexuality.

The development of ideas about homosexuality traced in this chapter reflects a shift from Freudian to Kleinian ideas about female sexuality. Deutsch's writings on female homosexuality, to which we now turn, remain more firmly within Freud's framework, albeit with many extensions of her own.

3

The Child and the Mother:
Deutsch and the Maternal/Erotic

*H*ELENE DEUTSCH – LIKE all other analysts of her time, but unlike later ones – developed her understanding of female homosexuality in the context of her ideas about female sexuality in general. Her main writings about female homosexuality consist of an article first published in 1932, and a chapter in her subsequent *The Psychology of Women* (1944).[1] The earlier article is based on her analyses of eleven homosexual women, of whom only two are discussed in detail. The chapter is more wide-ranging, and illustrated by a great variety of cases, although none is described with the earlier clinical detail.

Deutsch's writing is striking in several ways: her forceful disagreement with the notion that masculine and feminine roles are involved in homosexual relationships, her criticism of the idea that masculinity is a motive for female homosexuality, and the relative openness and vivacity of her descriptions of homosexual love and sex. Her account follows much more along the lines of Freud than those of Jones, which is hardly surprising in view of their respective positions concerning female sexuality, but it also represents an important amplification of Freud's ideas, particularly in the light of his later writings on female sexuality. Her similarity with Freud lies in the multifaceted account she gives, the twists and turns she describes between homosexual and heterosexual longings, and the interaction of post- and pre-oedipal factors, such that the foundation of later inversion is laid in the first period of infancy, but is crucially added to by later events at puberty. For the most part she also maintained Freud's distinction between inversion and perversion.

Homosexual love

Deutsch disputes (as Freud disputed) that there are any signs of physical masculinity in any of her first series of patients, suggesting that this was still an issue of some importance or contention. In her later book she still finds it relevant to mention several cases of sexual hermaphroditism, or apparent biological masculinity, but she also insists that most forms of homosexuality are psychogenic in origin.

She describes her first patient as 'fair' and 'feminine', and as not having a masculinity complex. She came to analysis suffering from depression and anxiety. During the course of the analysis the woman – who was married, and had not until then been actively homosexual – formed a relationship with a woman. This relationship Deutsch describes as 'extraordinarily blissful and uninhibited' and as being, on the patient's account, 'a perfectly conscious mother-and-child situation, in which sometimes the one and sometimes the other played the part of the mother'. She continues:

> In their homosexual caresses they derived gratification,
> especially from the oral zone and the external genital organs.
> In their relation there was no sign of a 'masculine–feminine'
> opposition of roles, but the antithesis between active and
> passive played an essential part. One received the impression
> that what made the situation so happy was precisely the
> possibility of playing *both* parts.[2]

It is striking how open Deutsch is to the woman's own experience, and how appreciative she is of the love involved. One could even read into this last passage a note of mild envy. She is able to convey the positive aspects of the woman's experience even though, as she says, she would have regarded a turn towards men, and a renunciation of homosexuality, as a more favourable resolution. She also acknowledges how much happier this previously suicidal woman was in other respects. Paul Roazen comments – although it is not clear on what evidence – that Deutsch was surprised that Freud (who had sent her this patient) had no objection to this outcome of the analysis.[3] By 1944, however, her comments had become more severe: 'It goes without saying that the experience fell far below what psychoanalysis demands of an adult personality . . . '

It is also apparent from this account how it was the analysis and the transference to Deutsch that allowed this woman to overcome her anxiety and hostility sufficiently to form a 'positive' libidinal relationship with another woman. Deutsch was clearly able to facilitate and work with a homosexual transference to herself, which was then carried over to another woman. We might suggest that this is due to a combination of her theoretical position and clinical and personal skills. Her adoption of a Freudian framework, particularly in relation to bisexuality, allows more space for homosexual positions as a normal variant of sexuality than does that of, for example, Horney, Jones or Klein. She seems more able to discern the positive and loving elements in homosexual relationships, as well as any conflictful or regressive aspects, than are other analysts. Her criticisms of the tendency to see homosexual love in terms of heterosexual replications of masculine and feminine roles suggest an ability and willingness to think outside prevailing frameworks, and the absence of a need to impose conventional categories on her clinical material. She appears able to allow homosexual love to be, and to work with homosexual transferences without unduly defensive reactions – something which is relatively unusual, as we show in Chapter 9.

Deutsch claims that all the other cases she analysed showed this mother-and-child relationship with the love-object, and again stresses the double role of each partner. In her book she presents a variety of homosexual relationships: women whose relationships are a continuation of adolescent best friendships; married women who act as confidantes for each other; women with more complex and ambivalent relationships, developing after puberty and often showing signs of unresolved bisexuality; women with thwarted heterosexual infatuations whose passive desire to be loved is converted into active desiring; and many others. This description of variety, albeit a limited one, is a refreshing contrast to the typifying and generalising accounts of 'the' homosexual given by many other analysts. Deutsch also presents a complex picture of eroticism in such relationships:

> Homosexual love is usually more passionate and more
> violently bound to the object than heterosexual love, even if it
> lacks the desire for direct sexual gratification . . . Woman's
> propensity to sublimate her sexuality into goal inhibited
> eroticism manifests itself especially in her homosexuality.[4]

Here Deutsch is describing female homosexual erotic experience in terms of features she deems to be typical of women generally; that is, she attempts to understand such eroticism as specific to women, and as an aspect of what we would now call gender. In this she anticipates subsequent feminist attempts to view lesbian experience in terms of 'women's psychology'. Although she compares homosexual to heterosexual love in terms of a relative lack rather than as a difference with many various aspects to it, some of which might constitute advantages, none the less she does not describe this lack in phallic terms. We might dispute the generality of her assertion concerning the supposed lack of desire for direct gratification, but it is still important that she is able to conceive of female homosexuality without reference to the phallus, and as taking place between two women. Again she is relatively unusual in this. She is also pointing in this passage to conflicts about sexuality which have found a voice in much more recent writing about lesbian experience – conflicts which we discuss in Chapters 9 and 10.

— *Oedipal and pre-oedipal issues* —

Whilst Deutsch advances so emphatically the sense of union with the mother that she sees in homosexual relationships, she maintains that the father also plays a part.

In her earlier article she describes in some detail the case of a second patient, but makes no further mention of the remaining nine. This second woman suffered from intense envy of a sister only nine months younger, and when she grew up she let her sister take precedence in feminine matters. When her parents divorced, she stayed with her mother. Analysis apparently revealed very strong aggressive impulses towards the mother and sister, and much of her life was taken up with a struggle against these. Although she developed with difficulty what Deutsch describes as a normal oedipal position, this intensified the aggression against her mother, and her guilt about this could be lightened only by 'over-compensation, by renouncing the father and remaining finally arrested in the mother-fixation'. After a fairly long description of some of the patient's dreams, Deutsch sums up:

> It is difficult to say whether the longing of her early infantile period (a longing that she never mastered) to be the sole possessor of her mother and to be nursed and tended by her had the effect of inhibiting the patient's normal libidinal development; or whether the further vicissitudes of her sexual life were determined by difficulties arising out of the Oedipus complex and familiar to us from other cases. I have tried to shew, in studying her dreams, that her return to her mother did not imply the renunciation of her longing for her father and that her relation to him was one of perpetual, terrified flight, which forced her into repression of her feminine attitude towards men.[5]

Deutsch quite clearly sees female homosexuals as having reached the oedipal position (something that was to be disputed by other writers); she puts this account of homosexuality into her general theory of female development, and particularly her perception of the difficulties and dangers of heterosexuality for girls. Such perils can mean that the libido turns back in a 'retrogression' to earlier experiences once enjoyed. The advantage of this to the girl lies not just in liberation from guilt towards the mother, but also in the protection it affords her from the wounds to her self-esteem caused by her father's rejection of her love for him. Deutsch describes a process of bisexual oscillation between the two parents and its outcome in neurosis, heterosexuality or inversion, and emphasises again how homosexuality is not a simple fixation but a complex process of retrogression. In her later writing she argues that homosexuality affects those who could easily have gratified their heterosexual wishes; but either they did not have such wishes or doing so did not yield happiness, but instead a greater yearning for someone of their own sex.

In her earlier article Deutsch asks whether there are cases where the libido has known only one object, the mother; these are cases she considers to be quite special and to show general psychic infantilism, and a highly adhesive transference full of anxiety. But this is not a line she follows; indeed, she subsequently asserts that every act of homosexual love expresses an unfulfilled heterosexual hope. She sees the final outcome as resting on a struggle between the primary tie to the mother, which gains strength at puberty, and the 'biological demands of heterosexuality'. With this latter phrase she is departing markedly – as she does in many other places – from Freud's eschewal of any natural heterosexuality, and aligning herself more with other psychoanalytic views of gender differences conceived of in terms of biological principles. She also considers the actual father's influence, favourable or unfavourable, to be decisive, and cites reasons why a girl may turn away from rather than towards the father.

Masturbation

Deutsch argues that in order for a full inversion to develop, the 'biological summons' to the father must be annulled. She sees this happening through the mother's active concurrence in the daughter's sexual pleasure from masturbation, which she had formerly forbidden:

> This sanctioning of activity and permission to masturbate constitutes a motive common to all forms of homosexuality . . . in this new edition of the mother–child relation the pregenital frustration must also be annulled, and this is what largely happens in the activities from which homosexuals derive their gratification.[6]

Deutsch's highlighting of the importance of masturbation is striking; we must ask why she does this, and what its implications are. It is also noteworthy that she was the first writer on female homosexuality to introduce this idea, which has been widely taken up. In her first case history, Deutsch describes how the child's very active masturbation between the ages of three and five was severely punished by her mother, who tied up her hands and feet, and jeered at her. This produced both furious anger towards her mother and also a 'violent sexual excitement'. To the child the most terrible thing was that her father remained a passive observer of this scene, and did not help her. Deutsch argues that this memory, which came to light only in analysis, was the centre of the woman's 'perversion'. She is careful to say that she does not think that this scene alone was causative, but rather that it brought together several ongoing trends in the child's life, and became the 'prototype' of later occurrences. In the patient's subsequent adult relationship with a woman, once she had overcome her enormous anxiety and hostility towards her mother, her infantile mortification by her mother could be wiped out by sexual gratification.

Deutsch's second patient provides much less obvious support for her general claims about masturbation. One dream is interpreted as showing the patient's desires for Deutsch to sanction her masturbatory activities, which is hardly specific to homosexuality. No childhood memories explicitly concerned with masturbation are presented, although one that is interpreted as implicitly so is described, but the interpretation is certainly questionable. Furthermore, none of this rather scanty material is related to the patient's actual homosexual activities.

Thus Deutsch's claim that the sanctioning of masturbation is a motive 'common to all forms of homosexuality' is based on only one clearly illustrative case, and the other nine cases are not described at all. Deutsch also puts considerable weight on her description of homosexual lovemaking to substantiate her claim:

> In all cases the forms of sexual gratification were the same:
> sleeping in close mutual embrace, sucking one another's
> nipples, mutual genital and, above all, anal masturbation, and
> *cunnilingus*, mainly in the form of sucking, practised inten-
> sively by both parties.[7]

Whilst the attribution of mutually masturbatory activities to homosexual lovemaking may (or may not) have a basis in actual experience, it does not follow that this can be assimilated to the solitary masturbation of childhood, or seen without question as necessarily pregenital. This assumption of psychic equivalence has gone largely unquestioned, but there are important distinctions that should be drawn. 'Masturbation' connotes sexual activity both carried out by the hand and also directed towards the subject herself – that is, autoerotic. When masturbation is mutual, or involves another person in some way, it is only the organ in question, the hand, that constitutes the basis for saying that it is masturbation. A central aspect of it, the autoerotic aspect, no longer holds, and this difference, whether solitary or part of an exchange with another person, will lend quite different psychic meanings to the activities in question – differences which are obscured by the assimilation of all uses of the hand in sexual exchanges to the infantile autoerotic paradigm.

It is also more than probable that people try to annul all kinds of infantile frustrations in adult sexual relationships, but this hardly distinguishes homosexual from heterosexual intercourse.

─────────── *Orality* ───────────

A parallel problem applies to Deutsch's description of homosexual activities as oral, and her claim that her case material confirms Jones's theory of an oral-sadistic disposition. The grounds for this attribution are the reported involvement of the mouth, which she describes as used in sucking nipples and genitals. Whilst sucking may well be involved, it is hardly the only form of oral activity – what about kissing, nibbling, licking, for example? The choice of 'sucking' as the supposed prototype of oral activity immediately conjures up images of babies at the breast, and hence biases the description towards the infantile. Deutsch assumes – as do Jones and Freud – that all oral satisfaction is necessarily pregenital, so that there is no conception of adult oral activity that is not determined by pregenital motives.

Once again the argument is dominated by the organs in question, so that the use of particular parts of the body is held to imply particular psychic stages, and therefore meanings. The implicit hierarchy is always the more genital (for which read penis and vagina), the more mature, so that there is no space for any mature form of sexuality that involves other components, except as 'foreplay'. The quality of the actual relationship between the owners of these organs recedes into the background. These genital and ultimately reproductive criteria of maturity are not confined to Freudian thought, as will become apparent.

─────────── *Masculinity* ───────────

As we have said, Deutsch is emphatic throughout that homosexual relationships between women do not involve feminine and masculine roles; and she also disputes that masculinity is in any way the motive for homosexuality. She claims that masculine tendencies in a woman, where these exist, are seldom responsible for her homosexuality. Rather, masculine appearances represent a façade, concealing more infantile wishes. The masculine gesture, she contends, is only a means of wooing, and is a pretext. The desired sexual goal completely excludes the masculine, because it involves gratification which no man is capable of giving a woman. Quite what this is she does not say, but presumably she is alluding to her view of homosexual relationships as involving the re-creation of mother–child dynamics, and also possibly to the involvement of the breast. This also underlines the way in which she conveyed her understanding of the attractions of homosexual relationships as having something that heterosexual relationships lacked, even though she ultimately regarded this as pathological. Deutsch's perceptiveness in not taking masculine appearances or behaviour to denote a masculine character or identification is striking, especially in view of the weight of both contemporary and subsequent writings on this subject – an issue we pursue further in Chapter 6.

Although Deutsch freed herself from the confines of seeing lesbians as stereotypically masculine, she replaces one reductive move with another – that of seeing lesbians as oral, infantile and seeking annulment of early frustrations. Her account is contradictory in this respect, because she also acknowledges that both the participants in this supposed mother–child re-enactment are capable of taking – and take – the position of the mother as much as that of the child. All her subsequent theorising, however, is concerned with the infantile position, not the seemingly more adult one, so we are left with the impression of female homosexuals as only infantile. What of the motives, capacities, feelings and gratifications that accompany the complementary role? Why not give these more prominence? And what about her description of the flexibility involved in adopting both positions; does this not contradict one of the features that is often regarded as a main characteristic of perversions, namely rigidity and restrictiveness in sexual encounters? It is this very flexibility that is commented on by later writers who adopt a more open position (see Chapter 10).

Deutsch was faithful to Freud, not just in adhering to most of his theoretical framework, but also in her respect for clinical detail and for the variety and complexity of what she was trying to understand. Yet despite her often sympathetic understanding of what she describes as a 'painful and tender longing for feminine love', by 1944 she is compelled to label it a 'pathologic distortion'. She thus eventually went much further than Freud in so unambiguously seeing homosexuality as a form of pathology – a reflection of the growing conservatism of the psychoanalytic world at that time, especially in America, where Deutsch had moved. This conservatism, which had many roots, was to lead to an intensification of pejorative and prejudiced theorising about homosexuality.

4

Klein:

The Phantasy that
Anatomy is Destiny

M ANY FEMINISTS HAVE been impressed by Melanie
Klein's emphasis on the centrality of the mother in
the infant's early development. It has signified a move
from Freud's phallocentrism, and the language of instincts and
their satisfaction. For Klein, the baby's unconscious phantasies
in relation to the breast initiate and underpin her relationship
to others. These are initially 'part-objects' identified in relations
of anxiety and satisfaction from oral, anal and genital positions; if development proceeds 'normally', relationships to
whole objects are established in which both 'good' and 'bad'
feelings towards the object can be sustained together.

Susie Orbach and Luise Eichenbaum, feminist psychotherapists and founder members of the Women's Therapy
Centre in London, praise Dorothy Dinnerstein for showing us
how Kleinian theory explains the misogynist nature of 'all our
psychologies'.[1] Dinnerstein (1978) uses Klein's concept of envy
to argue that women are the objects of oppression, hatred and
destructiveness because of the power of the baby's earliest
feelings towards the mother:

who was half human, half nature – we feel torn between two
impulses: the impulse, on the one hand, to give free rein to

the nursling's angry greed, its wild yearning to own, control, suck dry the source of good, its wish to avenge deprivation; and the impulse, on the other hand, to make reparation for these feelings, which threaten to destroy what is most precious and deeply needed.[2]

This reading of Klein recognises that psychoanalysis is not only a theory of individual suffering and development but also a social theory which has moral and political effects. However, these feminist psychotherapists and psychologists have failed to discuss Klein's specification of female homosexuality as oral-sadistic, destructive, fixated at the paranoid-schizoid position. There is no critique of the normativeness of Klein's metapsychology, notably her privileging of heterosexual dynamics.

It is relevant and important to analyse Klein's metapsychology, the way in which she constructs her theories, in order to highlight its implicit and explicit value judgements regarding psychic health and illness. Such value judgements can generate social and political judgements regarding morally correct behaviour and relationships. On this issue Teresa Brennan succinctly distinguishes Klein from Freud by pointing out that for Klein and ego-psychoanalysts:

> heterosexuality, potency, monogamy, and absence of perversion are listed as desirable outcomes of psychoanalysis. This would have been foreign to Freud, who recognized the force of social sanctions in causing unhappiness, but did not think it was the analyst's task to induce conformity.[3]

Like any social theory – and this holds true of those theories we have already described – Klein's theory of psychoanalysis embodies certain notions of truth, reality and value from a value-laden perspective. Klein claims to present the 'objective' truth of human development without sufficiently addressing the issue of her own inevitable historical, cultural and psychic biases. Often what is regarded as the truth of the patient's intrapsychic relationships results from an analyst's own strongly held views of the normal, which remain unquestioned for her/him.

Klein, unlike some of her followers (see Chapter 5), does not provide specific clinical examples of lesbianism. Instead, references to the 'female homosexual attitude' are intertwined with her accounts of the progress and vicissitudes of early male and female relationships to the mother/breast and father/penis. Thus it is not possible to extricate her position on solely the aetiology – the family background – of lesbianism. For this reason we present a general outline of her position on the Oedipus complex and the pre-oedipal psyche in order to set the context for understanding her position on homosexuality and lesbianism. Our exposition illustrates how Klein – along with earlier psychoanalysts, as we have shown – retains stereotypical gender descriptions which she assumes to be present from earlier infancy. Sexuality is theorised as intrinsic to gender differences. There is an assumption of a natural causality connecting sex, gender and desire, such that sexuality and desire are presented as the 'natural' expression of a given gender. In every scenario, as we will show, female homosexuality is regarded as 'oral-sadistic', pregenital and immature.

Klein (1950) specifies 'heterosexuality' as a major criterion for the termination of an analysis – that is to say, heterosexuality is a criterion of being psychically healthy, 'cured' of pathology. Thus in 'On the Criteria for the Termination of a Psycho-Analysis' she writes:

> The question arises how far the approach I am suggesting is related to some of the well-known criteria, such as an established potency and heterosexuality, capacity for love, object-relations and work, and certain characteristics of the ego which make for mental stability and are bound up with adequate defences.[4]

Although Klein differs from Freud's emphasis on the role of instincts at the pre-oedipal developmental stage she does, nevertheless, retain Freud's alignment of gender and sexuality. As well as arguing in favour of two distinct gender 'identities', masculine and feminine, whose characteristics are knowable and natural, she attributes appropriate – normal – sexual desires to each gender. In fact, sexual desire is postulated as intrinsic to gender identity. She maintains (1928):

> The next determining influence upon the mental processes is that of the anatomical difference between the sexes.
>
> The boy, when he finds himself impelled to abandon the oral and anal positions for the genital, passes on to the aim of penetration associated with the possession of the penis. Thus he changes not only his libido-position, but its *aim*, and this enables him to retain his original love-object. In the girl, on the other hand, the *receptive* aim is carried over from the oral to the genital position: she changes her libido-position, but retains its aim, which has already led to a disappointment in relation to her mother.[5]

Thirty years of clinical practice did not alter Klein's alignment of gender and sexuality:

> There are great differences in the Oedipus complex of the girl and of the boy, which I shall characterize only by saying that whereas the boy in his genital development returns to his original object, the mother, and therefore seeks female objects, with some consequent jealousy of the father and men in general, the girl to some extent has to turn away from the mother and find the object of her desires in the father and later on in other men. (1959)[6]

As in Freud, homosexuality is designated as a negative choice and results from a failure adequately to negotiate oedipal conflicts. Klein does not question the fundamental assumptions of her developmental theory but bases changes and variations in her theories on 'empirical' clinical practice.

Klein, like Freud, bases her metapsychology on the assumption of 'life' and 'death' instincts. She (1958) criticises Freud for not giving sufficient weight to the importance of aggression in emotional life.[7] She argues that from the beginning of life the two instincts attach themselves to objects, primarily the mother's breast, and thus initiate the various processes constitutive of psychic development. The primal process of projection results from deflecting the death instinct outwards. Klein stresses the importance in every analysis of considering the internal processes in relation to constitutional and relational factors – that is to say, 'external' factors.

— *Splitting of internal and external* —

For Klein, female homosexuality is to be understood in terms of its cause or causes. It occurs because of unresolved difficulties at the paranoid-schizoid position. Preceding the depressive position, when the baby becomes able to relate to whole objects, this position (at age three to four months) is characterised by part-object relations involving processes of splitting, denial and idealisation. According to Klein, female homosexuality can therefore be only a relationship of part objects.

Introjection of the mother's feeding breast is foundational for all internalisation processes. This relation to the mother determines the emotional and sexual development for both sexes.[8] Gratifying experiences of the breast allow the child to internalise a good object. When bad experiences are felt, they are projected on to the breast as a bad object. Klein emphasises the 'fact' that, from the beginning, the libido is fused with aggressiveness; this generates anxiety. To master the persecution anxiety derived from phantasies of the breast as destructive, the baby splits breast and mother internally and externally into a loved and, on the other hand, a hated object. This splitting of the breast into a good and a bad object is, Klein argues, the expression of the innate conflict between love and hate, and the anxieties generated by this.[9] Furthermore, this splitting is a precondition of the infant's relative stability because the ego (the self), which is initially unstable, gets rid of its destructive impulses and persecutory anxieties.

The infant achieves relative stability by turning a 'good' object into an 'ideal' one as a protection from the 'bad', 'persecuting' object. It is in phantasy that the infant splits object from its 'self'. As a result of this phantasised split, feelings and relations are cut off from one another.[10] These early processes are also the origin of transferences. Klein maintains that the life and death instincts are closely interconnected and so, therefore, are love and hatred. Negative and positive transferences are thus closely connected, and both require analysis 'in depth'.[11]

The paranoid-schizoid position is characterised by oral desires. Satisfaction from the breast allows the infant to find other gratifying objects, the secondary primary object being the father's penis. The penis is also the focus of the conflicting 'good' and 'bad' attitudes to the breast. According to Klein (1945), oral libido allows for the establishment of images of mother's breast and father's penis in the ego, and these form the nucleus of the superego.[12] Along with the anxiety, guilt and depression of libidinal development an urge towards reparation is also operative. This urge lessens persecutory anxiety towards the object, and is linked to gratitude and love.

Klein argues that the child expects to find the father's penis, excrement and children as edible substances within the mother's body. The infant phantasises excreta as dangerous weapons. This is in line with her assumption that the Oedipus complex originates at an early stage of development dominated by sadism. In fact the first relation to reality is constituted by sadistic phantasies directed against the inside of the mother. This sadism activates anxieties regarding excrement, organs, objects, and things which are equated with one another. Anxiety is not an exclusively negative concept but, argues Klein, a sufficient 'quantity' of anxiety is necessary for symbol formation and phantasy – that is, for the subject's relation to reality. The satisfactory resolution of this developmental stage or position depends on an adequate capacity to tolerate these anxieties.

Female development

Klein maintains that the girl's wish to possess her father's penis, stolen from the hated mother, is a fundamental factor in female sexual development. She assumes that the girl wants a penis as an object of oral satisfaction rather than as an attribute of masculinity,[13] as Freud had proposed. Klein argues that this desire for the penis is not the result of the castration complex, but expresses oedipal desires. The girl is directly influenced by oedipal impulses as a result of her feminine instincts rather than indirectly through her masculine tendencies. She unconsciously believes that her mother has incorporated her father's penis, and she envies this. The equation of penis and breast activates oral-receptive qualities in the girl, and is the foundation of her sexual development in that it prepares the vagina to receive the penis. Girls' oedipal impulses are much more dominated by oral desires than boys'. The girl's sadistic omnipotence over her parents produces phantasies of destroying the inside of the mother's body and its contents, including the penis. Feminine masochism is based on fear of the bad objects the girl has internalised; she turns her sadistic instincts against these.

Sensations are felt in the vagina as soon as oedipal impulses emerge. The girl identifies with her father shortly after identifying with her mother, and because of this her masturbatory phantasies constitute her clitoris as a penis. Klein claims that 'onanism' in girls does not provide as adequate an outlet for excitations as it does in boys. The girl experiences greater lack of gratification, which can cause complications and disturbances of her sexual development.[14] The girl's development is disturbed by the fact that while the boy actually possesses the penis which allows him to rival his father, the girl 'has only' the unqualified desire for motherhood. This is why Klein concludes that jealousy is more common in women than in men; it is reinforced by deflected penis envy.

Klein's theories rely heavily on anatomical similarity and difference. She argues that the girl has more problems in the formation of her superego because of her anatomical difference from the father and she has difficulty in identifying with her mother because the internal organs of sexual functioning and the possession of children are not open to reality testing.[15] Klein concludes that in men the ego and relations based on reality are psychically dominant; men, therefore, have the capacity for objectivity. In women the unconscious, with its sadistic and masochistic elements as well as maternal wishes, dominates. This is the basis for her claim that women are closer to children than men are, and that adult women have a stronger desire for children than for a sexual partner.

Female homosexuality as a defence against psychosis

Because Klein characterises female homosexuality as originating from the paranoid-schizoid position, the implication is that lesbians have not achieved adequate ego development: their relationship to reality therefore, is that of the psychotic. Their relationships are part-object relationships, driven by envious destructive phantasies arising from their failure to achieve the depressive position and the capacity for whole-object relationships.

In *Envy and Gratitude* Klein discusses female homosexuality in the context of her discussion of penis envy and its oral origin.[16] She specifies envy as the angry feeling that another person possesses something which is desirable, and the envious impulse is to destroy or spoil it. While she maintains that it is rooted in the earliest relation to the mother, the feeding breast, Klein praises Freud's 'discovery' of penis envy in women and his emphasis on the analysis of the girl's attitude to her mother as determining her subsequent relationships with men. Since, according to Klein, full oral gratification resulting from a satisfactory relation to the mother forms the basis for full genital (heterosexual) orgasm, envy interferes with this.

Three specific scenarios involving the 'female homosexual

attitude' emerge in Klein's account. In one, the father's penis becomes the target of envy originally experienced at the breast. This is a defensive move, an attempt to assuage the anxieties which would allow for the depressive position, whole-object relations, and subsequent reparation:

> Freud has shown how vital is the attitude of the girl to her
> mother in her subsequent relations to men. When envy of the
> mother's breast has been strongly transferred to the father's
> penis, the outcome may be a reinforcing of her homosexual
> attitude.[17]

In the second scenario, restitutive tendencies can also reinforce female homosexuality. In *The Psycho-Analysis of Children*, Klein claims that where the girl has focused her sadistic phantasies on the destruction of the mother by identifying with her father's dangerous penis, 'she will feel urged to restore her mother by means of a penis with healing powers and thus her homosexual trends will become reinforced'.[18]

In the third scenario, Klein claims that if envy of the mother's breast is not so strong, idealisation of the father's penis can offer women the possibility of combining envy of the mother with love for the father, and consequently for other men. Disappointment with the mother's breast, however, may lead to the search for a 'mother substitute'. She concludes that 'Friendship with women and homosexuality may then be based on the need to find a good object instead of the avoided primal object.'[19] She warns that expressions of good object relations in homosexual women are 'deceptive', and that 'the underlying envy toward the primal object is split off but remains operative and is liable to disturb any relations'.[20]

Klein's cure

Klein emphasises the necessity for the patient to 'co-operate' with the analyst, and to be determined 'to discover the truth about himself if he is to accept and assimilate the analyst's interpretations relating to these early layers of the mind'.[21] Every utterance of the patient is interpreted in terms of early pre-linguistic phantasies related to the breast. Her meta-psychology presents these interpretations as ahistorical 'psychic' facts. Lesbians in emotionally fulfilling relationships are thus in flight from the truth, the facts of the schisms in their psyches. Klein stresses the impossibility in every psyche of ever achieving complete and permanent integration: there are always residues of paranoid and schizoid feelings and mechanisms. This, however, does not imply that homosexuality is any the less pathological within her schema.

In her focus on the infant's early relationship with the mother's breast, Klein assumes the existence of an 'inner world' that lies outside language. Analysis of the patient's positive and negative transference in relation to the analyst revives these earliest object relations. Through the processes of projection and introjection the ego becomes strengthened, and this allows for the retention of a good inner object. The introjection of the analyst as a good object, not idealised, can provide a good inner object where one had earlier been lacking. Klein points out that a strong positive transference can be deceptive, since it is based on idealisation, which denies anxieties related to hate and envy. She found that patients often experience depression following recognition of an interpretation which heals splits in the self, but these depressive feelings involve relating to a whole object, and are thus a necessary step towards integration and cure.

In assuming the existence of an 'inner world' Klein ignores all twentieth-century advances in hermeneutic theory which 'systematically criticise divisions between thought and language, and spatial metaphors of 'inside' and 'outside' arising from that dualistic split.[22] Wittgenstein's critique of Freud's analysis of dreams[23] can be fruitfully related to Klein's arguments on 'early' psychotic positions which, as it were, 'remain' in the psyche and are triggered off by later adult experiences. This is an analysis of intentionality which relies on a later reaction caused in daily life by a later situation. The implication is that the later reaction not only points to the original desire or meaning but is a logically necessary and sufficient condition of the truth of the statement that the person originally desired or meant such a thing. In separating thought and language, Klein postulates an 'inner' world of mechanisms without language, but mysteriously available to 'knowledge'. This is in line with many essentialist, universalist, foundational theories.

Klein's genius was to have charted the desolate hinterland of psychosis; going beyond discrete conceptions of the life and death instinct, she explores the somatic/psychic territory of anxieties, persecution, splitting, loss, disintegration, phantasy. By thematising psychotic states or 'positions' she developed psychoanalytic technique in such a way that it has seriously challenged psychiatry's pretension to total 'expertise' in this area; she also challenges the primacy of pharmacological treatments of psychosis.[24] The paradox of such psychoanalytic theorising is that while it claims to be attentive to the individuality of each person's speaking, it simultaneously vitiates singularity. This is operative in Klein's *a priori* refusal to consider that two men or two women in sexual relationships can have happy, fulfilled lives and, furthermore, may be happier than many of those struggling in apparently 'successful' heterosexual relationships.

In subsequent chapters we shall discuss the developments in Kleinian theories further, and analyse their implications for their claims regarding reality, knowledge, happiness and the 'normal' human being.

5

Spoiling
the Perverse
Gratification:
Narcissism and Metapsychology

W E NOW FOCUS on recent psychoanalytic texts which analyse lesbians and homosexuals in terms of symptoms of a more serious psychic disturbance such as, for example, psychosis. Such texts present the aetiology of homosexualities in terms of perverse developmental schemata. Our strategy is to allow the texts to speak for themselves in order to elucidate their psychoanalytic and psychotherapeutic assumptions and conclusions regarding lesbians. This will illustrate the intertwining of what they term 'clinical' evidence with the universalist claims of their metapsychology. Many of these texts – published in the past twenty years, or even the past three – are used in training psychoanalysts and psychotherapists. Their stark conservatism stands out against contemporary developments in philosophy, and in cultural, social and political theory. These latter disciplines fruitfully influence one another and advance our appreciation of the limitations of imperialistic knowledge-claims as well as our respect for the complexity and ambiguity of our 'identities'.

Khan and Limentani

In his paper on 'Female Homosexuality', Masud Khan sees himself as continuing the work begun by Deutsch. Female homosexuality is perverse, he argues, because it is the expression of a:

> false situation, where the secondary gains have become too
> rigidly integrated into the superstructure of personality and
> its modes of dealing with anxieties and instinctual conflicts.[1]

This 'false situation' arises in the adult woman because of unresolved pre-oedipal conflicts. For Khan these conflicts originate in the perversity of the early mother–baby relationship. Latent and hypochondriacal depression in the mother predispose the child to perversion.

Consequently, the child's anxieties are unconsciously centred on the need to remain identified with the mother's body, with the fear of separating from her. Such identification acts as a defence, unconsciously relieving anxiety, depression and paranoid feelings. Khan quotes Deutsch:

> The decision in favour of the mother as the attracting magnet
> lies naturally in the old powers of attraction, but also in the
> repelling forces of other magnets – denials, anxiety and guilt
> reactions.[2]

Thus, in Khan's view, female homosexuals' experiences of satisfactory relationships result from the mobilisation of infantile satisfactions as a defence against the anxieties of loss, abandonment, anger, and guilt at separating from the mother. Because such satisfactions are, for Khan, a defence, they function as a 'false', a 'secondary' satisfaction or gain which must be abandoned in order to release the unconscious conflicts, which can then be analysed and allow for normal maturation and the 'primary' satisfaction of heterosexuality. Khan's quotation from Deutsch expresses his own starting point for analysing female homosexuality: 'Every individual act of homosexual love expresses a non fulfilled heterosexual hope.'[3]

Khan argues from his own clinical work that there is confusion in the inner world of the female homosexual between the defence mechanisms of isolation and those of splitting. Confusion, he claims, drives her to seek instinctual gratification with another woman in order to share her confused state – put it 'outside' her (in her partner) and then reabsorb it into her adult ego.[4] Khan interprets homosexual intimacies as an attempt to undo the split between the body and affective (ego) experiences resulting from the disturbed primitive relation to the mother.

For Khan, the female homosexual has 'exaggerated penis-envy', a masculinity complex that is a defence against what he terms a 'deeper sense of genital inadequacy'.[5] He argues that the female homosexual may have had preconscious vaginal sensations which intensified her penis envy: he accepts unquestioningly the psychoanalytic doctrine of the centrality of penis envy for female identity. He argues that because of her distorted body-image, the female homosexual is driven to seek symbiosis with another woman. This initiates what he calls the 'perverse practices' involving the erotic cathexis of mouth, anus, tongue or vagina. He stresses the significance of the tongue and its identification with the penis in the aetiology of female homosexuality, adding that this 'tongue–penis equation also made restitution to her self body image'.[6]

According to Khan, the task of analysis with female homosexuals is to uncover and analyse repressed instinctual needs. He points to the importance of the analyst's vigilance towards patients' defensive relations to the mother, which emerge as either masochistic submissiveness or affective deadness. Ironically, like other analysts whom he cites, he offers admonitions regarding the importance of listening to the patient:

> We have to start, as Freud did, in 1895, by giving a true
> phenomenological account of our clinical encounter with our
> patients, without paralysing the ambiguities of the therapeutic
> exchange by coercing them into the strait-jacket of our
> metapsychological preconceptions.[7]

Adam Limentani's work on homosexuality derives from his clinical work at the Portman Clinic, London. Although he talks of 'clinical' types of homosexuality, his arguments and claims refer to homosexual relationships generally, and he specifies homosexuality as a perversion. He argues that homosexuality is a syndrome and, as such, is not an adjustive process – rather it is a problem in itself. Limentani has 'found' that homosexuality may be the cause of alcoholism and drug addiction, in that hysterical and obsessional personalities are commonly homosexual. He stresses the complexity of homosexual aetiology which can best be understood, he claims, by using psychiatric as well as psychoanalytic models.[8]

Limentani describes homosexuality as repressed, sublimated, fantasied or manifest. He specifies that there are three groups: in the first group, homosexuality is linked with a flight from the opposite sex, which is perceived as dangerous and threatening. In the second group, homosexuality functions as a defence mechanism 'aimed at warding off overwhelming separation and psychotic anxieties, a dread of mutilation and even 'disintegration'.[9] The third group includes those 'truly bisexual individuals' where there is a 'severe dissociation' between male and female parts of the personality in which projections, splitting processes and multiple identifications are dominant. Although he stresses the complexity of the homosexual syndrome, Limentani claims that immaturity and narcissism are common personality features, as are denial and projection of emotional difficulties.

Limentani's female homosexuals are characterised by severe mother dependency, a turning from the father, in order to resolve oedipal feelings:

> It is particularly in the true lesbians that the mother–child
> relationship is sought and re-enacted between partners.
> There is here a very special type of mother fixation where
> there has been too little gratification combined with intense
> hatred, leading to over-emphasis of love for the object, and
> aimed at neutralizing guilt feelings. The hatred of mother is
> replaced by love of women, just as too much love or hatred

for father will drive the lesbian to seek consolation with her own sex.[10]

In his quest for psychoanalytic knowledge and truth, Limentani warns of the dangers for homosexuals of manic defences against depression which can, he stresses, result in a denial of reality and the creation of a mistaken group morality.[11] The task of the analyst, he maintains, is to guide the patient towards knowing the truth about himself and his 'inner world'. Limentani's analysis of lesbianism claims to know its truth in such a way that lesbians themselves, while remaining lesbian, can never know truth or 'reality' because, in his terms, they are locked into defensive denial.

Hanna Segal: lesbianism as an attack —— on the parental couple ——

Hanna Segal, who was analysed by Klein and is a training analyst of the British Institute of Psycho-Analysis, is one of the most prominent psychoanalysts in Britain today. In an interview with Jacqueline Rose (1990) she states:

> the price of normality is overcoming omnipotence and it is a heavy price to pay . . . I think that reality sense means being in a state of mind where you know yourself and you don't project so that you can assess reality . . .[12]

She goes on to say that she does not consider the giving up of 'polymorphous sexuality' a heavy price to pay, since 'the rewards are so much greater and . . . because the perversion in fact exacts a much higher price'.

Segal specifies homosexuality in terms of part-object relations of the paranoid-schizoid position. Although she expresses uncertainty as to whether or not she would call homosexuality a perversion, she nevertheless concludes that

'. . . all homosexuals that I have analyzed did have a perverse personality structure'.[13]

Segal shares with Khan and Limentani the view of female homosexuality as a denial, and a failure to think properly and know 'reality'. She conceives of thinking as that which puts 'a limit on the omnipotence of phantasy'.[14] In her view lesbians are caught in a phantasy, in a necessarily narcissistic condition: 'as the name itself betrays. Loving homo – the same as me not hetero – the other, different'.[15] She maintains that narcissism is dominated by projective identification and envy. She asserts the 'reality' of the basic 'truth' of the Oedipus complex as recognising the hate, jealousy and envy of the parents; 'the couple as a creative relationship because that is what produces the baby'.[16]

Segal holds that the lesbian is caught in the phantasy of envious attack on the heterosexual couple:

> I think that there is some reality sense and some innate idea
> about the parental couple and creative sexuality which is
> attacked by homosexuality.[17]

'Creative sexuality' as she conceives it is particularly attacked by lesbian parents:

> Two lesbians adopting a baby . . . what the hell is going to
> happen to this boy when he reaches adolescence?[18]

Does Segal, with her penchant for epistemological and ethical reflections, wonder what the intellectual and social limitations of her theory will do to this little boy?

Segal grasps a metapsychological nettle entitled 'Psychoanalysis and Freedom of Thought':

> Psychoanalysis belongs to the great scientific tradition of
> freeing thought from dogma, whether religious or arising out
> of an established scientific tradition itself.[19]

She asserts the emancipatory character of psychoanalytic 'freedom of thought' as that which necessitates the move from the narcissistic omnipotence of phantasy to the knowledge of our own thoughts. Since, for Segal, lesbians remain and relate in a state of narcissistic omnipotent phantasy, they cannot 'know' their own thoughts. Central to her bizarre theory of knowledge is the unquestioned link between her notion of the normal – that is heterosexuality – and 'reality'. Her conclusion is that the failure to 'achieve' heterosexuality is, as such, the failure to 'know' 'reality'.

Harry Guntrip echoes Segal's linking of perversion and reality:

> Prostitution and homosexuality are clear cases of schizoid compromise in their evasion of the full commitment to the real relationship of marriage.[20]

Ismond Rosen, a Member of the British Institute of Psychoanalysis, offers a general psychoanalytic theory of perversion. Specifying homosexuality as a perversion, he quotes Michael Balint (1965), who writes of the 'pretense and denial' involved in homosexuality, the denial of 'what they all know – that, without normal intercourse, there is no real contentment'.[21] In Rosen's view, homosexuals do not have sufficient ego strength to enable them to achieve the regression necessary for heterosexual intercourse; he argues that such intercourse is felt to be a psychotic threat to the homosexual's inadequate ego.

Clear metapsychology —— and polymorphous perversity ——

Donald Meltzer explicitly sets his analysis of homosexuality in the context of developing metapsychological theory:

> A term like 'homosexual' can now be given a clear metapsychological significance, if desired, to distinguish it from the manifestations of infantile bisexuality, although there is much to be said in favour of throwing it out . . . in favour of a more definitive elucidation of the terms *polymorphous* and *perverse*.[22]

Meltzer claims that Klein's concept of projective identification provides for more extensive understanding of destructive forces, especially those of envy. Following Klein, he holds that envy creates psychic states of confusion between good and bad. He argues that this differentiation of good and bad is applied to sexual life:

> Internal and external, narcissistic and object-related, part- and
> whole-object, at all levels of the mental life, we can establish
> the terms *polymorphous* and *perverse* as having definitive
> reference to good and bad sexuality respectively.[23]

He also argues that there is no one single cause of adult homosexuality. Rather, it can emerge from the variations which he specifies in perversions and polymorphism. For Meltzer, perversions can be either expressions of narcissism or defences against depression; polymorphism can be expressed as inhibitions or immaturities such as the retention of infantile zonal confusions or inadequate genital responsiveness. By contrast with the homosexual, the 'mature' heterosexual has been able to achieve an introjective identification with the internalised coital parents in both masculine and feminine roles.

For Meltzer, the sexual relations of homosexuals remain stuck at the level of 'foreplay', infantile and/or perverse. He contrasts this with heterosexual intercourse:

> The definitive act of coition is serious . . . It is work, not play,
> and has a sense of urgent and immediate relation to the
> stresses of the day, week, era, as the introjective identification,
> with its cosmic scope, takes hold of the mind–body.[24]

Like many other writers, Meltzer makes a special plea for the status of his text – that it can have little significance for, or be properly understood by, anyone who has not experienced the analytic process as a patient, an analysand. His terminology derives from the technicalities of Kleinian analysis: splitting, internal and external objects, part- and whole objects, projective identification. He emphasises:

> Nothing could be more dangerous to the development [of psychoanalytic work] than a split between the 'doing' and the 'talking', between the practitioner and the theorist.[25]

Meltzer claims to avoid such 'splitting' by using language to hold together parts of the personality which tend to recede from one another. In other words, he conceives of language as a tool which labels already-assumed existing processes or mechanisms. He aims to uncover what he calls 'the structure of the mind' which produces the analytic process.[26] However, Meltzer produces a circular argument whereby he 'discovers' the 'structure of the mind' by means of the analytic process, which is, in turn, produced by the 'mind'. The concepts of transference and countertransference are central to his account of the psychoanalytic process, and he interprets these concepts as mechanisms which link what he assumes to be infantile experiences in the 'minds' of analyst and analysand.

The analyst's expertise consists in enabling the patient to verbalise rather than act out his feelings and desires. Analytic interpretations emerge from the analyst's ability to hold the infantile features of the patient's mind, and to constitute them objectively by speaking about them. This is a 'search for the truth about the patient's mind',[27] which is claimed to be a scientific enterprise. Yet despite his scientific pretensions, Meltzer, along with other psychoanalysts cited in this book, does not offer any critique of his self-referential terms, or of his circular argument based on what he claims to be the *tabula rasa* of his own 'mind' in clinical observation and practice. Meltzer's characterisation of lesbians and gay men as polymorphously perverse, infantile and immature derives from the circularity of his metapsychological research. He 'discovers' that all lesbian and gay sexuality is immature, because he interprets and assumes it to be so.

Classification of homosexuality in terms of perversion is not confined to British analysts. Charles Socarides, an American analyst, is acknowledged by Adam Limentani, Joyce McDougall and others to be a leading expert on homosexuality. Socarides defines his task as elucidating a structural theory of homosexuality, examining therapeutic problems in treating homosexuals, and analysing the connection between sexual instinct and object choice:

> From the outset, therefore, homosexuality was considered to be a recognized form of perversion along with fetishism, voyeurism, paedophilia, transvestism, and so on.[28]

Homosexuality, he argues, is perverse because one component of infantile sexuality replaces genital sexuality:

> Perverse acts are distorted exaggeration and have a quality of uniqueness and stereotypy which does not appear in normal persons, except as introductory activities prior to intercourse.[29]

Socarides provides an aetiology of homosexuality. He argues that in the pre-oedipal type, failure to negotiate separation-individuation from the mother successfully leads to a 'deficient' and 'distorted' sexual identity. For Socarides, the pre-oedipal stage for the girl is dominated by fear of both parents; she feels rejected by her father because she is female, and by her mother, who is felt to be both hateful and hated, because she too is female. Problems of gender identity arise when the girl persists in identifying with the hated mother from whom she cannot separate because she has not had enough love. Separation, in so far as it does occur, happens when the infant girl identifies with father whom mother is felt to love. Socarides claims that a masculine identification becomes superimposed on the hated earlier feminine identification. This masculine identification arises in order to 'secure' the good mother which, in adult life, is the homosexual partner.

Socarides quotes Freud to support his view that in homosexuals pregenital, archaic and primitive characteristics predominate in the ego. His evidence for this is his experience of homosexual patients who replace remembering with acting out. He insists that homosexuals are driven to sexual acts as a way of reconstructing a sexual identity: 'The female achieves "resonance" identification and anxiety relief, but she also creates the "good" mother–child relationship.'[30] He outlines the oedipal causes of homosexuality: failure to resolve oedipal conflicts; castration fears leading to a regression to oral and anal conflicts. He claims that female homosexuals take the role of the male in relation to the mother and to other women, substituting oral for genital acts. Homosexuality resulting from oedipal conflict is, he argues, more flexible (i.e. heterosexual acts can be performed), in contrast to the fixed, driven character of homosexuality arising from pre-oedipal conflict.

Socarides is insistent that homosexuals require treatment – whether analytic or behavioural. Of the forty-four overt homosexuals he has analysed, two-thirds were, he claims, of the pre-oedipal type, and one third of the oedipal. Fifty per cent were 'cured' – that is, they developed full heterosexual functioning. Three lesbians were 'cured'. Despite his evident pride in such 'success', Socarides does admit that there can be problems in analysing homosexuals because:

> Homosexuals bear and carry with them characteristics that
> are present in most individuals who suffer from impulse
> neuroses; addiction, delinquency and narcissistic personality
> disorders. Because of their pathological narcissism, they seem
> unable to maintain a continuity of analysable transference
> relationships . . . they often suffer from poor object relation-
> ships and/or lack of object constancy.[31]

Socarides does not allow that a homosexual leaving analysis with him may be expressing a healthy desire not to be confined and reduced to naive, generalising interpretations. He presents an unquestioned *a priori* position masquerading under the guise of clinical evidence. Cross-references to the work of other analysts abound in his work as validation of his position – for example, Edward Glover's classification of 'improvements' arising from his survey on success rates in the treatment of homosexuality carried out at the Portman Clinic, London, in 1953;[32] as well as Michael Balint, Herbert Rosenfeld, and others. Despite the American Psychiatric

Association's deletion of homosexuality from its list of classifi-
able pathological illnesses, Socarides, psychiatrist and psychoanalyst, persists in classifying homosexuality in both men and
women as an illness. Analysts who share his view frequently
refer to each other's published work with homosexual men
and women as a way of endorsing and 'scientifically verifying'
their discoveries of pathology. Socarides sees himself as the
guardian of the truth of homosexuality as pathology, and
warns against viewing it as having a biological origin or being
a matter of sexual preference. He is emphatically against any
attempts to view homosexuality as in any way an acceptable
sexuality.

Elaine Siegal, another American analyst, shares a platform
with Socarides.[33] She argues that early psychosomatic confusions, split-off anxieties in relation to the breast, the mother,
cause the girl to sexually desire a body the 'same' as her own.
This narcissistic object choice is an operative denial of difference, of otherness. This is to claim that the imperialism of the
'same', lesbianism, is an attempt on the woman's part to repair
a defective body-image by searching for someone like herself. According to Siegal, in lesbians there is a failure of inner
representation of the vagina:

> A woman whose body is her own, that is who has success-
> fully integrated her sexual organ and her sexual self within
> her total inner self representation, is able to meet a potential
> male partner without either resenting him or competing with
> his maleness.[34]

Siegal maintains that for lesbians, when schematisations of the
body were 'laid down' in the psyche, the vagina, 'inner space',
was not included. This failure, she claims, is proved by her
findings that her lesbian patients feared penetration. Although
fingers and other devices were used in homosexual 'loveplay',
they were experienced masochistically: 'Penetration, when it
did occur, aroused murderous fantasies which were then
secondarily sexualized and elaborated.'[35] Siegal's 'objective'
clinical interpretations of lesbians have the same status as

interpretations of male homosexuality: homosexual men are expressing a need to find a penis because of their failure to 'identify' with their own.

Early in her book *Female Homosexuality: Choice Without Volition*, Siegal stresses the difficulty for female homosexuals of establishing the transference because of their tendency to 'act out'. She argues that in the transference, when it does occur, the analyst is seen as the ideal mother. There are hypochondriacal preoccupations in the analysand – her attempt at healing her distorted body – and body-image distortions are projected on to the analyst. In Siegal's counter-transference she found that her patients' oral-aggressive phantasies evoked slight nausea and unease in her. She says that her patients produced these symptoms in her because of the combination of hurt and rage in them.[36]

Because female homosexuals cannot, initially, imagine a 'good-enough' mother, they attempt, in Siegal's view, to heal themselves with homosexual lovers. But, she asserts:

Theirs was always a narcissistic object choice that was doomed to failure because in refinding themselves, they also refound the death-dispensing, coercive, preoedipal mother. To deal with this to them catastrophic event, they denied that such internal happenings could exist.[37]

Siegal's position is that of a naive biologism linked to rigidity of gender identity and sexual identity. She uses the trappings of psychoanalytic interpretations to support her view of the truth – we know what women are, we know what men are, and each can be truly 'itself' only in procreative activity with the other.

We might summarise the various perspectives of these analysts as follows: lesbianism is the result of a distorted body-image which drives the woman towards symbiosis with another woman; it is narcissistic, and cannot tolerate that which is other or different; it results from infantile zonal confusions; lesbian sexuality is not genital but confined to foreplay; lesbianism is oral-sadistic; lesbians have a confused gender identity and identify with their fathers; lesbian sexuality is a defence against psychosis.

Is it possible that these analysts have identified lesbianism with borderline psychosis on the basis of women presenting to them who are experiencing painful borderline states, including their phantasies of lesbian relationships – which concur with psychoanalytic phantasies of such relationships? François Roustang describes somebody experiencing such a state:

> Her sexual life, as a radical expression of what constitutes her perceptual world, is going adrift and can become anything whatsoever and for any reason whatsoever, without consequence or consistency. She goes off with anyone to make love with him or her . . . but none of this has any significance for her, she is absent from it all, having neither a self nor a personal history.[38]

Or is it that lesbians are *a priori* defined as borderline psychotic because they challenge stereotypical psychoanalytic identifications of gender and sexuality?

Clinical complexity

In our analytic work with lesbians we have not, as we stress throughout, concluded that there is a universal aetiology, or character structure, or psychology, of 'the' lesbian.

B. came to therapy because she wanted close friends; each time she got close to someone, either as a friend or a sexual partner, she would become terrified. Her father died when she was one, and her mother, who remarried, was depressed for many years and was treated with Largactil, a major tranquilliser. She had an older brother who cared for her and tried to protect her from attacks by her stepfather. B. said she wanted lesbian relationships; she had phantasies of 'perfect merging' with a woman; there, she felt, she would be safe, and the fear would leave her. She had relationships with men in which she felt intense sexual excitement and total dependency, and she regressed in order to be spoon-fed by them.

B. initially experienced very positive transferences to the therapist – this was expressed as feeling both fed and held, and 'in love' with her. Gradually her dreams became cauldrons of broken bodies, mutilations and relentless terror. This coincided with a sexualising of the transference coupled with increased paranoid feelings. The paranoid feelings extended to work colleagues and neighbours, but decreased in relation to the therapist. B.'s recurrent phantasy of maintaining her 'lesbian self' served to protect her from breakdown. Through years of therapy she came to integrate the repressed pain and anguish of her life, loss of her father and her mother's psychosis. The sexualising of her pain-filled, bodily existence decreased to the point where she could tolerate friendships, but she expressed herself as not ready for an intimate sexual relationship.

B.'s phantasy of herself as lesbian is similar to cited psychoanalytic interpretations of lesbianism; the crucial point, however, is that both B. and these analysts are describing a phantasy of lesbianism as it can arise in borderline states. It is on the basis of this phantasy that some psychoanalytic writers establish their pathological theories of lesbianism as such.

M. presented for therapy because she was frightened; she was experiencing panic attacks and constantly crying because of her father's death. She was thirty-two years old, French, a widow with three children. Her father had died two years previously; her husband five years previously. She said that as a child she had had a close relationship with her mother, but she felt closer to her father as she grew up, married and had children. M. spoke longingly of her husband, who had died suddenly but had been suffering from heart disease. Since her husband's death she had developed a successful public career; previously she had worked in the home. M. felt guilty that her grief was affecting her children, and could not understand why she was unable to get on with her life. It emerged that she felt in an acute state of conflict between her feeling of freedom after her husband's death, her professional ambitions, and her grief over the loss of his love. She described her marriage as very happy.

In the course of therapy, M.'s panic attacks stopped and she spent a long time exploring how she had transferred her feelings towards her father on to her husband. Identifications with the therapist emerged as allowing her permission to accept promotion in her work, since in M.'s view the therapist had a successful career, a husband and a family. Gradually M.'s friendship with a woman friend developed into a sexual relationship. She struggled greatly in the transference with what she perceived to be the therapist's negative or pathologising view of lesbianism. She wondered how the therapist could accept that she, M., could be happy in her new partnership with a woman.

M. began to realise that she could acknowledge her past love for her husband, and be a woman different to both her mother and her therapist. In her final session she said, 'Even though it's been painful admitting to myself and to you that I am happier with J. [her lover] than I have ever been with anyone, I think that as a therapist you probably had the sensitivity to recognise that women can happily love women.'

M. had had relationships with men since her husband's death, and liked them; she did not reject men or 'fly' from them; her struggle was to accept her loving and sexual feelings for J. M. came to lose her panic at experiencing herself as strong and independent – she found that she could be both independent and yet loved and loving, which, she reflected in retrospect, had not been the case in her marriage. There, she now felt, her loving and being loved had depended on her compliance with well-defined stereotypes of being a wife.

L. cried throughout her first therapy session that she did not know who she was, and was she mad? She was living with a man, and had two children. She said she had fallen in love with a woman friend who did not reciprocate her love. Her partner knew about it and was very hurt and angry with her, and repeatedly said to her: 'You have always enjoyed our sex together; how can you say you are in love with E., that she means more to you than I do? She can't give you what I can.' This expressed L.'s own confusion about her feelings for E. and for her partner, whom she had loved for many years; also her concern for her children and her future.

In the early stages of therapy L. expressed incredulity that the therapist could tolerate her being, as she constantly repeated, 'so confused'. She felt that she was hateful – neither desirable to the woman she longed for nor desiring the man she had loved for many years. She felt that she had failed both of them, was not a proper mother, and deserved to die. L. came to accept that the therapist tolerated her with all her confused longings and pain; this allowed her to remember her first love affair with a girl, when she was sixteen. In this relationship L. felt both joy and helplessness – joy at discovering the pleasure of sexual intimacy, yet frightening feelings of dependency on her friend. She felt trapped in a symbiotic relationship, unable to live without her lover but full of painful shadows that obscured the light. However, neither L. nor her friend thought that their relationship was a real-life possibility; their futures would be as wives and mothers.

L. began to enjoy relationships with boys, then with men, and initially she felt very happy with her partner. Gradually he became more and more dependent on her, just as she had felt with her first lover. L. felt suffocated in the relationship, yet stuck. Painful, self-hateful and abandoned feelings emerged for her in her relationship to the therapist. In the course of these transferences L. experienced desolate abandonment by the therapist. She eventually became angry and came to realise that her mother had been symbiotic in relationship to her, and had expressed both love and hatred of her daughter throughout her childhood and adolescence. Hatred and anger were particularly directed at L.'s attempts to separate from her mother. L.'s father was very warm and encouraging to her, and supportive of her independence, yet weak in many ways, failing in business and not strong enough in protecting L. from her mother's narcissistic demands. L. had been protective of her two younger brothers in the way that she had wished her father could have protected her.

Recognising and integrating the painful ambivalence of her earlier relationship – especially to her mother, but also to her father – in the therapy enabled L. to separate from her symbiotic relationship with her partner, and also from the unrequited longing for such a relationship with her woman friend. She began to feel good about herself; she left the business which she ran with her partner and went to college to study art, which she had always felt she wanted to do. She fell in love with a woman who reciprocated her love, and embarked on a healthy partnership which facilitated the growth of both women, and their children.

In this brief case study we can again see that lesbianism does not always involve a flight from men and, most importantly, that a symbiotic mother–daughter relationship can give rise to symbiotic relationships with other women, but does not determine lesbianism as necessarily symbiotic.

In describing therapeutic work with these three women we are not attempting to establish pseudo-scientific evidence to counter psychoanalytic identifications of lesbianism and perversion empirically. Rather, these examples serve to highlight the complex situations of women we have worked with over many years. Our aim is to preserve such complexity without reducing it to 'known pathology', and to hold open the ambiguity of women's sexual relationships.

6

'Truth' and 'Reality':
McDougall and Gender Identity

J OYCE MCDOUGALL'S WRITING on female homosexuality constitutes part of her interest in various forms
of perversion, in psychosomatic disorders, and in other
phenomena, all of which she sees as neither neurotic nor
psychotic. Her theorisation of homosexuality is complex,
dense and many-levelled, and draws on various sources as
well as her own richly described clinical material. Her detailed
consideration of female homosexuality, especially in 'The
Homosexual Dilemma' (McDougall, 1979),[1] and her standing
in the analytic community generally, make it particularly
important for us to examine her work in both its theoretical
and clinical aspects.

A universal theory?

The first thing we notice about 'The Homosexual Dilemma'
is that it is in a textbook entitled *Sexual Deviation*, alongside chapters on male homosexuality and on phenomena
such as fetishism, voyeurism and transvestism. Whatever
the refinements of McDougall's position in relation to the
status of homosexuality, the message this context conveys is

uncompromising. We might also wonder about the title of her chapter, in particular the confident use of 'the'. This usage recurs throughout – for example '*the* homosexual relationship' (p. 207) – and in her other writings – '*the* homosexual response' (McDougall, 1989a, p. 206; emphasis added).[2] In some places (McDougall, 1986a)[3] she advocates the use of the term homo-sexualities as well as heterosexualities, but this is not a recom-mendation she follows in the main body of her work. Instead she puts forward what purports to be a universal theory of female homosexuality, and this enterprise rests on the gener-alisations she feels she can make on the basis of her clinical work with five homosexual patients. There is no discussion of the appropriateness of this method, or of the status of homo-sexuality as a phenomenon that merits grouping people together in this way. There is no acknowledgement of the exis-tence of non-clinical populations of homosexuals – a relevant consideration if the aim is the development of a universal the-ory. Nor is there any tentativeness about generalising on the basis of such a small sample. Instead we have the confident assertion of extraordinary resemblance:

> In spite of their individual differences, these women showed striking similarities in their ego-structure and in their oedipal background. Their violence was particularly evident . . .
> Equally striking was the fragility of their sense of identity as expressed in periods of depersonalisation, bizarre bodily states, and so on.[4]

Furthermore:

> In homosexual men and women, we find a family romance of a specific kind . . . My female homosexual patients might all have been of the same family, so much did the parental portraits resemble one another.[5]

There is a problematic mixture here of psychoanalytic and natural science principles. The method employed is that of grouping together apparently similar phenomena (homosexual patients) and trying, on the basis of further observa-tion and investigation (the psychoanalytic treatment process), to find further resemblances (ego structure and family background), and then to use these to explain the original phenomenon (homosexuality). The model appears to be that of the inductive sciences, such as zoology, with its classificatory basis. However, the parallel is not really valid, even supposing the enterprise made sense. No account is taken of the method of selecting the objects of investigation. Psychoanalytic treatment does not (nor should it) resemble scientific observation, and the conditions for reduplication do not exist. Furthermore, there are no comparison groups of any kind. If such a natural scientific enterprise were seriously engaged in, then much larger numbers would have to be used, with particular attention to methods of selection, otherwise it is just pseudo-science.

Where this has been attempted, as in the many studies of male homosexuality, there are still huge difficulties in methodology and also massively inconclusive results. Richard Friedman (1988),[6] in his extensive review of the attempts to ascertain common personality characteristics and family backgrounds for male homosexuals, concludes that no such commonalities have been established, that homosexuality coexists with all kinds of character structure and personality, all degrees of pathology, and is connected with no clearly distinctive pattern of family dynamics. Studies which appear to show one characteristic are contradicted by others, and in many cases the methodology is flawed. There are many fewer studies of female homosexuality, but attempts to discern either physical or mental characteristics in common have also been inconclusive. None of these issues, however, is addressed by McDougall in her grouping together and generalising from five patients.

Why do psychoanalysts attempt to group homosexuals together and find common characteristics at all, especially since it flies in the face of one of the hallmarks of psychoanalysis – namely, the claim to treat individuals as individuals rather than as members of a group, to respect individuality and difference? Why the concern to find supposedly typifying features amongst a group of homosexual patients rather than to record and understand their diversity and difference? The attribution of sameness to a group of people, at the expense of individuality, is one hallmark of stereotyping ('They're all alike'). When we look at McDougall's theorising in this light, we might well wonder how convincing her assertions of similarity actually are: what do they rest on, and what differences are ignored? These issues will be addressed in more detail below, but as a preliminary some basic starting points of her investigation must be considered.

Real desire?

McDougall sees female homosexuality as an attempt to resolve conflict between identity as a separate individual (subjective identity) and sexual identity. She summarises her theory thus:

> The manifold desires and conflicts which face every girl with regard to her father have, in women who become homosexual, been dealt with by giving him up as an object of love and desire, and by identifying with him instead. The result is that the mother becomes once more the only object worthy of love. Thus the daughter acquires a somewhat fictitious *sexual identity*; however the unconscious identity with the father aids her in acquiring a stronger sense of *subjective identity*.[7]
> [original emphasis]

So McDougall's theory comprises a range of developmental issues: oedipal and pre-oedipal dynamics; questions of identity as well as questions of sexual desire. It contains both Horney's and Jones's emphases on identification with the father, and also Freud's and Deutsch's notion of return to love of the mother. Her understanding of why the young girl gives up the father as an object of love is much more elaborate than the older notions of fear of incest and disappointed desires, as we show below. However, there is a similar logic to that of

Horney and Jones in her claim that a lost love-object is replaced by identification with that object, although she does see the consequences of this, and the role of the mother, very differently. In particular, her claim that the resulting sexual identity is 'fictitious' marks a new step, and seems to imply that homosexual identities are inevitably imaginary, unreal or invented, in a way that heterosexual identities are not – that there is no possibility of a non-fictitious homosexual identity. McDougall subsequently asks: 'How is it possible to maintain the illusion of being the true sexual partner to another woman?', thus defining all experiences of desire between women as illusory. This is an astonishingly strong move, similar to the Kleinian claim that any experience of happiness in homosexual relationships is deceptive (see p. 81).

The underlying assumption here seems to be that real desire is possible only between a man and a woman, not between people of the same sex – which may well be a widely held but not explicit psychoanalytic assumption. In other writings McDougall does imply this, along with the claim that not to accept the 'truth' of this 'reality' is perverse, albeit a necessary defence against an unbearable realisation. In her wider writings on perversion,[8] she describes the pervert as denying that there is any significant difference between the sexes, and in particular that the difference is the cause or condition of sexual desire. This, she says, is a denial of a vast order, and includes the denial of the primal scene (sexual intercourse between the parents). It constitutes a disavowal or destruction of 'sexual truth'. The perverse solution to this unbearable knowledge about parental sexuality (which she carefully distinguishes from neurotic and psychotic responses) is contained in the 'mythical sexual act [which] permits some illusory recovery of the paternal phallus'.[9] The denied knowledge has been retrieved in the form of an illusion, and whilst she claims some specificity for homosexuality, McDougall also incorporates it in her general understanding of perversion.

McDougall takes it for granted that what she describes as 'sexual reality' and 'sexual truth' are incontestably just that – reality and truth. But how do we arrive at these judgements of what is reality, and what kinds of reality are meant? Our conceptualisations are not simple givens, but constructions. Psychic and material reality do not neatly or necessarily coincide, and the significance we give to aspects of material reality is a human creation – this applies to all pronouncements of what is reality. Here biological phenomena, the division of people into male and female, and the necessity for a male and female in some form to ensure conception and reproduction have been made into assertions about sexual reality – namely, that the genital differences between the sexes are the source of sexual desire. So strong is the conviction that real desire exists only between male and female that any claim otherwise has to be rendered as illusion or disavowal of the 'true' state of affairs. But another denial is involved here: McDougall's denial of the possibility of 'real' desire between two women or two men. Instead of this denial being seen and examined for what it is – a reliance on fundamentally bio-logistic conceptions of sexuality – it is projected into homosexuals themselves, and seen as their denial of what is supposedly 'reality'.

To point out these difficulties with notions of sexual reality and truth is not to dispute the clinical importance of the issues McDougall discusses, such as problems relating to the denial of the parental sexual relationship, failure to establish sufficient separate identity from the mother, difficulties with gender identity. These clinical issues recur again and again, with heterosexual as well as homosexual patients, but they do not in themselves mean that no 'real' desire is possible in homosexual relationships.

This discussion also raises the question of what is meant by 'real' desire. How is this different from illusory desire? What does being a 'true' sexual partner to someone else, of whatever gender, mean? McDougall describes homosexual desire as illusory, not because of any supposed feature of the desire itself, such as falsity, pretence or superficiality, nor even because the partner might be an object of fantasy. Instead the desire is seen as illusory because the position from which the desiring is supposedly done, that of unconscious identification with the father, is held to be fictitious. It is the supposed nature of such identification that is held to determine and structure the desire itself.

The father

One distinguishing feature of McDougall's account of female homosexuality is her concern with aetiology. In pursuit of this, as we have seen, she tries to find recurring patterns in family structure, and also in the images of their parents that patients present. This concern with aetiology is not, on the whole, to be found in the earlier psychoanalytic writers we have considered; it represents a further step in the attempt to delineate patterns of abnormality in relation to homosexuality – a step that reflects the adoption of psychiatric and medical methods of understanding, combined with psychoanalytic ones. It is therefore important that we address McDougall's aetiological claims inasmuch as these are based on the clinical material at her disposal, and compare them with other sources.

In the image of the father presented by McDougall's lesbian patients, there is no expression of desire or love for him:

> If not totally absent from the analytic discourse, he is despised, detested, or denigrated in other ways. Intense preoccupation with the noises he makes, his brutality, insensitivity, lack of refinement, and so on, all contribute to giving an anal-sadistic colouring to the portrait. Furthermore, his phallic-genital qualities are contested, since he is often presented as ineffectual and impotent; there is no feeling of a strong loving father nor of a man whose character might be considered as essentially virile.[10]

Instead, physical closeness to the father arouses fear and disgust, and an intense repudiation of him has taken place. McDougall maintains that regression and repression have been used to deal with any sexual interest the father might have aroused. Castrated, he is not desirable as a love-object, but the underlying image is of someone strong, dangerous and disgusting.

This picture of the father is derived from what the patients say about their fathers, and from the absence that McDougall notes, in the early stages of analysis, of any reference to the father's genital sexuality. The difficulty here – and it is also a general one – is to know how specific such descriptions are to lesbian patients, or how universal they are amongst lesbians. In our clinical practices we have heard comparable descriptions from heterosexual patients, and very different ones from lesbian patients, as well as some similar ones – for example:

'I have only contempt for my father; he was always telling lies and playing mean tricks, to disguise his pathetic inadequacies. And he was repulsive to look at, especially his nose and his hair. He really played very little part in our family life.' (Heterosexual woman)

'I was absolutely terrified of my father – I used to watch him beating my brother and sister and knowing I'd be next. Then he would crawl to us to ask our forgiveness like a disgusting slug, slobbering all over us. I used to desperately try to find something that I could admire about him.' (Heterosexual woman)

'All the best times were with my father. He was great at keeping me amused, and I felt he was really fond of me and proud of me. When I was a teenager, we were especially close, he helped me with all my school-work, and I missed him most of all when I left home.' (Lesbian)

'My father hardly existed for me when I was little, even though he was actually there most of the time. He was quite kind in a distant sort of way but I really thought he was irrelevant and also pretty incompetent at most of the things that seemed to matter. He was very shy and embarrassed about anything to do with bodies and I don't remember him ever doing anything physical with me, not even helping me get dressed. He never came swimming with me.' (Lesbian)

Whilst such descriptions are necessarily partial and incomplete, and mainly concern conscious material, they are equivalent to the kinds of descriptions McDougall uses to establish her paternal portrait. They underline how the specificity and uniformity that she claims for her paternal image is achieved only at the cost of ignoring significant diversity.

McDougall presents us with a composite picture drawn from what her five patients say; as a result, the differences between their pictures are ignored. But the composite may well be misleading. Those who are detested may be significantly different from those who are despised, and again different from those who are ignored or not mentioned, but all these aspects are rolled into one picture. Even allowing for the very real possibility that one aspect may be a defence against another, important differences may be lost between those fathers who are held in contempt, for example, and those who are terrifying.

It might also be argued that what McDougall is describing about the fathers of her homosexual patients is a widespread, though by no means universal, feature of fathers in our culture, particularly those with quite disturbed relationships with their daughters. Some of the descriptions in *Fathers: Reflections by Daughters*[11] resemble those that McDougall provides, as do those often given by sexually abused daughters. As McDougall says, the young girl has often had to find psychic defences 'to deal with the *unconscious problems of the father* regarding femininity,'[12] but this is hardly specific to lesbianism.

McDougall moves on from these descriptions to the unconscious identification with the father which she sees her patients as having constructed, in a part of her chapter that is particularly important, since this unsatisfactory identification is a cornerstone of her theory. No argument is provided to explain the movement from these descriptions of the father as an unsatisfactory love-object to the assertion of unconscious identification with him; instead, the underlying logic remains implicit as it does with Horney and Jones. The grounds for claiming an unconscious identification with the father are aspects of the patients' presentations and self-descriptions. One patient, whom McDougall describes as 'always dressed in stained jeans and vast thick sweaters', feels herself to be 'scruffy . . . like a grubby boy', and also 'dirty, clumsy and disgusting'.[13] In this, according to McDougall, she is applying the 'identical' terms to herself that she applies to her father, and this identity of terms is taken as grounds for her identification with him. Perusal of the text supplied, however, shows that the only identical term is 'disgusting', in reference to his noises and facial movements; the other terms do not appear at all. This patient also found her father frightening, and McDougall takes her wearing of a wristband, to give herself an appearance of strength and cruelty, as further evidence of her unconscious identification with him. A second patient's self-description as 'a piece of shit', and as not caring if she was smelly, is also adduced as evidence for unconscious identification with her father, although no attempt is made to link it to what she says about him. McDougall does, however, directly link the sadistic intentions this woman feels her father has towards her with her own violent fantasies of killing men. A third patient describes herself as having similarly misogynist views as her father, and as feeling uncomfortable, 'like a castrate', if she is wearing a dress rather than trousers. A similar point is also made about the first patient – that she feels ridiculous dressed up like a woman.

That is the extent of the argument for unconscious identification with the father; the remaining two patients are not mentioned in this connection, and we are given no indication why not – whether there is no relevant material from them, or they do not fit the perceived pattern. The grounds given for the supposition of unconscious identification are thus twofold: similarities in description of self and father, and certain aspects of clothing and appearance. The first, perhaps, is fairly usual evidence, but the amount of it provided by McDougall is not great, and especially in the second two cases the extent of the identity described is slender and difficult to evaluate. The question of what clothing, and attitudes to conventionally feminine clothing, mean psychically is more complex and controversial, and liable to subjective bias on the part of the analyst. What is striking here, however, is that dislike of dresses is seen as evidence for a masculine paternal identification, and there is no room for any more complex understanding of what clothes may represent, especially for those whose sexualities are not conventional (an issue we consider further in relation to questions of masculinity and femininity); nor, indeed, is there much room for cultural variations in fashion.

McDougall continues by describing how, behind the conscious wish to eliminate or denigrate the father, lie narcissistic wounds linked to the image of an indifferent father who has failed in his parental role of enforcing separation from the mother: 'The father has become lost as a love-object, and equally lost as a representative of security and strength, *which bars the way to future genital relations*'[14] (emphasis added). The mother's contribution to this destruction of the 'masculine' image of the father is considered subsequently. What is notable here is not only the conventional image of the father as the representative of security and strength (does none of these qualities ever come from the mother?), but also the exclusive equation of genital with heterosexual. Homosexual relationships, apparently, are not counted as genital. Here we have another strong but undiscussed foreclosure on the possibilities conceived of for homosexuality.

The effects of this assumed paternal identification upon the girl's ego structure are seen as profound: the renunciation of the father as a libidinal object is not like the heterosexual relinquishing of the male oedipal object. Instead, the identification, whilst it prevents further ego-dissolution, is extremely ambivalent, for the image is a mutilated and disagreeable one, and the ego is subjected to internal attacks from the superego for such identifications. This leads to impoverishment or paralysis of the ego's functioning – something which may lead to difficulty in work and creativity. This is a feature McDougall holds to be typical of many of her homosexual patients, but it could hardly be substantiated as a wider generalisation about lesbianism.

We would suggest that there are some individual lesbians to whom McDougall's description of unconscious identification with an unsatisfactory father does apply, but others to whom it does not. In the former instances, however, we would not see such an identification as necessarily fictive, nor would we see it as part of the explanation for someone's lesbianism. Rather, such difficulties as do arise would appear to stem from the unsatisfactory features of the father that are identified with, rather than the fact that it is the father *per se* – something which is confused in McDougall's account. The unsatisfactory nature of these identifications can contribute in different ways to the felt possibilities for sexual, and other, expression. Such an identification, when it becomes conscious in the therapeutic process, may be accompanied by all kinds of fearful and self-hating feelings; that is, depending on the perceived nature of the father, it may be experienced as an extremely unwelcome and disturbing identification, one which is inhibiting to the expression of sexual desire and the forming of satisfactory relationships. Just as the father's sexuality may have seemed repulsive, unwelcome and frustrated to the child, so to the adult her own sexual desires may seem unacceptable and damaging to others – an image of the self that may be massively reinforced by the cultural disapproval of lesbian sexuality. This in turn may effectively inhibit or diminish the possibilities for any more positive experiences to facilitate the evolution of a different self-perception, leaving such an adult with a very stuck and restricted experience of her own sexuality. Therapeutic progress – which, for the most part, McDougall does not discuss – can consist in the lessening of this unconscious identification with the feared and hated aspects of the father, and a consequent decrease in the degree of self-hatred surrounding the expression of lesbian desire.

The image of the mother

McDougall presents a picture of mothers who are idealised but not identified with:

> Invariably these mothers are described in idealized terms –
> beautiful, gifted, charming and so on. The mother is felt to be
> possessed of all the qualities which the daughter lacks . . .
> There is no conscious envy of the mother. Furthermore she
> emerges as the sole safeguard against the dangers of living,
> dangers coming from the father as well as the outside world.[15]

Identification with the mother is difficult – partly because of the idealisation which has to be maintained in order to repress hostile wishes, and partly because of the disavowal of the parents' sexual relationship. Behind this 'denial of sexual realities' are sadistic and frightening images of parental sexuality; thus there is no wish to identify with the mother's 'genital role'. McDougall sums up her patients' wishful fantasy as 'a desire for total elimination of the father and the creation of an exclusive and enduring mother–daughter relationship', in which the mother is maintained as a non-conflictful object. She then cites as evidence of this picture what two of her patients say about their mothers, but again we are left wondering about the other three.

Another 'unfailing regularity' which McDougall discerns is that of 'a rigidly-controlling mother wielding omnipotent power over the body of her child, meticulously preoccupied with order, health, and cleanliness'.[16] Such a mother left the child with a sense that her body, and indeed her whole physical self, was severely rejected, and McDougall notes her patients' violent rejection of their own bodies. Furthermore, all her patients 'unconsciously regarded themselves as an indispensable part or function of the mother',[17] with a consequent terror of becoming separate or independent: 'there can never be *two* women; to separate from the mother (or later substitutes) means to lose one's identity'.[18] McDougall again sees, as an additional result of this family constellation, an inability to work constructively, to make decisions, so great is the fear that independent activity is dangerous, with corresponding feelings of being an incomplete entity, ill-defined, incapable and vulnerable.

A large number of different characteristics are thus being

attributed to the mother, and the mother–daughter relationship, and seen as leading to and typical of homosexuality in women. But once again the clinical picture seems to us much more various and less specific to lesbianism than McDougall claims. We are aware, as the following vignettes illustrate, of partial aetiological pictures similar to those McDougall describes, and also of pictures which are substantially different.

In one case, the patient felt that her relationship with her mother was the only relationship she had throughout her childhood, despite the fact that she had three other siblings – an older sister and two younger brothers – and a father who seemingly did not have any markedly disturbing features. It was as if for her, only she and her mother existed, and she looked back at this time as one of utter security and simplicity – of, as she said, 'constant sunshine'. This encapsulating world was devastated for her by a serious accident her mother had when she was an adolescent, but she devoted herself to her mother's many physical needs, and felt that only she could keep her mother alive and cared for, and stave off her depression. She felt as if she lived inside her mother's injured and disabled body, and indeed developed many physical symptoms herself. Her ensuing conflict when she did eventually leave home and form friendships, and a sexual relationship with a woman, was enormous; she still felt that her life was really of any use only if it served her mother. She vacillated between a murderous hatred for the mother who kept her so tied and guilty, a continual need to keep constantly in touch with her, and a despairing longing for what she felt she had lost.

This patient's history does illustrate McDougall's descriptions of a symbiotic tie to the mother, who was extensively idealised, with a failure to recognise her as having any relationship with the father, and an extreme difficulty in developing any sense of separate identity. Whether the nature of her relationship with her mother could be said to explain or be the cause of her adult lesbian sexuality is a further question. She certainly did reproduce many of the features of her maternal relationship with her first woman lover, in particular the totally enclosed and enmeshed world, and the only solution to this symbiosis was a violent and sudden ending to the relationship. In therapy she expressed many desires to adhere to the therapist, and the working through of her often expressed assumption that the therapist thought exactly what she thought was extremely painful to her, and long-drawn-out. Such reproductions of a symbiotic tie, either in relationships or in therapy, are not in themselves specific to lesbianism, and their eventual dissolution does not necessarily lead to a change of sexuality. This patient did eventually develop another lesbian relationship in which she managed to remain significantly more separate, with her own independent views and feelings; one where both conflict and more sexual engagement were experienced.

It is possible, therefore, that McDougall's theory applies at a descriptive level, not to all lesbians, but to some; and that what is involved is a difficulty in the capacity to have lesbian relationships without undue symbiotic enmeshments, rather than that the desire for lesbian love is in itself a consequence of an unresolved symbiotic tie to the mother. In other words, what McDougall may be describing is a particular difficulty that may characterise some lesbians or some lesbian relationships; she sees this difficulty as being the root of the patients' lesbianism, rather than considering that it may be a difficulty in being and loving as lesbian. To consider this latter possibility is to conceive that such difficulties could be resolved within a lesbian framework, and also that there could be other, less problematic ways of being lesbian: in particular, expressions of lesbian love that do not involve such painful symbiotic wishes.

In another case the patient, a self-identified lesbian for all her adult life, had a mother who was harsh, rejecting and preoccupied with her first dead child. She grew up with a strong sense that her mother's happiness was not something she, her father, or other siblings could contribute to; and she was the target of much scorn and envious disparagement from her mother. She felt that her only importance to her mother was as a repository of depression and complaints about the hardness of her life, and grew up with a sense of her mother as useless to her, hateful, and failing to protect her from her drunken and abusive father. Her only source of hope as a child was an aunt who intermittently provided her with some sense of herself as worthy of love and respect, but emigrated when she was six. Her mother was also extremely controlling of her bodily functions, instituting toilet training at a very early age and creating enormous anxiety about the undesirability of her body products.

Her sexual relationships with women were characterised by the choice of unavailable partners who, she felt, held her in contempt in various ways. She often hated these other women herself at the same time as experiencing them as essential to her survival, but very unreliably so. In this illustration there is no marked idealisation of the mother, and none of the kind of symbiosis that McDougall describes, although there was a different kind of taking in of her mother's depression. There were, however, the features of rigid control of bodily functions and a rejection of the bodily self as in any way desirable, so that this patient illustrates some of the features McDougall claims for the mother, but not others.

In a third example, the patient, an only child, was brought up by her father's mother, in a separate house, until she was three, and then with her mother and father, in one household, until she was ten; then her grandmother died. Her grandmother took primary care of her, and seems to have been experienced as a consistent but somewhat controlling figure. Her mother she felt as unavailable, rejecting, and preoccupied with her work, and also with the father's career. He was often away, but kindly and interested in the patient when he was present. In therapy she was very preoccupied with the relationship between grandmother and mother: she felt that her mother despised and denigrated her grandmother, but had also been very jealous of her daughter's attachment to her, ridiculing the patient's grief when the grandmother became ill and eventually died. The patient felt that her mother relegated all care of her to someone who was seen as inferior, and that she was never of great interest to her mother; she would

117

long to feel that she could arouse her mother's interest, and hold her attention. As an adult her choice of female partners represented many of her wishes for this unavailable exciting mother, and her fearful anticipation of rejection; available seemingly loving women were felt as uninteresting, unerotic, and somewhat inferior, although important as a source of security.

In this case the family background is quite different from any McDougall describes. The patient had three effective parental figures, of whom the two most salient were women and the primary one was not her mother. In many ways the actual mother figured as the classic father of psychoanalytic theory, the exciting second parent: relegating the care of the child to a woman who was seen as essential but inferior, and also intruding into this dyad, and constituting herself as someone more desirable in her unavailability and access to the outside world. The painful and unsatisfactory split that the patient, as an adult, experienced between seemingly different kinds of women is not unlike the splits between eroticism and affection that have so often been described in heterosexual contexts.

We have given these illustrations to indicate the kind of clinical diversity that has to be apprehended in terms of the parental images presented by various lesbian patients: there are undoubtedly many more that we have not recorded.

— *A deviation in gender identity?* —

We have seen that McDougall regards the unconscious identification with the father that she attributes to homosexual women as unsatisfactory, because of the problematic image of the father, but she also calls it 'fictitious'. It seems that she does this because these identifications do not correspond to the seemingly appropriate gender rather than because of any intrinsic quality of the identifications themselves – that is, as especially false or defensive. This supposition that the fictitious attribution is to do with the way gender and gender difference is understood is borne out by a consideration of McDougall's later (1989)[19] theorisation of homosexuality, where she squarely locates it on a continuum with transsexualism, despite the various arguments that have been put forward against this by, for example, Robert Stoller.[20] In placing homosexuality in such a context she implies that it arises from anxiety about gender difference, although not as 'extreme' an anxiety as that seen to underlie transsexualism. Here McDougall describes homosexuals:

> Others again, [homosexuals] while accepting their biological sex as an inescapable reality, refuse the sexual role that society attributes to masculine and feminine identity. This is the homosexual response to an internal conflict regarding sexual role and object choice. The reasons for this deviation in gender identity are various and highly complex.[21]

In this somewhat scrambled and confusing passage, homosexuality is named as a deviation in gender identity, and heterosexuality (the sexual role which 'society attributes' and homosexuals 'refuse') is tied to the respective gender identities. Homosexuality is located within a framework of issues about genital and gender differences, with a somewhat unpsychoanalytic reliance on the notion of sexual roles.

From the outset, therefore (this is the theoretical preamble to a clinical article about a lesbian patient), it is assumed that female homosexuality does involve conflict about feminine identity; there is no conceptual or conceivable room in this theory for a woman to be homosexual and also to be confident and relatively conflict-free in her femininity – at least as much as any woman could be. This restrictive split between the gender of the object and the gender identity of the subject is also expressed in McDougall's formulation of the homosexual oedipal drama as involving the double aim of *having* exclusive possession of the same-sex parent and that of *being* the parent of the opposite sex' (original emphasis).[22] Here again, and as in earlier writings (see Chapter 2), sexual desire and identification are split apart along gender lines, and a

119

woman cannot be conceived of as desiring to possess another woman from the position of also fully being one.

McDougall attempts to resolve the problem presented by lesbian desire to this version of psychoanalytic theory by making such a woman into an imitation or fictive man. Desire in a homosexual form is seen as meaning that the identity as feminine is thrown into question, and indeed that this 'deviant' identity helps to construct the desire – a step that earlier writers did not take. This formulation blocks the exploration of what it means to desire another woman from the position of being a woman, what the nature of this desire could be, yet this is actually an issue which is expressed and explored in many lesbian relationships, in various ways. The question of the desire and the identity of the other partner, the object of the fictive man's love, is totally ignored, as if she did not exist. McDougall's formulations of lesbian desire also illustrate what Judith Butler (1990) has described in her consideration of the production of categories of gender and sexuality:

> 'Intelligible' genders are those which in some sense institute
> and maintain relations of coherence and continuity among
> sex, gender, sexual practice and desire . . . The cultural matrix
> through which gender identity has become intelligible
> requires that certain kinds of 'identities' cannot 'exist' – that
> is, those in which gender does not follow from sex and those
> in which the practices of desire do not 'follow' from either sex
> or gender . . . Indeed, precisely because certain 'gender
> identities' fail to conform to those norms of cultural intelligi-
> bility, they appear only as developmental failures or logical
> impossibilities within that domain.[23]

Here it is the lesbian with the masculine identification who is seen as a developmental failure, and the one who desires a woman from a feminine or female position who is the logical impossibility. It is what Butler calls the heterosexualisation of desire that 'requires and institutes' the kinds of oppositional feminine and masculine identities that are seen, for example, in McDougall's formulation of oedipal issues.

Before turning to McDougall's clinical illustrations pertaining to gender identity, we should acknowledge the theoretical minefield that surrounds this area. 'Gender identity' is itself a problematic concept within a psychoanalytic framework, since it does not possess the kind of psychoanalytic specificity that 'object choice', for example, has. Rather, contained within it are a range of conscious and unconscious referents, behavioural, social and subjective meanings, some incorporated from the wider psychological literature. Gender identity refers to a person's sense of themselves as male or female, and is typically distinguished from 'core gender identity', which is seen as the knowledge that one is either male or female: which sex one belongs to. 'Gender identity', therefore, makes reference to perceptions of what it is to be male or female, and how a person situates him- or herself in relation to this. 'Masculinity/femininity' are frequently the terms used to describe this relationship.

Jean Laplanche and Jean-Bertrand Pontalis (1973)[24] define masculinity/femininity as 'the way the subject situates himself [sic] vis-à-vis his biological sex' – this being the 'variable outcome of a process of conflict'. They point out the indeterminate position of masculinity and femininity between the social and the biological, with its 'psychosexual' significance interlocking with these other two dimensions – especially, they claim, the social one. They, like Freud (1920)[25] before them, warn of the socially conventional and often confused and superficial nature of the distinction between masculinity and femininity. They also underline, with an example, its historical and cultural specificity, which they accuse psychoanalysis of too often ignoring. They maintain that what is of decisive importance for a psychoanalytic perspective is an individual's unconscious phantasies in relation to this dichotomy, rather than any externally imposed criteria, but the history of psychoanalysis we are examining suggests that this definition has seldom been adhered to. Rather all kinds of social norms have been incorporated into psychoanalysts' judgements of their patients' femininity. McDougall in particular does not show any of Laplanche and Pontalis's caution; for her, these concepts have an unquestioned and universal status, with an unreflective acceptance of what she takes to be prevailing social norms.

Furthermore, the scope for subjective and personal bias in perceptions of femininity is very great, especially in psychoanalysts' not uncommon reliance on the patient's appearance and style of dress to form such judgements. We have seen how prominent descriptions of her patients' clothes were for McDougall in her attributions of paternal identifications. In 'The Dead Father' she describes her patient in the following terms:

> Her face, framed by short curly hair, bore not a trace of
> make-up; her tight blue jeans and well-cut cashmere sweater
> revealed an attractive feminine silhouette.[26]

Into this apparently objective language a large number of personal and social values are being incorporated unremarked. Some norm of female presentation is being appealed to in the noting of the absence of make-up. The writer also assumes that we all know and agree what a feminine shape is, and also what makes this an attractive one; as well as what constitutes a well-cut sweater. McDougall assumes that there is a universal readership which sees things from the same position as she herself does. This passage leaves us in little doubt that McDougall approves of this woman's feminine shape, and that something about it makes her attractive in McDougall's eyes.

McDougall is by no means the only psychoanalyst who describes women patients in terms of their attractiveness, finds femininity in women attractive, or draws conclusions about their inner worlds from their clothes or appearance. Thus Enid Balint (1986)[27] sees a boy-like shape as a sign of difficulty with femininity; and Thomas Ogden (1987)[28] sees his patient's eventual wearing of a skirt and blouse, rather than trousers, as a progressive step into the Oedipus complex. Given the psychoanalytic commitment to understanding individual experience in terms of its subjective and unconscious meaning, the crudity of some of these observations is baffling. Such a departure from psychoanalytic methods suggests, again, powerful countertransference reactions, and defences against anxieties aroused by aspects of these patients' self-presentations.

In making these kinds of observations about appearances, psychoanalysts need to be aware in what a complex socio-psychological field these issues of clothes, identity and sexuality exist, as regards both their patients and themselves. This is particularly the case for identities and sexualities that are as marginal as lesbianism. Inge Blackman and Kathryn Perry (1990),[29] for example, emphasise the multiple and changing meanings that style and appearance may have, and the pitfalls in reading off from appearance and presentation anything about a person's identity or other characteristics. They describe the different relationships they perceive lesbians as having to their appearance: for some, it may be an expression of their sexual identity, a way of being recognised as sexually interested in women rather than men; for others, their appearance may be designed to conceal rather than reveal their sexual identity, with a style that says as little as possible about the wearer. For yet others, appearance may be a field of play and experimentation with different expressions of femininity and masculinity, something that uses the various social meanings attached to different images for individual purposes. As Blackman and Perry say: 'Being aware of how style is used to identify, lesbians may confound expectations by subverting the image they project.'

These considerations may make us wary of McDougall's pronouncements about the deviant gender identity of her lesbian patients, but she does also adduce clinical evidence about their experience of their bodies and their femininity. In several of her writings she describes how her lesbian patients 'lacked femininity'. They compared themselves unfavourably to their mothers, who were seen as attractive to men, and as possessing all the feminine attributes that they lacked. In this way, femininity is construed as indissolubly linked to hetero-sexual attraction. Furthermore:

The image of womanhood held by these patients is divided
into a highly idealised and a totally castrated one – so
idealised that it is felt to be inaccessible, and so castrated that
they must disguise their femininity by all the psychic means
at their disposal.[30]

McDougall also sees her patients as exhibiting various forms
of distress about their own bodies, as finding themselves 'ugly
and deformed, physically weak or unhealthy'.

Our own clinical experience does not suggest the homo-
geneous picture of disturbed gender identities that McDougall
presents. Rather, we are aware of a huge range and diversity
of conflicts that lesbian patients may have in relation to themselves as women, or about their bodies, but these do not
invariably amount to serious gender identity conflicts, and
they are not necessarily specific to lesbians; they may also be
experienced in various ways by some heterosexual women.
This range and diversity indicates a need for much subtler
clinical differentiation in this area, and also for greater sophistication in determining what such conflicts may mean. It is,
important, therefore, to distinguish clinically between those
lesbian patients who do have difficulties in the area of gender
identity and those who do not, or only to a lesser extent, and
to consider how these conflicts relate to sexual identity and the
expression of sexuality. Of course, it is difficult to prove an
absence of conflict, since it can always be argued that further
or different analysis would reveal currently hidden or unrecognised unconscious conflicts, but this is a risk that has to
be taken in presenting any material. Furthermore, these issues
concerning gender identity represent only a part, often quite a
minor part, of the material presented in therapy, so the condensation and distillation necessary to select just these must be
borne in mind. What follows is, therefore, a very preliminary
exploration of different ways in which some lesbians have
represented themselves in therapy in relation to issues of fem-
ininity/masculinity, and how this representation has been
seen by the therapist. The purpose is to draw out a significant
diversity that has been ignored, and to explore further issues

of how lesbians can and do represent themselves as women and as sexual women, and the difficulties they may face in doing this.

K. had a childhood of severe social dislocation and ostracism; her parents were refugees who never learned to speak the language of their host country, and never wished to 'fit in' to what they regarded as a hostile and inferior culture. K. longed to 'fit in', but felt that she did not know how to. Her experience of oddity and difference she ascribed – amongst other things – to the unfashionable clothes her mother provided for her, and increasingly, as an adolescent, to what she felt to be her 'unfeminine' appearance. This distress about her appearance was focused on her thin, short body and her relatively large hands and feet, but underlying this was a horrified sense, which emerged in therapy, that there was something freakishly abnormal about her, embodied in some way which she could not articulate but which, she was convinced, meant that no one could find her attractive or desirable.

In therapy she would repeatedly return to the feeling that she 'couldn't decide to be a woman – it's too difficult a decision, too decisive'. She knew she was a woman, but she couldn't feel that other people did; she would often wonder whether the therapist could 'see her as a woman'. Like McDougall's patients she attributed the monopoly of femininity to other women, particularly her various women partners, whom she envied for their apparent ease with matters of attractiveness and dress. However, her mother did not present the kind of image described by McDougall; rather, she conveyed to K. a minimal, depressed and despised sense of femininity which K. feared to be like, but felt convinced she was like. Her two older sisters, by contrast, appeared to K. to possess all the feminine attractiveness that she and her mother lacked and were, she felt, of much greater interest to her father. K. often expressed her 'indecision' about her status as a woman in terms that suggested she saw herself as male or masculine: she felt that she achieved any desirability only by being in some ways male or masculine, although she greatly disliked these aspects of herself which, she felt, were abnormal. To her 'masculine' meant taking the initiative, organising and fixing things. This 'indecision' lessened greatly in the course of therapy, as she came to feel that perhaps her therapist could sometimes see her as a woman, even if she herself often couldn't.

It would be insufficient, however, to see K.'s difficulties with her status as a woman, which were considerable, simply in terms of a repudiation or lack of femininity. Rather, they seemed to the therapist to be linked to other areas of massive 'indecision' in her life – whether she wanted a male or a female partner (though in fact she had exclusively female ones), or indeed anything much else. Involved in this inability to want was a terrifying sense of the impossibility of being a person at all, in particular in relation to others. She had frequent experiences of not really knowing if she existed: she felt that the therapist's words could obliterate her, and that when she spoke she obliterated the therapist; such obliteration of the other was the only alternative, for her, to being extinguished. It meant that no two people of whatever kind could coexist, nor was any reciprocity or mutuality possible for her. She felt utterly constructed by what she imagined to be others' views about her, which extended to other areas apart from her femininity. To have recognised herself as definitely female and not male would have been to establish herself as more of a person, with wants and desires, than she felt able to be. Keeping herself in a state of 'indecision', though it was acutely painful, allowed her to avoid the immense risks associated with being a desiring subject of any kind. From such a position any kind of engaged sexuality was impossible, and her difficulties in being lesbian, in sustaining relationships, reflected this.

It would have been easy to be misled by K.'s frequent references to herself as male, by her activities which she regarded as masculine, and also by her self-presentation, to think that she did really construct herself in this way. However, she was no more able to be masculine than she was able to be feminine – or, indeed, anything much else. The 'masculine' rather described for her what she felt she could not be – a person of a specific kind, a woman. Therapeutic progress for her consisted in part in coming to feel that her masculine attributes were real ones for her, not just a sign of failure and undesirability – that they indicated something strong, admirable and creative about her, something that was likeable. This positive identification with her masculinity – and also, indirectly, with more benign aspects of her somewhat feared father – allowed her to feel there was more, not less, possibility of also being a woman, of being desirable and likeable as such.

K. felt that she could be neither a woman nor a man, neither masculine or feminine. Another woman, T., who had had involving relationships with both men and women at different points in her life, felt that she had to try to be both. She was the only child of upper-class parents who had both wanted her to be a boy so that she would inherit the family title and land. She experienced her father's disappointment at her being a girl as more acute, since it was his inheritance that she could not carry on, and would try desperately to do what she saw as boyish things to please him. As an adolescent she also felt her mother's disappointment that she was not feminine enough, and as an adult she felt that she had failed her mother by not getting married and having children, so that her mother could at least have grandchildren to compensate for not having been able to produce more children herself. To T. the differences between men and women seemed enormous, stark and acutely painful; she wished there were none, then it wouldn't have mattered so much what she was – her parents would have loved her more, and perhaps their marriage would have been happier. In therapy it emerged how, throughout her life, she had evolved a way of – as she said – 'trying on' being both a boy and a girl, although she never doubted that she was a girl. All positions felt impossible – she couldn't be a boy for her father, because she wasn't one; she couldn't be a girl for him, because he hated her as that. It felt unsafe to be fully a girl, and also acutely painful not to be a 'better' one, especially in relation to her mother. T.'s attempted solution to these perils was a certain kind of androgynous presentation, a mask in relation to her mother. T.'s attempted solution to these perils was a certain kind of androgynous presentation, a mask of seemingly confident offbeat femininity which, she felt, was attractive to both men and women. This hid how unsafe it felt to be a woman, and how important it was not to be too much of one. Her perilous status as female, although she found a certain stability in her various modes of expression, prevented her from resolving her other conflicts about intimacy and trust. Feeling so fundamentally the wrong kind of person, she could allow little genuineness and security in anyone's love for her, male or female, and this contributed to the difficulties she experienced in being a woman with another woman. She felt, as she felt with her mother, that she was a great disappointment to her partner – not a 'proper' woman or lesbian, yet not wanting to be a woman for a man either.

In T.'s case her overwhelming conviction that she was wrong and bad was focused on her gender, but also importantly extended to many other areas of her being, the many other ways in which she felt greedy, wicked and evil. We will now describe several women with areas of conflict about their status as women, which are not of the acute or overwhelming kind described above, but were nonetheless significant, all in quite different ways.

C. was a woman who had identified herself as lesbian for most of her adult life. She had also had some relationships with men. Her parents, especially her mother, had very much wanted a boy, and indeed almost expected her to be one. As a child she felt constantly inferior to her younger brothers, one of whom was adored by her mother, who generally considered women inferior to and less interesting than men. C. recurringly wished to be a boy until she reached her twenties, but felt that it was hopeless to try to be like one in any way – she just couldn't play games, be tough, get a penis, mend things, which seemed to be the characteristics that excited her mother. She also felt very anxious that she wasn't feminine and attractive enough as a girl, finding it hard to identify with and participate in the other girls' concerns with clothes, boyfriends and appearance.

As an adolescent and young adult she did manage to be what she considered feminine enough with men, and got considerable enjoyment from being seen as attractive and interesting by them, but this always felt false and precarious to her. Although she became attached to the father of her child, her persistent fantasies and dreams were about women whom she knew and loved. In her subsequent lesbian relationships she achieved a degree of sexual satisfaction and involvement that she had never experienced with men, and also a great lessening of her anxiety about being feminine enough. She felt confirmed in her sense of herself as female – as she said, 'more of a woman', at last loved as a woman by a woman, with a woman who wanted a woman and didn't prefer a man, and much more able than she had ever been to appreciate her body as attractively female. Such a resolution of anxieties about being female – in which a woman is enabled, through relationships with women, to feel more securely and positively female than she is able to with men – is one aspect of lesbian relationships that is missing from conventional psychoanalytic accounts, where femininity can only ever be realised through heterosexual engagement.

C.'s anxieties about being female had been acute at various points in her life, and contributed to her depressed sense of herself, and the differences she perceived between boys and girls were extremely painful to her. None the less this does not, in our view, amount to a disturbance in gender identity as such. Her concern was to find a way of being female that was not so injurious to her self-esteem as that which she had experienced as a child, and this she did – partly through her adult heterosexual development; partly through her engagement with feminism, which brought her into contact with women who valued women; and partly through her developing lesbian sexuality. The resolution of many of these conflicts about her femininity allowed her then to engage with other areas of difficulty relating to dependency, trust and intimacy in her sexual relationships, which had previously been warded off.

In both these last two cases, of T. and C., the painfulness of its immediate origins within the families concerned (in one case the father, in the other the mother, who wanted the girl to be a boy), but it has clear reverberations with the general social position of women. The usual psychoanalytic conceptualisation of sexual difference, especially as supposedly apprehended by the child, tends to treat the two categories as of equal significance, posing the psychic issues for the child only in terms of the narcissistic wounds involved in not being able to be both sexes, and having to acknowledge itself as belonging to only one. Perversion in its various forms is seen as stemming from a denial or disavowal of this monosexual status, as representing a wish to deny sexual difference; and difficulties or conflicts with conventional femininity (or masculinity in the case of men) are too readily understood or interpreted as perverse in this sense.

But there are many other sources and forms of difficulty with sexual difference – not the least of which, for women, is their often devalued status, either within a particular family or more generally. It is virtually a cultural norm in our society for young girls at some point to wish to be boys, but not for most boys to wish to be girls – certainly it is a very widespread phenomenon, according to existing research. The source of such a wish is seldom a perverse desire to deny all difference (indeed, as far as psychoanalytic and psychiatric evidence goes, men are massively more likely to engage in perverse activities than women are), but rather the perception and experience of what this difference brings with it for the women concerned, and the conflicts it creates with desires for self-esteem, activity, a place in the social order, safety. Both T.'s father and C.'s mother, from their different positions, were transmitting their own and society's evaluation of being a girl to their daughters in a particularly virulent way, thereby making it difficult for them to achieve an acceptable sense of themselves as women. To have difficulty with the way in which this difference is represented within a particular family or society is very different from the refusal of any difference at all, although of course the former can seem very like the latter from the position of someone who accepts the conventional

and contemporary forms in which these differences are represented as unequivocally 'reality', or how things should be.

Another woman, O., had experienced strong sexual attraction towards women from adolescence, and had openly identified herself as lesbian since her twenties. As a child she had
been left temporarily by her mother, who greatly preferred her
two younger brothers. As far as she was concerned, they were
given vastly preferential treatment. O. saw herself as stupid
and worthless compared to them, but never had any conscious
desire to be a boy; rather, she wanted to get more for herself
as a girl – something she would demand incessantly of both
her parents. As an adult she felt that her sexuality was second-
rate, hated and despised by others, whom she experienced
as unremittingly hostile towards her; she insisted that this
hostility was due to her lesbianism. Her conviction about the
badness of her sexuality was very great and found ample con-
firmation in the world around her, but even with more accepting friends whom she eventually found she continued to feel
extremely bad – this time a bad lesbian compared to others.

Through therapy this degree of persecution, and her need
continually to provoke and re-experience the rejection that she
most feared, lessened. What transpired was a conviction that
her love and her sexuality were highly damaging to others; she
felt that she had caused her mother to abandon her as a baby.
Her conviction of her own badness was focused on her sexuality rather than her femininity: though she was outraged by
what she saw as unfair treatment of herself and other women,
she also felt that being female was one of the few good things
about herself, a source of much-needed solidarity and support
which she could get at times from other women, although they
also let her down. Her difficulty with being female stemmed
from a sense of difference from other women's preoccupations, which she could not identify with, because, she felt, of
differences in sexuality which left her marginalised and isolated. This she connected to a feeling that she never shared
her mother's feminine preoccupations, that she was too awk-
wardly different from her mother. Although for a long time
she did not know how she could connect to other women,

except in a demanding, insistent way, she never experienced this as throwing doubt on her femininity.

S. was a woman who had her first relationship with a woman in her late twenties; she had always felt very 'rooted', as she put it, in being female, and never had any desire to be male. This, however, was a fairly anxious 'rooting' in that she put considerable energy into presenting herself attractively, in choosing clothes and jewellery. She had experienced some adolescent shame and doubt about her body, but as an adult, on the whole, she enjoyed herself as a woman, taking pleasure in her female form, her breasts, which she came to consider as beautiful, her pregnancy and breastfeeding her child. She experienced some lack of self-confidence sexually, in that she felt she did not know how to show her sexual interest or respond to overtures, but once engaged with a partner sexually, she had considerable capacity to enjoy herself, despite many fears of loss of control which affected other areas of her life. She had a close, somewhat idealising but also ambivalent relationship with her mother, from whom she felt she had inherited her capacity for sexual enjoyment. Her mother had always implied that this was one of the satisfactory areas of the relationship between her and her husband, S.'s father, in what was in other ways a very problematic marriage. S. felt intensely identified with her mother, especially in her interest in clothes and appearance, and in a tendency to compulsive eating and smoking. She was also very ambitious and successful professionally, having managed to deal with her anxieties about surpassing both her parents. Although she experienced her lesbianism as painful, in that she hated the sense of being marginal, an outsider, and possibly disliked because of it, it did not, for her, make her doubt her status as a woman. She did not regard any of her attributes or activities as especially male, even though her work meant that she was often the only woman amongst men, in situations of considerable power and responsibility.

We have described here a range of illustrations of the ways in which difficulties with gender identity, with the experience of being female, can present themselves. Some of these would amount to the kind of serious difficulty described in the psychoanalytic literature; some are of a different order; and there are yet others where such difficulties are not so evident. We have tried to show how the relationships between gender-identity difficulties – where these exist – and lesbian sexuality are much more complex and various than McDougall's formulations suppose, and these complexities may make us question the simple attribution of 'deviant' gender identity to lesbians. More fundamentally, however, as we have indicated – and as we explain further in Chapter 11 – the whole framework in which such an attribution is cast rests on various assumptions that render it inevitable and problematic within the terms of psychoanalytic theory.

7

Promises and Contradictions:
Lacan and Language, Irigaray and Kristeva

W E SHALL NOW consider the work of French psychoanalysts Jacques Lacan, Luce Irigaray and Julie Kristeva in order to evaluate their contributions to the understanding of lesbianism. As with other psychoanalytic texts we examine, we shall also show how their general theory of psychic development generates their theorising of lesbianism. Lacan's work has been greeted favourably by many feminist writers, who see it as providing guidelines for a comprehensive analysis of patriarchy in that it allows for an analysis of the constructions of psychic identities within social and cultural contexts. François Roustang, a contemporary French analyst, highlights Lacan's attraction for feminists:

> The Lacanian psychoanalyst does not try to reintegrate the
> analysand into the society as it is. He sees this society as
> based on the misapprehension of the subject's desire, and
> believes it exists only through the repression of desire . . .[1]

However, Lacan also stresses that the alienation of desire can occur by revolution as much as by adaptation.

Feminists are attracted to Lacan's work because he acknowledges cultural issues, linking subjectivity, sexuality and language in a way that, for example, Kleinian analysts do not. Elizabeth Grosz puts it succinctly:

> His decentring of the rational, conscious subject (identified with the ego), his undermining of common assumptions about the . . . purposiveness of the speaking subject's 'rational' discourses, and his problematizations of the idea of a 'natural' sexuality, have helped to free feminist theory of the constraints of a largely metaphysical and implicitly masculine, notion of subjectivity – humanism.[2]

Similarly, Juliet Mitchell points out that:

> In the Freud that Lacan uses, neither the unconscious nor sexuality can in any degree be pre-given facts, they are constructions; that is they are objects with histories and the human subject itself is only formed within these histories.[3]

Lacan is critical of naive biologism, and elaborates psychoanalysis in terms of Saussurian structural linguistics. This offers a strategy for understanding the emergence of subjectivity as gendered in such a way that it allows for the analysis of the hierarchical dualism operative in the distinction of masculinity and femininity. The problem with Lacan, however, is that his theory remains universalist in that he argues for the cross-cultural, ahistorical primacy of the phallus as the signifier of difference, which he equates with the signifier of sexual desire. We shall examine the paradoxes of his theory and, in particular, the contradictions between his claims for the precariousness of subjectivity and identity and his maintenance of a binary gender identification.

Lacan's work contains few references to lesbians. However, in outlining his account of language, of the unconscious, and of the practice of analysis, we aim to highlight its implications for women's desires for one another. We shall focus particularly on the problematic of Lacan's phallocentrism, then go on to consider the feminist readings of Lacan offered by Irigaray, who deconstructs his theory, and Kristeva, who criticises it from within the 'Law of the Father'.

135

— *Language and the unconscious* —

Our exposition of Lacan's account of language, the unconscious, and the practice of analysis is particularly important in the light of the unfamiliarity of his theories to many British analysts and therapists. His view of psychoanalysis has often been characterised as abstract, too philosophical and lacking in clinical rigour by comparison with the 'concrete' steps to health achieved by analysing phantasies of destruction, aggression, envy and reparation in relation to the breast and the penis. However, Lacan and his followers offer extensive and detailed accounts of analytic practice.[4]

Against the Kleinian assumption of two-body psychology, mother and baby, Lacan returns to Freud's emphasis on the centrality of the unconscious for subjectivity. Following *Beyond the Pleasure Principle*, Lacan emphasises the repetition compulsion which surpasses the principle of pleasure/ unpleasure:

> Lacan linked the repetition of the unconscious repressed to the insistence of the signifying chain . . . the chain of unconscious purposive ideas.[5]

This is to stress the element of the beyond, the gaps, errors in speech which cannot be fixed by referring to a mechanistic developmental moment such as, for example, the paranoid-schizoid position in pre-oedipal conflict. Lacan maintains that beyond speech is always another speech:

> The schema which places the object relation at the heart of theorisation of analysis misses the mainspring of the analytic experience, namely that the subject gives an account of himself.[6]

Lacan argues that Klein's theory of development in terms of object relations misses the central analytic experience because she does not offer an adequate account of language and speech. According to Lacan, Klein's dialectic of phantasied objects rests on the notion of identification: the subject is destroyed by or incorporates the objects or part-objects of breast, phallus, excrement – 'above all he *is* these objects'.[7] Speech is reduced to one single meaning. Against this Lacan claims that speech occurs within the semantic world of language, in which speech has several meanings and functions. It is not a matter of language conceived as signs, where each sign designates a signified, but, rather, a chain of signification: language as a field of complexity and ambiguity. Against object-relations theorists' emphasis on the 'mechanisms' of the psyche, Lacan privileges the subject's experience of speech. Such an emphasis on speech as involving the complexity of signifying chains – rather than, for example, the Kleinian notion of language as a sign pointing to an alinguistic or prelinguistic psychic process – seems to offer more scope for recognising and hearing analysands' own speaking, and for questioning fixed interpretations of normal and pathological development, love and desire.

For the mechanistic notion of defence in relation to repression Lacan substitutes the linguistic categories of metaphor and metonymy.[8] Desire is expressed in metaphor in the passage from one signifier to another, in the substitution of words. Emphasis on the play of metaphors challenges the notion of a fixed truth expressed in literal speech. This is the place of the symptom which both reveals and veils. Metonymy refers to the linear character of syntax, with one word following another. This linearity of the linguistic order replaces the subject's lack of being:

> In metonymy an original splitting is represented, whereby the order of language replaces the subject's lack of being. It is from this original splitting that desire for the lacking object arises . . .[9]

The meaning of a word emerges from describing its usages in practice, not by pointing to some equivalent.

Lacan in practice

Lacan differentiates between 'full speech' and 'empty speech'. Empty speech is the speech of the ego, the demand of the patient that the analyst fall in with it by providing, for example, a cure, love, hate, reassurance. The task of the analyst is to recognise and interpret this speech. The analyst must be attuned to the full speech of the patient, that which is unconscious and which:

> aims at, which forms, the truth such as it becomes established in the recognition of one person by another. Full speech is speech which performs. One of the subjects finds himself, afterwards, other than he was before.[10]

This is not a matter of a subject having a dual relationship with an object but, rather, of objects acquiring meaning in relationships between subjects – the object is named; its presence is invoked, and sustains its identity through time.

For Lacan the subject's truth is outside the matrix of certainties by which the human recognises his/her ego. It is to be found elsewhere, in what Lacan calls the locus or place of the Other. The subject of this speech is the subject of the unconscious. It is not the emission of a unitary ego with only one 'I', rather, in Lacan's terms, the 'I' is a shifter; yet-to-be-spoken dynamic possibilities are spoken from different positions which are irreducible to one synchronic, fixed identity.

How does this kind of analysis work? Lacan claims:

> That the subject should come to recognise and to name his desire, that is the efficacious action of analysis. But it isn't a question of recognising something which would be entirely given, ready to be coapted. In naming it, the subject creates, brings forth, a new presence in the world. He introduces presence as such and . . . hollows out absence as such. It is only at this level that one can conceive of the action of interpretation.[11]

Transference occurs because the subject puts herself in the position of acknowledging herself in her speech, and the meaning of her speech to the analyst is her 'existential relation before the object of [her] desire'.[12] The central issue, then, is not that the subject-patient comes to have her hitherto unmet needs satisfied (as, for example, Guntrip holds) but rather that, in speaking with the analyst, the unconscious, the otherness, of her speech emerges and moves her beyond a narcissistic demand for a completion that denies loss and death. The ego of the subject speaks, and the task of the analyst is to respond to the irruptions into the linear narrative – to point to the gaps, the displacements, the errors. The unconscious, for Lacan, is structured like a language; it is not a container holding our life traumas under the lids of defences until the repetition compulsion is activated in the analysis. Thus Lacan's view of psychic historicity is quite different from that of object-relations theorists. Each of us has a unique subjective history emergent in the ongoing dialectic of our being, from birth, 'thrown into language', the language of our family, class, culture, epoch – in a sense we are carried by language. We are carried, for example, by the stories of our grandparents, and we live our lives finding our way by speaking against this background. Gaps, errors, omissions, slips of the tongue, the displacement and condensation of dreams, constitute the 'other side' of language – that is, the language of the unconscious which the analyst addresses.

The analyst continually strives to put his/her own ego aside in order to hear and point to the limits of the analysand's speech, where it is in thrall to his/her egoistic closures; places in which he/she is frightened, blocked, inhibited. Lacan emphasises the fact that progress in analysis involves placing the subject's speech in the wider discourse of the subject's history.

Lacan distinguishes the domains of the real, the imaginary and the symbolic, and situates analysis on the borders between the imaginary and the symbolic. For Lacan the real is similar to Jean-Paul Sartre's notion of the in-itself – the facticity, the 'being-there', which we constantly try to grasp with images and symbols, but which eludes us. The imaginary is the world of mirror-images with which we identify, through which we fix and so alienate ourselves.[13] The irruption of the irrational, the breaks and gaps in the discourse, that which is beyond the ostensive narration of the analysand, opens out space for the exploration of the symbolic value of the images. Again, this is stressing the fact that we do not own language but are thrown into it, and are continually developing by finding our way within it. The unconscious challenges the circle of certainties by which the human recognises itself as ego.

The privileging of images of the human body by object-relations analysts is, in Lacan's view, a perversion of the meaning of psychoanalysis:

> It is . . . the exercise of the dialectic of analysis which should
> dissipate this imaginary confusion, and restitute to the
> discourse its meaning as discourse.[14]

Analysis consists in the unfolding of revelations specific to each subject:

> There is a readiness to the transference in the patient solely by
> virtue of his placing himself in the position of acknowledging
> himself in speech, and in searching out his truth.[15]

Analysis occurs in the realm of intersubjectivity, the symbolic rather than the imaginary realm of object relations.

For Lacan the criterion for the termination of an analysis is a matter of the analysand's recognition that the analyst is not the 'one who knows' – that beyond the analysand's ego and the ego of the analyst there are the others whom one addresses:

> The analysis must aim at the passage of true speech, joining
> the subject to another subject, on the other side of the wall of
> language. That is the final relationship of the subject to a
> genuine Other, the Other who gives the answer one doesn't
> expect, which defines the terminal point of analysis.[16]

This brief account of psychoanalysis from our reading of Lacan stresses the place of analytic discourse as one of a struggle against the patient's fear of death, loss, suffering, vulnerability, while expressing such gaps and breaks in his/her speech. The unconscious, structured like a language, challenges the patient's initial egoism in her/his transference to the analyst as the 'one who is supposed to know'. Dissolution of the transference occurs when the patient moves beyond certainties, the narcissistic identification of the mirror stage, to the full speech of the symbolic in which the subject emerges.

—— *Lacan's subjection to Oedipus* ——

Lacanian analysis might appear to be an appealing prospect for lesbians, gay men, heterosexual men and women who want to find happier lives through working with an analyst but do not want endless interpretations of their sexuality as 'the root of the problem'. Subjectivity and intersubjectivity are presented in terms of complexities that surpass the notions of human nature construed as psychological properties which can be essentially known and universalised. Lacanian psychoanalysis is compelling in that it might be seen as carefully avoiding *a priori* pathologising, and emphasising the originality of the patient's expressions. But as we indicated above, the problem remains that all Lacan's elucidation of speech and language is theorised within his notion of the phallocentric 'Law of the Father'.

So far, in discussing Lacan's analyses, we have avoided references to the Oedipus complex, the feminine as other, the castration complex, penis envy, the libido as unitary, the primacy of the phallus as signifier, the Law of the Father. Lacan – in line with earlier analysts, including Melanie Klein – conceives of human beings as masculine and feminine, with an appropriate alignment of gender and sexuality. The Oedipus complex retains its centrality as the place of the emergence of masculinity and femininity which arise from identifications and denials *vis-à-vis* mother and father. For Lacan, however, the Oedipus complex is a linguistic structure, unlike Freud's account of it in instinctual terms. This has crucial implications for accounts of lesbianism and homosexuality – whether they are characterised as pathological.

Stuart Schneiderman highlights the nexus of the Lacanian enterprise, albeit central to psychoanalysis – namely, the relationship between bodily and psychic linguistic development:

> When there is a failure of psychosexual or psychosocial
> maturation, relating it to a moment in a developmental
> process is secondary to analyzing the specific signifiers that
> the patient uses to talk about it.[17]

For Lacan, the resolution of the Oedipus complex is crucial for the child's entry into language as symbolic.

In the pre-oedipal stage the child is narcissistic, caught in identifications in which she/he imagines the body as whole, as complete. The child is in an ambivalent relationship to the mother in that, for Lacan, desire is desire of the other's desire. Thus in the mirror, imaginary, stage the child wishes to be the object of the mother's desire – that is, the phallus. With the child's awareness of mother's desire for father comes the anxiety of castration, because of father's prohibition of the desire, and the anxiety of loss and incompleteness.

Castration anxiety introduces the challenge of moving into the symbolic – recognising that the primary love-object is irretrievably lost. The primary signifier of the phallus emerges because the father is signified by the penis and is simultaneously signifying the mother's desire. Castration anxiety moves the child, boy or girl, out of narcissism, imaginary wholeness, into the symbolic, governed by the Law of the Father.

Are there contradictions in Lacan's structuralist claims about the Oedipus complex, castration anxiety and the primacy of the phallus as signifier? He appears to be trapped in a paradox. As Jacqueline Rose skilfully points out, he:

> rejoin[s] the place of 'non-knowledge' which he designated
> the unconscious, by the constant slippage or escape of his

speech, and thereby to undercut the very mastery which his own position as speaker (master and analyst) necessarily constructs.[18]

This contradiction is evident in Lacan's account of the Oedipus complex and his emphasis on its negotiation within a socio-cultural matrix. Consequently masculinity, femininity and heterosexuality are not biologically given. On the face of it, Lacan would seem to be subverting any claims that there is a knowable, appropriate sexual desire for each gender. In Lacan's view, however, the symbolic order pre-exists the sub-ject as a universal structure. It is through resolution of the Oedipus complex that the individual is inscribed within this order.

The subject – neither masculine nor feminine, but under the Law of the Father – recognises the lack (of a penis) in the mother and, through identifying with her desire, recognises death and the lack in his or her subjectivity. The paternal metaphor breaks the dyad, and introduces the third term which is essential for symbolisation. Masculine and feminine are the markers of difference in our languages. Although Lacan argues that there is no fixed psychic representation of masculine/feminine, he does attribute different values to them.

For Lacan, the question of the feminine is posed as the question of difference. He lays the ground for this by citing the much-criticised anthropologist Claude Lévi-Strauss, who maintains that woman defines the cultural order as against the natural order because she is the 'object of exchange':

> The fact that the woman is thus bound up in an order of exchange in which she is the object is really what accounts for the fundamentally conflictual character . . . of her position – the symbolic order . . . transcends her.[19]

Lacan uncritically accepts Lévi-Strauss's account of the uni-versality of the elementary structures of kinship, based on the exchange of women. Lacan and Lévi-Strauss interpret such structures as the fundamental basis of communication, as the foundational social 'fact'.

Lacan's crucial point, following the linguist Ferdinand de Saussure, is that although woman is an 'object of exchange' between men, nevertheless, the sexual difference of masculinity and femininity occurs only within language because 'difference' is a distinction, an interpretation. This is not to deny anatomical and biological differences, but to stress that such differences are specified within the discourses or language games of biology and anatomy. He emphasises that our identities as men or women are precarious and challenged by the unconscious, the slips and breaks in language which reveal their fictional character, pointing to that which always escapes the subject (the breast or phallus), the 'objet petit *a*',[20] in his/her demand for completion.

Lacan appears to want it both ways. While he claims that sexual difference and identity is precarious, he nevertheless assumes the structural invariants in language in which the phallus occupies the privileged position. As Rose points out:

> Sexual difference is then assigned according to whether individual subjects do or do not possess the phallus, which means not that anatomical difference *is* sexual difference (the one as strictly deducible from the other), but that anatomical difference comes to *figure* sexual difference, that is, it becomes the sole representative of what that difference is allowed to be.[21] [original emphasis]

For Lacan there cannot be sexual difference, or desire, without the phallus. Because the phallus signifies difference, there can be no symbolisation without it. He is not saying that women or feminine desire do not exist, but he is stressing the unitary character of libido as phallic, the primacy of phallocentric discourse which, he argues, characterises language; and that femininity is subject to this. Despite Lacan's insistence that the phallus is symbolic, and not equated with the biological penis, nevertheless, as the privileged signifier it:

stands out as most easily seized upon in the real of sexual
copulation . . . One might also say that by virtue of its
turgidity, it is the image of the vital flow as it is transmitted
in generation.[22]

Lacan's elaboration of sexuality, desire, and the unconscious is
expressed in his repetitious insistence on the dialectic of our
human desire to know, and the equal knowledge that we do
not know. As 'exchange object' woman is the object of ascriptions, of fantasies, of needs, yet it is in so far as the otherness
of feminine *jouissance* (enjoyment) displaces men's egoistic
pretensions that sexual desire can arise. This *jouissance* exceeds
phallic knowledge; it cannot be spoken because discourse is
phallocentric, and its function is to enthral the man with the
fiction that in relation to it he can possess himself. However,
despite his constant exhortations to women to tell him about
it, it always eludes him.

Lesbian desire

The elusiveness of women's *jouissance* is highlighted by lesbians, women desiring women. Lacan is forceful in his accu-
sation against Freud of being unable to face Dora's
homosexual desire, suggesting that:

> this has to be ascribed to prejudice, exactly the same prejudice
> which falsifies the conception of the Oedipus complex from
> the start, by making it define as natural, rather than norma-
> tive, the predominance of the paternal figure. This is the same
> prejudice which we hear expressed simply in the well-known
> refrain 'As thread to needle, so girl to boy'.[23]

As we have said, for Lacan the Oedipus complex is structured
within language; it is not a 'natural' phenomenon. Lacan
seems to assume that this eliminates the prejudice for which
he criticises Freud. However, his own reading of Dora leads
him to conclude:

the problem of her condition is fundamentally that of accepting herself as an object of desire for the man, and this is for
Dora the mystery which motivates her idolatry for Frau K.[24]

Lacan regards disappointment as central to 'feminine homosexuality'. Since the lesbian's love has been thwarted in the
real, it is idealising, 'taking on the airs of a courtly love'.[25] He
therefore claims that lesbians deny sexuality as such because
they assume the phallus and act 'as though' they are it, but
deny castration and hence sexual difference:

In that such a love prides itself more than any other on being
the love which gives what it does not have, so it is precisely
in this that the homosexual woman excels in relation to what
is lacking to her.[26]

Situated in the realm of the imaginary, lesbians' love is 'soul-
ful' and ultimately hysterical ('acting the man') in structure; it
is 'outside sex'.[27] Lacan's desexualisation of lesbian sexuality,
as Judith Butler suggests, arises from the assumption that sexuality is heterosexual. She emphasises that Lacan's viewpoint
is that of the heterosexual male who is being refused:

Indeed, is this account not the consequence of a refusal that
disappoints the observer, and whose disappointment,
disavowed and projected, is made into the essential character
of the women who effectively refuse him?[28]

Lacan's view of homosexual love echoes Sartre's account of
the futility of love in human relationships. Sartre conceives of
human relationships in terms of conflict; each subject desires
freedom and is attracted to the freedom of the other whom
she/he wishes to possess, but in the surrender of the sexual
caress the other surrenders his/her freedom, and is thereby no
longer desirable.[29] Although Lacan stresses that normality
itself is an ideal fiction, nevertheless in homosexuality:

the other subject is reduced to being only the instrument of
the first, who thus remains the only subject as such, but the

latter is reduced to being only an idol offered to the desire of the other.[30]

Can Lacan's position really be regarded as any less prejudiced than Freud's? As we have said, Lacan's structuralist account, with its emphasis on language and culture, might have appeared to hold promise for lesbians and gay men. However, although Lacan rejects the notion of 'natural', his adherence to a universalism and his privileging of the phallus as primary signifier pose contradictions that once again deny the possibility of satisfying and fulfilling lesbian (and gay) relationships.

Irigaray, lesbian desires —— *and sexual differences* ——

Luce Irigaray is one of the most powerful contemporary French writers. She brings a wealth of expertise in linguistics and philosophy to bear on her reading and practice of psychoanalysis. Although her work is well recognised by literary critics and feminist theorists, it is not much appreciated by British psychoanalysts. This is partly because of the positivistic traditions of British psychoanalysis, which shares the traditional British intellectual distrust of continental thinking as 'poetic' rather than 'empirical'. In addition, given what we have seen of general psychoanalytic views of lesbianism, it is not surprising that Irigaray's work has not been psychoanalytically influential. While working as an analyst and directing research on schizophrenia, she has also criticised psychoanalysis, situating it as a dominant patriarchal discourse, and she has emphasised the importance of erotic desire between women. Irigaray places lesbian desires at the forefront of psychoanalytic theorising.

Irigaray's work interweaves an analysis of gender differences with differences in sexuality.[31] She argues that because gender differences are not adequately recognised, masculinity operates as the impoverished dominance of male-identified abstraction. Men bond and compete with no regard for their bodies and their sexualities; cut off from the earliest bond with the mother, they are also cut off from developing genuine relationships with each other and with women. This situation validates an inadequate model of heterosexuality which simultaneously denies the values of homosexualities.

We have seen how feminists have been attracted to Lacan's work because he acknowledges cultural issues, addressing subjectivity, sexuality and language more than, for example, Kleinian analysts. But how can Lacan maintain that we must hold open the questions of identity in terms of gender and/or sexuality, and simultaneously argue for the primacy of the phallus as essential or necessary to explain sexual difference and sexual desire?

Irigaray provides one of the most scathing critiques of Lacanian psychoanalysis by focusing on the claim that his inability to hear about women's desire undermines his account of masculinity, and hence of sexual differences and desire as such:

> Given *your* universal – the Lacanian code – one knows *a priori*
> how you will interpret 'the most particular desire of the
> subject'.[32]

She argues that Lacan's claim to have discovered the law of the unconscious means that every analysis becomes no more than an application of that law, and leaves nothing new to be said.

For Irigaray, analysis is primarily the task of recognising its irreducibility to pre-established knowledge, and she links this openness to the focus on the finitude of sexed bodies. In her view, Lacan has been more concerned with establishing a theory of truth – for example, the Law of the Father and the primacy of the phallus as signifier – than with the singularity of the speaking sexed body. Irigaray accuses Lacan of remaining within a medical discourse of organs rather than developing a discourse of sexuate bodies.

Irigaray has often been criticised for substituting one essentialist model of gender and sexuality – female sexuality and desire between women – for those she criticises. However, she explicitly rejects such criticisms, and argues that:

> the issue is not one of elaborating a new theory of which woman would be the *subject* or the *object*, but of jamming the theoretical machinery itself, of suspending its pretension to the production of a truth and of a meaning that are excessively univocal.[33]

'Jamming the theoretical machinery' has involved her in major critiques of patriarchal power through her analysis not just of psychoanalytic writing but of Western philosophical pronouncements on the specification of reality, knowledge and justice.[34] Throughout these analyses Irigaray highlights the denial of sexual difference which emerges as the dominant discourse of the patriarchy in its claims regarding universal truths of the 'human'. She argues that Lacan denies sexual difference because of his assertion of the existence of only one libido, the Phallic, and that he therefore denies both masculine and feminine difference.

Although Irigaray is increasingly recognised for her critiques of patriarchy, it is significant that little attention has been paid to her analyses of women's sexual relationships. In order to counter Lacan's designation of the woman as lack, as object of exchange between men, Irigaray presents one woman's love song to another.[35] This love song challenges both the claim that lesbian desire cannot be spoken, and the claim that the meaning of women's desire can be designated only in the discourse of patriarchy, which denies sexual difference. Irigaray's strategy is to present the specificity of lesbian desire in bodily terms of touching rather than a univocal theory of truth as, for example, Lacan does when he designates sexual difference by the marker of the castrated phallus:

> They've left us only lacks, deficiencies, to designate ourselves
> . . . I love you who are neither mother . . . nor sister. Neither
> daughter nor son . . . What need have I for . . . persona, role,
> function? Let's leave all those to men's reproductive laws.

I love you, your body, here and now. I/you touch you/me, that's quite enough for us to feel alive.[36]

Here Irigaray pursues her narrative strategy of challenging universalising theories which claim to know the truth of sexuality without attempting to indicate the ways in which touching – in this case caressing – cuts through the mediation of the symbolic.

Irigaray, as we have already indicated, has been criticised for substituting essentialist feminine descriptions for the dominant psychoanalytic concepts of masculinity. However, her focus on the feminine body, and particularly on women touching each other, is her way of privileging differences in experiences of desire rather than the traditional univocal claims of philosophers or psychoanalysts regarding the truth of women's sexuality: 'Between our lips, yours and mine, several voices, several ways of speaking, resound endlessly, back and forth.'[37]

Irigaray is not alone in focusing on touching in order to challenge hierarchical dualisms such as that of reason over body. Philosophers such as Jean-Paul Sartre, Maurice Merleau-Ponty and Emmanuel Levinas share the view that in presenting theories of subjectivity one must acknowledge the individuality of each finite being. It is by focusing on our embodied subjectivity, with its needs and desires, that we can allow for differences, for otherness, for the fact that our lived bodily experiences are at one level irreducible to universal categories, even those of the psychoanalytic readings of the Oedipus complex.

Irigaray's descriptions of lips are evocative of both the vaginal lips and women's lips kissing and in this evocation she points to the fluidity and diversity of touching expressions. This 'bodily' speaking is an affirmation of continuity and multiplicity. Women, according to Irigaray, are not, as in Lacan's view, simply 'holes' to be filled, or 'objects' exchanged by male 'subjects': 'We are not lacks, voids awaiting sustenance, plenitude, fulfillment from the other. By our lips we are women . . .'[38] She stresses the self-definition of women in order

150

to counter common psychoanalytic truth claims regarding women's sexuality and its complementarity to men's, where this complementarity is frequently expressed in terms of organs such as the penis-in-vagina of heterosexual coitus, or the phallus in Freud's theory as the organ responsible for hier-archisation of the component instincts in infantile sexuality. Women touching each other in nakedness involves, for Irigaray, the stripping off of alienating representations:

> They have wrapped us for so long in their desires, we have
> adorned ourselves so often to please them, that we have come
> to forget the feel of our own skin.[39]

Irigaray emphasises that she is not developing the question 'What is woman?', since this would be within the patriarchal, universalist project of definitions. Rather, by her analyses of the grammar of discourse, its syntax, images and metaphors, she claims to indicate its silences – particularly regarding women. Irigaray conceives of the loving act not in terms of power but in terms of dwelling, lingering with the other in her separateness; she emphasises the quality of intensity, of sensation, colour and rhythm. The pleasure is the immediacy linking the lovers. Such analyses also provide a 'disruptive excess', a *jouissance* of diffuse sensuality which challenges the linearity of men's culturally sanctioned dominance in the possession of women.[40]

In her strategy of challenging psychoanalytic theories of sexuality, Irigaray highlights lesbian desires; in so doing she raises questions about sexual differences, gender differences and heterosexuality as well as homosexuality. She is not claim-ing to legislate for lesbian sexuality as the 'true' female sexu-ality because, she says, this would be to reinstate the very notions of sameness and univocity which she criticises.

Whereas Lacan, in line with most psychoanalytic writers, emphasises the importance of breaking the mother–baby dyad with the introduction of the third term, Irigaray maintains that stress on castration veils the cutting of the umbilical cord. In her view, such concealment has negative consequences for relationships to the body and desire, for both women and men. The Lacanian specification of desire as a function of the Law of the Father implies that men:

> are paralysed in their relationship with their bodies, in the
> living and desiring relationship with the mother, which has
> been censored.[41]

For women this censorship means that daughters cannot identify with a desiring woman, and women are designated as the effects of man's relations to his unconscious. Even for Freud, Irigaray argues:

> it is as a little man that the little girl loves her mother. The
> specific relation of the girl-woman to the mother-woman
> receives very little attention.[42]

Despite the fact that the maternal function is the basis of social order and desire, Irigaray maintains that fear of this powerful connection has resulted in relegating these relationships to the dimension of need and its fulfilment rather than desire. She argues that the fear of sexual desire for women is frequently represented in Western discourse as connected to the fear of madness, and particularly desire of the mother, who is designated the 'dark continent', the shadow of our cultures.[43] The fear is that:

> If the father did not sever this over-intimate bond with the
> primal womb, there might be a danger of fusion, of death, of
> the sleep with death.[44]

Irigaray argues that this severance is a denial of the mother's generative power. Furthermore, she stresses that such generative power is not reducible to the generation of children but also creates love, desire, language, the social and the political. Irigaray takes up the task of inventing the language which speaks the archaic relationship with the mother and with our bodies; she claims that acknowledgement of the primacy of the maternal relationship involves the recognition of women's archaic relationship to homosexuality. Following from this, women can acknowledge their love for other women outside the patriarchal economy of women as objects of exchange.

Irigaray is not denying rationality in favour of an intuitive, alinguistic 'sense' of the body. Two leading feminist commentators, Elizabeth Grosz and Margaret Whitford, reply to such charges against Irigaray:

> The image of the two lips, for example, of the four elements, must be seen as textual strategies, devices of writing and representation whose function is interdiscursive rather than referential.[45]

> Irigaray is proposing, not the abolition of rationality – she is after all adept herself in the manipulation of rational argument – but the *restructuring* of the construction of the rational subject.[46]

Whitford points out that Irigaray's project is similar to that of Merleau-Ponty's work on the phenomenology of perception – that is, a concern with the relationship of pre-discursive bodily experiences and conceptualisations. Furthermore, she is concerned with how, in the imaginary, these are characterised in relation to sexual differences – masculinity conceived as unity, linearity, self-identity; femininity conceived as plurality and fluid identity.

Irigaray's canvas is a broad one, situating gender differences and sexuality within the discursive histories of Western theorising and, most importantly, situating psychoanalysis, its ontologies and techniques, within such a historical context. This could be construed as collapsing the psychoanalytic field into the political or the sociological, and operate as a denial of the intrapsychic, the unconscious and transference. Thus, it could be argued that while Irigaray has provided a deconstructive analysis of patriarchy and its suppression of differences, nevertheless she has not advanced the field of psychoanalysis. Does her rehabilitation of the earliest bond with the mother's body, particularly women's 'archaic homosexuality' and men's 'archaic heterosexuality', answer such criticisms? How can she maintain the value of the vicissitudes of psychic development while denying the centrality of the oedipal conflict?

For Irigaray psychoanalysis is a cathartic journey, an exceptional task to be accomplished without 'amputation' or 'sacrifice' – that is, without interpreting development in oedipal terms which cut the girl and her body off from the mother, except in so far as the daughter emulates the mother by becoming a mother herself. She considers that in the oedipal scenario women have been sacrificed; therefore, a model for analysis between women has to be invented. For Irigaray the principal task of the analyst is to create room while listening to the analysand:

> That he or she gives the horizon, listening in a space made
> possible by his or her relationship with space–time . . . that
> should be the end of analysis – approaching the one and the
> other in their respective horizons, no longer constituted by
> rejection, hate or mastery, but moving and remaining open to
> the other.[47]

It is important to stress that Irigaray is speaking about the end of analysis, not denying the vicissitudes of anxious feelings of rejection, hatred and mastery as they variously arise in the transference. It is also important to note that moving and remaining open to the other does not imply an ongoing relationship with the analyst at the end of analysis but refers, rather, to an openness to the other(s) in one's life. Thus, in her view, relationships do not remain trapped in negative or positive transferences dominated by patriarchal power relationships.

In keeping with her project of tracing the matrices of the body, gender, sexuality and language, Irigaray points to the challenge of analysis between two women; she maintains that there is an immediacy, an openness within which transference and countertransference occur. She stresses that transference is not only the projection of a history but also involves the 'appropriation' of the other: the analysand takes what she needs to live well from the 'raw material' of the analyst. Irigaray emphasises the countertransferential elements of closeness and distance – the listening that opens the horizons of life and death. Beyond the limits of interpretation is the perception of the possibility of tranquillity, the calmness which allows for two to exist without strife or lethal fusion:

> a harmony which lets the other be, a sort of extra-
> transferential reserve which allows the analyst to ensure
> his/her own solitude and to direct the other in or towards
> his/hers.[48]

Within this context Irigaray considers that sexual difference constitutes the opening to an enigma, the complexity of questioning rather than either the discovery or the imposition of *a priori* value-laden classifications of masculinity and femininity.

It is clear from her reflections on transference that Irigaray is not confining her analytic work to analysis between women. She is not establishing the analytic relationship in terms of a rehabilitated mother–daughter relationship in which the daughter's needs are met by the 'good' mother-analyst. Neither is she proposing that lesbian relationships are, as many analysts hold, a regression to the mother expressed in sexual intimacy with women because of a failure of adequate maturation processes. Rather, in stressing the need for acknowledgement of our earliest connection to our mother's bodies, she argues that we can more creatively acknowledge our own bodily and sexual being-in-the-world as women and as men. Furthermore, such acknowledgement will free mothers from being designated dark, 'devouring', all-powerful places from which one must be severed, and allow for the recognition of mothers as women who love, create, work and generate in a myriad of cultural expressions.

Although Irigaray criticises psychoanalysis, she herself remains an analyst – acknowledging the transferential journey, fraught with its mortal dangers of destruction and incorporation and its creative possibilities for the move to tranquillity:

the recognition of non-assimilable duality within open-ended and developing horizons. Irigaray's analytic originality is that she has stressed the task of the analyst as providing not only transferential possibilities but a space for birth and growth, a space for gestation, and furnished a space for the analysis of lesbianism.

Kristeva on the disappointed ── *feverishness of the lesbian* ──

Julia Kristeva shares Irigaray's project of setting psychoanalysis within analyses of linguistics and philosophy: the relationships of subjectivity, language and sexuality. Like Irigaray, Kristeva elaborates the baby's early relationship with the pre-oedipal mother as the starting point of her psychoanalytic reflections. Unlike Irigaray, however, she remains within the dominant psychoanalytic framework, with its privileging of the notion of the Oedipus complex, and this centrally influences her theories of masculinity, femininity and homosexuality. Kristeva specifies subjectivity as a process, the intersection of the body and signification. Subjectivity is conceived in linguistic terms as semiotic and symbolic. The semiotic is not a stage which is surpassed but that which irrupts and challenges pretensions to closure in what Kristeva calls symbolic, patriarchal speech.[49]

Kristeva shifts the Lacanian emphasis on castration anxiety as the motivator into the symbolic order towards the analysis of the child's rejection of the pre-oedipal mother. This is the realm of oral and anal primary processes involving expulsion – what Kristeva terms the work of abjecting:

> The abjection of self would be the culminating form of that experience of the subject to which it is revealed that all its objects are based merely on the inaugural *loss* that laid the foundations of its own being.[50]

Abjection is a resurrection that has gone through death (of the ego). It is an alchemy that transforms death drive into a start of life, of new significance.[51]

Separation through abjection enables the subject to speak, which is simultaneously to recognise 'his' mortality – that is, to attain the symbolic order. Thus Kristeva maintains Lacan's primacy of entry into the symbolic as the place of the emergence of subjectivity under the Law of the Father.

Kristeva argues against what she terms essentialist notions of sexual difference which, she claims, postulate the feminine as a bodily specification outside the symbolic, the Law – that is, equalling language. Instead of Lacan's notion of the imaginary, Kristeva introduces the notion of the semiotic:

The *semiotic* [is] a psychosomatic modality of the signifying process; in other words, not a symbolic modality but one articulating . . . a continuum: the connections between the (glottal and anal) sphincters in (rhythmic and intonational) vocal modulations, or those between the sphincters and family protagonists, for example.[52]

The semiotic, although it is specific to pre-oedipal expressions, is similar to Klein's pre-oedipal positions in that such expressions are not a stage which is surpassed but a possible mode of relating which remains within the subject, along with the symbolic.

Gender differences are not the paradigm of relational differences for Kristeva, as they are for Irigaray. She situates 'masculinity' and 'femininity' within her analysis of the semiotic and the symbolic, which are distinguished by the oedipal axis. 'Femininity' is not confined to the biological female but refers to the 'pre-subject's' expression of the rhythmic, the intonational which emerges from the *chora* (the womb) – that is, from processes anterior to sign and syntax:

Once the subject has entered into the symbolic order, the *chora* will be more or less successfully repressed and can be perceived only as pulsional *pressure* on or within symbolic language: as contradictions, meaninglessness, disruption, silences and absences.[53]

Although Kristeva questions fixed notions of masculinity and femininity, she nevertheless retains common psychoanalytic alignments of gender and sexual desire:

> The girl . . . will retain the traces of that primary transference only if assisted by a father having a maternal character, who nevertheless will not be of much help in her breaking away from the mother and finding a heterosexual object. She will thus tend to bury that primal identification under the disappointed feverishness of the homosexual, or else in abstraction, which, as it flies away from the body, fully constitutes itself as 'soul' or fuses with an Idea, a Love, a Self-Sacrifice . . .[54]

> Beneath homosexual libido, which our social objectives catch and maintain captive, the chasms of narcissistic emptiness spread out; although the latter can be a powerful motive for ideal or superegotic cathexis, it is also the primary source of inhibition.[55]

Kristeva claims to present the originality of feminine speech, which she terms the semiotic, as a challenge to fixed, patriarchal, symbolic structures. Semiotic speech, the poetic, is defined as emanating from a primordial relationship to the maternal body, but also in constant challenge to the symbolic. Lesbianism, in Kristeva's theory, occurs outside a relationship to the symbolic, the patriarchal culture. This analysis points to the confusions in her descriptions between the semiotic and the symbolic. Because language and culture are, for her, defined by the symbolic, and language is meaningful, lesbianism involves a regression to a pre-linguistic psychic state, and is therefore psychotic. Contradictions in Kristeva's notion of lesbianism in terms of pre-given drives which are defined within the Paternal Law have been pointed out by Judith Butler (1992a) who argues that such a move precludes the subversion which Kristeva attributes to the semiotic:

If these drives are only manifest in language or cultural forms already determined as symbolic, then how is it that we can verify their pre-symbolic ontological status?[56]

Kristeva argues, on the basis of her psychoanalytic work, that there is a universal desire underpinning all speech – namely, to return to one's origin. The origin, in her view, is the archaic mother, who is unnameable and unpossessable. The analyst opens space for the unnameable, thus allowing analysands the freedom to express their desires. However, Kristeva, despite her claims, retains a reifying psychology of masculinity and femininity. As Elizabeth Grosz (1990b) points out:

> [Kristeva] . . . concedes the relevance of biological, physio-logical, genetic and chromosomal structures in her discussion of maternity. She is content to attribute an irreducibly biological basis to pregnancy while refusing an identity or agency to the pregnant woman.[57]

8

Jung:
The Waters and the Wild

W E HAVE SEEN how object-relations analysts' privileging of the Oedipus complex has resulted in their designation of lesbianism as immature. We have indicated how it is both arbitrary and restrictive to base theories of psychic development on the Oedipus myth. Jung and his followers, by contrast, have recourse to a myriad of cross-cultural myths, stories and legends. It might be expected that such richness and diversity would produce an analysis which recognises the diversity and differences of adult sexual desires and loves, including sexual love between women and between men. However, even though Jung roamed outside Greece, he nevertheless retains a dualistic metaphysics, an assumption of an oppositional universal notion of 'the masculine' and 'the feminine'.

Jungian interpretations of individuation (analogous to psychoanalytic notions of mature development) normatively legislate for the optimum psychic balance between masculinity and femininity. Such foundationalist norms of gender distinctions are reflected in many Jungian positions on lesbianism. In one of his few references to lesbianism, Jung maintains:

The main value lies in the exchange of tender feelings on the

one hand and of intimate thoughts on the other. Generally
they are high-spirited, intellectual, and rather masculine
women who are seeking to maintain their superiority and to
defend themselves against men. Their attitude to men is
therefore one of disconcerting self-assurance, with a trace of
defiance. Its effect on their character is to reinforce their
masculine traits and to destroy their feminine charm. Often a
man discovers their homosexuality only when he notices that
these women leave him stone-cold.[1]

This quotation expresses both an alignment of gender and
erotic desire and the common psychoanalytic claim that
lesbian desires necessarily imply a rejection of men and an
identification with masculinity.

Although Jung insists on the empirical character of his psychic research, he nevertheless recognises, in contrast to Klein,
the dangers of establishing psychic analysis as a doctrinal system:

Since it is my firm conviction that the time for an all-inclusive
theory, taking in and describing all the contents, processes,
and phenomena of the psyche from one central viewpoint,
has not yet arrived, I regard my concepts as suggestions and
attempts at the formulation of a new scientific psychology
based in the first place upon immediate experience with
human beings. This is not a kind of psychopathology, but a
general psychology which also takes cognizance of the
empirical material of pathology.[2]

However, Jung, like other psychoanalysts, accepts the alignment of gender, sexual desire and social role as the norm of
human development. Deviations from this alignment are
designated as lack, failure of integration or individuation.
Developmental failure, in Jungian terms, does constitute a
pathology but it is important to recognise the variable contexts of the term 'pathology' in his work. Andrew Samuels
points out that 'Jung's emphasis on teleology led him to propose that symptoms, and indeed, mental illness itself, may

often signify something of great psychological value for the individual'.[3]

The Jungian tradition exemplifies the vacillation between the phenomenological emphasis on interpretations of experience and meaning and the 'scientific' claim to establish universal norms of the psyche which can be empirically verified. The question of empirical verification in Jungian terms is as open to question as it is in any psychoanalytic claim – that is to say, the questions asked, the methodology used, structures the 'evidence' that is 'discovered'.

Like Freud and his followers, Jung claims to elucidate the 'inner' workings of the psyche, its processes and dynamics. But he does not reduce psychic events to early phantasies of biological entities; he analyses images and symbols which are antecedent to the individual psyche, yet arise within it. For Jung the unconscious has three tiers: the personal unconscious, the collective unconscious and the part of the collective unconscious that can never be made conscious. The personal unconscious consists of contents that are forgotten and repressed by the individual, and is continually replenished. The collective unconscious, in contrast, contains symbols which, he claims, are universal and cross-cultural. These he called 'archetypes', specifying that the archetype is synonymous with the Platonic universal idea.[4] He argues that there cannot be presuppositionless knowledge: 'There is an a priori factor in all human activities, namely, the unborn, preconscious and unconscious individual structure of the psyche.'[5]

These unconscious forms function as dispositions that influence our lives, our thoughts, feelings and actions. Jung stresses that the archetypes are 'forms', possibilities of representations, rather than fixed contents. We inherit them, and they are related to our instincts. They are collectively generated, emergent in individual psyches yet not exhaustively possessable by any one individual. Archetypal symbols emerge most powerfully in the individual psyche when we have problems that cannot be consciously or rationally resolved. This constitutes a central element of Jung's individuation process – namely, the integration of unconscious aspects of ourselves. The animus and the anima are archetypes that refer to the contra-sexual aspect of the masculine and the feminine within each individual. Many of Jung's references to male homosexuality are concerned with the man's relation-ship to his anima, his 'feminine' aspect. Although Jung distinguishes the personal unconscious from the collective unconscious, he regards them as inextricably linked. The symbol of the mother, for example, has both a personal and an archetypal aspect: 'the first carrier of the anima-image is the mother'.[6]

How is lesbianism viewed within Jung's schema? In his book *Jung, Jungians, and Homosexuality*, Robert Hopcke, a contemporary Jungian analyst, points out that discussion of lesbianism is strikingly absent from Jungian writings, given their preoccupation with the question of femininity.[7] Hopcke's project is to analyse Jung's account of homosexuality, and thereby assess his contributions to issues ranging across the social, political, cultural, intercultural and clinical dimensions. In our discussion we will rely considerably on Hopcke's research, since he provides an impressive and comprehensive survey of Jung's views on homosexuality. We shall highlight in particular Jung's shifting and often contradictory stance, and his adherence to dualistic notions of masculinity and femininity.

Early on Jung argues for 'a great mobility of the sexual components'.[8] He was also explicit in his criticism of the criminalisation of homosexuality.[9] However, as Hopcke points out, Jung never gives an example of a highly individuated person who is also homosexual.[10]

Hopcke's discussion of Jung's method of dream interpretation in 'The Synthetic or Constructive Method' (in *On the Psychology of the Unconscious*) exemplifies some of the contradictions in Jung's position. Since this also contains one of Jung's few references to female homosexuality, it is of particular relevance. Jung gives an account of a dream of a woman patient who 'had just reached the critical borderline between the analysis of the personal unconscious and the emergence of contents from the collective unconscious'.[11] The dream is as follows:

She is about to cross a wide river. There is no bridge, but she finds a ford where she can cross. She is on the point of doing so, when a large crab that lay hidden in the water seizes her by the foot and will not let her go. She wakes up in terror.[12]

The woman associated the dream with her conflicts with a woman friend – a friendship which Jung describes as 'bordering on the homosexual'. According to Jung, both women were very similar and their friendship, although it was 'ideal', also restricted them, and was marked by considerable quarrelling. Jung's patient, although she was exhausted by these arguments, seemed also to thrive on being misunderstood by her friend. He attributes this to her previously 'exaggerated, fantastic relation' to her mother, which she had transferred to her friend after her mother's death.

Jung goes on to compare a 'causal-reductive' interpretation of the dream, and of why the patient continues her involvement with her friend, with his own 'synthetic' or 'constructive' method. The former characteristically analytic method would interpret the woman's behaviour as expressing an unwillingness to relinquish an 'infantile wish' (accompanied by 'corresponding sexual fantasies') to identify with a masculine role in relation to her friend, seeking to re-create her relationship with her mother. Jung's critique of this approach as 'a severe depreciation of the patient's ideal of friendship' which 'tells the patient nothing new' does not, however, lead him to challenge the traditional psychoanalytic view of the woman's homosexual attachment as immature. Following another line of the woman's associations – that the crab reminded her of cancer, and then of a woman she knew who had died of cancer after 'a series of adventures with men' – Jung concludes that the woman's attachment is a defence against her 'frivolous streak' – that is, her own promiscuous feelings:

Accordingly, she remains at the infantile, homosexual level, because it serves her as a defence. (Experience shows that this is one of the most potent motives for clinging to unsuitable infantile relationships.)[13]

Hopcke discerns a number of strands in Jung's thinking in relation to homosexuality. First – as exemplified above, and characteristic particularly of Jung's earlier work – homosexuality is viewed as infantile. However, Hopcke also stresses that Jung's emphasis on the individual meaning of the person's homosexuality emerged at this time, citing his case history of an adolescent whose homosexuality represented a desire to enter into the world of adult men. Jung likens this to homosexual practices in Ancient Greece, which had an educational function. The analysis progressed 'beyond the mother towards masculinity', moving out of the 'relatively childish position' of homosexuality.[14]

This account, whilst it indicates a certain breadth of thinking, nevertheless crystallizes the way Jung sustains a number of contradictory threads. Hopcke rightly distinguishes Jung's emphasis on the individual meaning for each person of their homosexuality from the traditional psychoanalytic position. We would question, however, how far Jung really allows for such meaning to emerge when he simultaneously regards homosexuality as a 'relatively childish position'. His acknowledgement of cultural/historical factors is also somewhat at odds with his insistence on homosexuality as infantile.

In *Psychological Types* (1921) Jung introduced a major new perspective on homosexuality. He claimed that in many cases homosexuality arose out of identification with the contrasexual archetype of the anima (in men) or the animus (in women). The persona, which is consequently unconscious, is projected on to a person of the same sex. A woman's attraction to another woman would therefore be towards the femininity that she has rejected. He also attributes 'mother-transferences' in women to this process. He concludes:

> In such cases there is always a defective adaptation to
> external reality and a lack of relatedness, because identifi-
> cation with the soul produces an attitude predominantly
> orientated to the perception of inner processes, and the object
> is deprived of its determining power.[15]

As Hopcke points out, Jung is not claiming that animus or anima identifications are a universal cause of homosexuality. Neither does he restrict this explanation to active homosexuality; it also applies to a psychic state of same-sex attraction. However, Jung's analysis does adhere to oppositional and dualistic notions of masculinity as identified with men and femininity as identified with women.[16]

This dualism is particularly evident in 'Women in Europe' (1927). Jung is strident in his criticism of women who enter work and politics, areas previously dominated by men. He describes such 'masculinised' or animus-identified women as sexually unfeeling, frigid or aggressive, adding that 'a third possibility, especially favoured in Anglo-Saxon countries, is optional homosexuality in the masculine role'.[17] Once again, Jung does acknowledge the role of socioeconomic factors in the expression of homosexuality between women. However, this paper exemplifies a shocking insistence on dualistic notions of masculinity and femininity, and on identification of sex role with gender.

In his mature work Jung considers homosexuality as a move towards 'wholeness' or integration. In refusing to identify with a 'one-sided sexual being' the homosexual disposition preserves the archetype of the Hermaphrodite or the Self (the 'coniunctio'), the Jungian ideal of the union of opposites.[18] According to Hopcke, 'this view of homosexuality, therefore, looks beyond the anima/animus to the archetype of the Self, and sees homosexuality as a wrong-headed attempt to have psychological integration without personal cost'.[19] Hopcke points out that the archetype of wholeness, like all archetypes, can have both positive and negative aspects. It can function as regressive symbiosis with the mother, or as an integrated union between 'inner' and 'outer' reality. The Jungian emphasis on wholeness of the personality can allow homosexuality and lesbianism to be seen in terms of one aspect, among others, of a person's being-in-the-world rather than as a defining pathology.

So far we have concentrated on Hopcke's exposition of Jung's analyses of homosexuality and lesbianism. Later in this chapter we shall critically address Hopcke's reading of Jung and his allegiance to the archetypes. In order to set the stage for such a critique, we shall explore the backdrop of writings by feminist Jungians. It might be expected that the diversity of perspectives on homosexuality that emerge in Jung's work would offer contemporary feminist Jungian analysts fertile ground for opening out new considerations regarding lesbianism. However, their unquestioning acceptance of Jung's basic dualistic classifications of masculinity and femininity structurally restricts their thinking.

Many of them draw on a schema of four archetypal forms of the feminine which was developed by Toni Wolff, a colleague of Jung (see Figure 1).

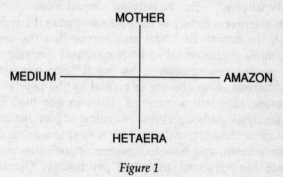

Figure 1

The four feminine types are identified as mother, hetaera, medium and amazon. Nor Hall explains:

> The mother pole opposes the hetaira, which is companion
> (concubine) to men . . . Wolff describes this axis as 'personally
> related'. The pole stretching from the medial (one who
> mediates the unknown) to the amazon (one who goes off
> alone) is impersonal in comparison. Every woman (and the
> feminine face of every man) lives primarily at one end of this
> structure.[20]

Each pole has its positive and negative aspects:

> The other face of the nurturing mother is the devouring
> mother; there is a heteira that is inspirational and another
> who leads to death, and so on.[21]

The advantage of this typology by contrast with, for example, Nancy Chodorow's and Susie Orbach and Luise Eichenbaum's analyses of women's psychology in mother–daughter terms[22] is that it offers wider possibilities for taking up feminine positions. Yet as Demaris Wehr points out, there are dangers in such naturalistic interpretations. She acknowledges that Jung's oppositional character typologies facilitate the recognition of the potential for conflict as well as the potential for balance. However, Wehr stresses the 'danger in this typology of "archetypalizing"' – that is, reifying – social roles.[23]

Wehr refers specifically to the heterosexism of the symbol of the self, the coniunctio.[24] She also argues that the religious and scientific traditions on which Jung draws generate unconscious gender assumptions in his work.[25] She suggests that Jung's analysis of spirituality as crucial to 'the psyche' offers a far more adequate account of development than that of psychoanalysis. Although Wehr is critical of patriarchal interpretations of 'the feminine', she does not explore erotic desires between women, and how recognition of such desires might influence her views of analytical psychology. She fails to recognise the effects of a theory expressed in terms of metaphysical foundationalism for the practice of psychotherapy, especially in its universal pathologising interpretations of lesbianism and homosexuality.

Nor Hall is concerned to distinguish between the stereotype ('a stricture') and the archetype ('an enabler'). However, her use of Wolff's schema in her understanding of lesbianism highlights the restrictiveness of her position. Her only references to lesbianism appear in her discussion of Artemis, an archetypal figure on the amazon pole whom Hall describes as:

> unconventional in any culture: she is wild mountain woman,
> woman alone, fighter, hunter, dancer, lover of animals,

protectress of all newborn suckling and roving creatures,
a sister to men and a teacher of women.[26]

Artemis's love, either for men or for women, is 'barren in the sense of not producing offspring', and she is a 'mannish woman' who 'encourages women to express their masculine natures'.[27] It is within this context that Hall refers to lesbianism, alluding to it in relation to the Korythalia, a festival in Artemis's honour in which women would dance with exaggerated phalli attached to their male costumes. Women 'may leave her for marriage, the way girls trained under Sappho left her and their circle of intimate friends'.[28] She suggests that later in life the desire to reconnect with the lost experience may '"come out" in a woman's recognition of her desire to form love relationships with women'.[29] Although this outcome is not viewed in a pejorative sense (as a pathology), Nor Hall's association of lesbianism with masculinity and also barrenness clearly reveals her firm adherence to dualistic and stereotypical notions of masculinity and femininity.

Sylvia Brinton Perera, another contemporary feminist Jungian analyst, presents a theory of feminine psychology and a therapeutic practice in line with her theory. Perera argues that women, as daughters of the patriarchy, have lost their connection to the repressed femininity of the mother. She outlines transferences of women clients to women analysts in terms of archetypes, and she focuses particularly on the archetype of the Goddess.[30] She analyses the Sumerian myth of the Descent of Inanna, queen of heaven and earth, in order to highlight its cosmic and psychologically transformative potential for women. Perera maintains that by interpreting her own and her analysands' experiences with reference to the myth, the repressed archetypal, instinctual femininity can be released.

Perera isolates four archetypally fruitful perspectives on the myth, which provides an image of rhythmical natural cycles, and also tells of an initiation process into the mysteries. Inanna travels to the underworld, to the darkness. Her openness to being affected is, in Perera's view, 'the essence of the experience of the human soul faced with the transpersonal. It is not based on passivity, but upon an active willingness to receive.' Perera maintains that this is an openness to the pre-verbal, affect-laden and transformative depths of the psyche. For her, this therapeutic regress leads to transformation. Thirdly, the myth provides a model of psychological health: the balance of opposites, earthly reality and the unconscious. The stripping away of persona-identifications can lead to the balance between the ego and the Self. Lastly, the myth provides a model of a return of the feminine from the underworld to Western culture, and the possibility of equal relationships between women and men.[31]

It is surprising that in her task of retrieving femininity, Perera does not refer to lesbians. In her consideration of what she terms 'incest with the mother or sister' she interprets erotic transferential fantasies in relation to the therapist as healing or substituting for a lack or loss of early mothering:

> The erotic bond [with the mother] permits intimate connec-
> tion to positive shadow qualities the woman may never have
> had conscious access to in herself. It is also a return to the
> possibility of being intimately reconnected to an other who is
> like herself and who can, therefore, validate her fully.[32]

Since she makes no mention in this text of fulfilling love relationships between women as lesbians, there is an implication that eroticism between women is regressive, a stage in the woman's journey towards wholeness.

June Singer presents something rare in analytic literature – a case study in which a successful therapeutic outcome of analysis recounts the patient as being happy and mature in a lesbian relationship. She describes her patient:

> She had discovered in her female lover all the well-
> disciplined, self-activating qualities that women as a rule
> expect from men. In addition, this woman had a perception
> of Ms. B's longing to be able to be sexual in the traditional
> feminine way, without fear of being taken advantage of as

men had taken advantage of her in the past. Therefore, the woman as lover could bring her to ecstatic heights of sexual pleasure such as she had never imagined it would be possible to achieve with a man.[33]

Singer maintains that difference is essential to individuating erotic desire, but she argues against differences being defined and confined to biological gender differences. She does, however, retain what she calls the archetypal masculine and feminine. Singer claims to follow Jung in her stress on the interplay of masculine and feminine in the individual psyche. In her case study she analyses her patient's difference from her lover: Ms B. could be her feminine self and experience her sexuality 'as a woman' because of the 'masculinity' in her woman lover. Singer claims to open the boundaries of sex and gender, and to focus on the individual. She argues that the ideal of psychic integration is expressed and achieved through the archetype of androgyny. The androgyne is the symbol of the self, the principle of wholeness, and is present, at least potentially, in each individual. Singer's notion of the 'natural self' involves the integration of masculinity and femininity. She distinguishes androgyny from bisexuality, which is, in her view, an interpersonal rather than an intrapsychic event. The 'inner process' of androgyny does change behaviour to allow individuals 'the freedom to be her or his most natural self'.[34]

Singer argues that the traditional conflation of gender roles and sex necessitated the suppression of the contra-sexual element; as a result, the potential of innate androgyny was repressed. Despite her questioning of the alignment of gender and sexuality, Singer fails to move away from universal foundationalist notions of the human as natural, having a nature which, at least in principle, can be known; being typified in terms of masculinity opposed to femininity, and joined in the union of androgyny. Notwithstanding her valuing of the cited lesbian relationship, Singer prioritises heterosexual intercourse as the ultimate expression of the bodily experience of androgyny:

171

In this act are combined the potencies inherent in the union of the cosmic Masculine and Feminine, with those generated in the union between two human beings, in each of whom the 'mystical marriage' has come to pass. Androgyny expresses itself through coitus in a dissolution of gender identity.[35]

Conclusion

Hopcke, like Singer, privileges Jung's notion of the coniunctio, the marriage of masculinity and femininity as the symbol of the ideal self. He agrees with the notion that a primary erotic relationship with another person symbolises the potential 'wholeness', the Jungian ideal of the human. Hopcke argues that Jung's theory of the multifaceted archetypal phenomena allows for the recognition of erotic desires between people which are not confined to the common Western divisions of homosexuality and heterosexuality. He denies that there is an archetype of homosexuality, defining sexual orientation as the result:

of a personal and archetypal confluence of the masculine, feminine, and Androgyne . . . bisexual men and women are not . . . sexual anomalies . . . but individuals whose masculine, feminine and androgynous energies merge and flow in a particular individual pattern in response to certain archetypical and personal experiences.[36]

Hopcke maintains that his theory of sexual orientation, as the co-presence of archetypes of masculine, feminine and androgyne in every sexual expression, is dynamic, and acknowledges shifting attractions rather than postulating a static condition. He claims that his focus on Jung's teleological view of erotic attractions surpasses the causal emphasis of psychoanalytic theories of sexual orientation.

Hopcke criticises the ethnocentrism of Jung's work, his descriptions of non-Western cultures as primitive and undifferentiated. Nevertheless, he asserts the universality of the foundational archetypes of the erotic, arguing that the specific combinations of masculine, feminine and androgyne acknowledge the differences of gender categories, sex roles, throughout the world. Given his stress on the complexity and fluidity of erotic desires, it is surprising that he insistently retains the notion of archetype to universally define the human and human relationships.

What does Hopcke's analysis of sexual desire in archetypal terms add to his sensitive and complex descriptions of sexual attractions? Why should homosexuality have a 'purpose', as he maintains in the last line of his book? Hopcke's allegiance to archetypal metaphysics and teleological notions of human relationships results in his establishing, in a similar way to psychoanalysts, notions of meaning that are independent of language. Archetypes are postulated as 'forms' which are available only through various representations but are themselves unknowable: 'the masculine', 'the feminine', 'the androgyne' are not acultural, ahistorical and extra-linguistic terms; they occur within language contexts; they are not independent entities. Retaining the archetypes of 'the masculine' and 'the feminine' and the composite 'androgyne' as foundational sets them up as ideals against which gender conformity and related erotic desires can be measured. Hopcke's scholarly research is valuable in its expansion of Jungian theories of homosexuality. However, his adherence to foundationalist and universalist categories must be questioned.

9

Eroticism and Countertransference

*I*N THIS CHAPTER we look more specifically at issues concerning sex and sexuality. It is evident that psychoanalysis has had enormous difficulty in the area of lesbian eroticism: there are very few clinical observations and descriptions of sex involving two women, even where lesbianism is the focus of concern. Deutsch's (1933)[1] account is probably still the most extensive (see Chapter 3). Furthermore, the two main models of lesbian sexuality – as heterosexual imitation or pre-oedipal immaturity – impose great limitations on what can be envisaged. We are also aware, from various sources, of difficulties in therapeutic practice in relation to lesbian eroticism, and here we aim to address these practical and theoretical issues, and also the origins of these psychoanalytic difficulties.

We have seen, especially in Chapter 6, the limitations of a psychoanalytic understanding in which a woman has to have a fictitious male identification in order to be conceived as desiring another woman. As we noted there, what is strikingly missing in this perspective is any account or analysis of the 'other' woman, the supposedly feminine one, who desires another woman. What are her desires? And how does she come to be a lesbian in the first place, if not by the route of supposedly deviant gender identity? Whilst within this paradigm of heterosexual desire the 'masculine' woman's attraction to another woman can be explained as a replica of heterosexuality, the 'feminine' woman's cannot. As Judith Roof (1991)[2] says in her account of various configurations of lesbian sexuality, she 'remains the impossible space, in and out of culture, unaccountable', and is widely ignored in most theoretical discourses, including psychoanalysis.

The advantage of the mother–baby paradigm is that it does not involve the problematic notions of masculine and feminine identifications as definitive for lesbian relationships. However, it consigns lesbian relationships to the pre-oedipal, with all the connotations this carries in psychoanalytic theory of the infantile, the enmeshed or symbiotic, the immature, the insufficiently genital or phallic: a failure of necessary separation from the mother. What is foreclosed upon is any idea of a mature sexuality between two women. Both models – which are often used in combination, as in McDougall's writings – contain an essential appeal to the phallus, either as fictively possessed by the 'masculine' woman, or as missing in 'immature' pre-oedipal sexuality. Sex outside the phallic field appears to be inconceivable as 'proper' sex, and this impression is borne out by an examination of contemporary psychoanalytic texts on the subject.

Sexual silences

Jean-Michel Quinodoz (1989),[3] in an article on five lesbian patients, confirms the impression of psychoanalytic silence in relation to lesbian sexuality: 'The psychoanalytic literature has little or nothing to say about the nature of erotic and sexual exchanges between homosexual women.' He continues:

> The patients have little or nothing to say about them.
> Eroticization of the skin is particularly important, and is often
> a form of defence against the painful feelings connected with
> mourning and separation. Some women confine themselves to

exchanges of this kind, while others use the fingers or the
tongue as a substitute for the penis.[4]

This, a recent description in one of the most prestigious
psychoanalytic journals, is notable for its crude phallocentric
assumption that some parts of the body function *as substitutes*
for the penis, as if the penis were the uncontestable standard
by which sexual activity is to be judged. Quinodoz approv-
ingly cites Jones's (1927)[5] article as 'memorable', and quotes
his view that female homosexuals' use of the tongue to achieve
identification with the penis can reach 'a quite extraordinary
degree of completeness', such that it can be an almost entirely
satisfactory substitute. Without a penis, or penis substitute,
these authors cannot conceive of any sexuality.

It is also evident how Quinodoz describes eroticisation of
the skin, which he sees as a predominant feature of lesbian
sex, only in terms of its supposedly defensive and infantile
aspects. The implication is not only that lesbian sex is insufficiently genital, but that the non-genital aspects detract from
the possibilities of real genitality rather than being in themselves substantial sources of adult pleasure, which might be
missing from more narrowly focused genital sex. The criterion
of genitality as an indicator of mature sexuality does seem to
be very tied to the presence of the penis, so that the ways in
which lesbian sex is thought to be genital are seen only as
heterosexual imitations, and the ways in which it is not are
seen as infantile. This appears to be another instance of organ-
dominated thinking, where inferences are drawn from the
presence or absence of particular parts of the body in lovemaking to the supposedly equivalent stage of development or
degree of psychic maturity.

In such a context, Quinodoz's report that his lesbian patients
had very little to say about sex comes as no surprise, but he
provides no explanation for this state of affairs. The effect of
this is to blame the patients – to convey that their lack of articulation about sex is their defect alone and, furthermore, a
defect that has to do with the nature of their sexual expressions. It does not occur to him that it might have something

to do with himself, with other aspects of the psychoanalytic relationship, or be connected to the general lack of representation of lesbian sexuality and the manifold cultural inhibitions and suppressions of erotic sensibilities between women.

Given his mainstream clinical background, it is hardly surprising that Quinodoz does not take such cultural forces into account. What is more surprising is that he does not consider how this silence in the consulting room may have something to do with the relationship between himself and his patients, with transference and countertransference issues, and with the assumptions of his theoretical stance. He claims instead that analysis of manifest homosexual women has been and is difficult, with frequent failures, despite greater analytic sophistication in interpreting the negative transference. Quinodoz says that *all five* of his patients showed a 'negative therapeutic reaction' – that is to say, they were resistant to the treatment in various ways. Most practitioners, if they encountered five patients with such negative reactions, would be led to consider what part they themselves played in this situation, and to examine possible countertransference contributions to both it and the lack of expression in relation to sex. Examination of countertransference is so commonplace nowadays that it is startling to find a clinical article with this kind of material where it is not considered; its absence is as remarkable as the patients' silence about their sexuality. That this has something to do with the subject under consideration is borne out by the realisation that countertransference issues are strikingly absent from almost all psychoanalytic considerations of female homosexuality, modern ones as well as older ones, as we discuss further in Chapter 10.

It is also likely that Quinodoz's theoretical position contributed to the silencing of his patients, and their negative reaction to the treatment. He sees homosexuality unequivocally as a failure of heterosexual development. He casts this failure in generally Kleinian terms, and sees manifest homosexuality as reflecting a borderline situation, with dual defences against both paranoid and depressive anxieties preventing a backward turning to psychosis and a forward direction to the Oedipus complex. Heterosexuality is a desirable end of both development and the treatment.

Within such a framework, which Quinodoz elaborates in some detail, the patients feel unconsciously empty, deprived and impoverished in their femininity, unable to identify genitally with the mother. Their main identifications are at the oral stage, with the aim of avoiding excessive amounts of anxiety associated with separation from the mother. Primitive defences are developed with the aim of gaining omnipotent control over the mother, and eliminating the father. These attacks on the mother aim to destroy in her everything that is inconsistent with what they want. Such attacks on the parental couple engender tremendous fear of retaliation, with the consequent sense that the inside of their own bodies may be spoiled and destroyed. The homosexual partner is seen as fulfilling many possible functions: as a fetish, who is used to disavow the lack of either male or female identity, and to sustain the omnipotent phantasy of being able to provide everything a couple may wish; as supporting 'excessive' projective identifications, so that the partner is used as a narcissistic mirror; as a defence against but also an acting out of envy, in which possession of another woman protects against the feelings of envy and also destructively ensures that the partner is deprived of her heterosexual possibilities, such as having a husband and children (which assumes that this is what all women should optimally want, and lesbians cannot have).

It is at least plausible, and important enough to warrant further consideration, that Quinodoz's holding of such a highly normative theory is one ingredient of the total analytic situation. Such a theory, depending on how it is adhered to and expressed within the therapeutic relationship, is, for most patients, unlikely to be facilitative and enabling, especially of expressions relating to sexuality. The holding of such a theory by the analyst is much more likely to stimulate defensiveness, distrust and negativity of various kinds, and may well account in part for Quinodoz's experience with his patients: that all five showed negative therapeutic reactions. The fact that such

178

a possibility is not even a subject for reflection compounds the deleterious effect of heterosexual normativity.

– *Defences against lesbian eroticism* –

So far we have considered mainly theoretical issues that may limit how lesbian sexuality is seen. There are also more personal or subjective factors, such as the analyst's or therapist's own comfort or discomfort in the area of sex, especially lesbian sex, and the strategies that may be employed to reduce any anxiety that is aroused by erotic material. Such anxiety is also likely to contribute to the silences about lesbian sexuality, and it raises further issues both about how lesbian eroticism is seen psychoanalytically and about how any such material is dealt with in terms of transference and countertransference. In discussing the nature and impact of erotic transferences, we are not thereby assimilating all lesbian sexuality to what transpires in the transference, which probably, by its very nature, manifests the most infantile, unresolved and conflictful aspects of anyone's sexuality.

We very much doubt that most psychoanalytic and psychotherapeutic trainings facilitate sufficient consideration of such issues for trainees – in relation to erotic material generally, and most particularly in relation to homosexual eroticism. Our grounds for thinking this are the absence of countertransference considerations generally with homosexual patients (Kwawer, 1980)[6] and the evident inability of many practitioners to enable erotic material to emerge in therapy with lesbian patients. One of the very few comments in this area is made by Roy Schafer (1983)[7] in his survey of analytic practice and the analytic relationship. He claims that any vulnerability on the analyst's part to homosexual erotic transferences is most likely to be shown by blind spots and defensive displacement of analytic interest, rather than by conscious sexual arousal or acting out. Ethel Person (1983)[8] maintains that erotic transferences of all kinds are often blurred and never fully worked through, and the limitation of erotic material in the analysis often lies with the therapist. She also claims – albeit with no substantiating material – that erotic transferences with homosexual women and female therapists are often particularly intense, difficult to manage and interpret, and that this can lead to disruption of the treatment; but she does not discuss what susceptibilities on the therapist's part might make this more probable. This is clearly an important area which has been virtually ignored, to the detriment of the patients involved.

One of the few examples in the existing analytic literature on this subject – albeit with a seemingly heterosexual patient – is to be found in McDougall's (1986b)[9] reflections on her countertransference responses at a point where she felt that the treatment had become repetitive. A manifestly homosexual dream of her own, which she connected to aspects of the patient's previous session, made her realise that she had overlooked the patient's homosexual attachment to her mother, and her wish to have a mother who sexually desired her. This McDougall saw as due to her own need to keep in repression her homosexual wishes in relation to her own mother, which meant that she had not been listening properly to the patient's wishes, nor had she been able to understand the patient's difficulty in talking to her about masturbation. These analytic shortcomings she describes variously as countertransference deafness and unconscious complicity; once they were recognised and understood, the treatment proceeded much more fruitfully. This example is interesting for the unusual analytic scrutiny in this area; but it also underlines the paucity of such material generally, especially in relation to lesbian patients, with whom McDougall, in other writings, does not consider such possible countertransference reactions.

More recent psychoanalytic work examines countertransference responses to what is considered to be early maternal erotic material. Thus Judith Welles and Harriet Wrye (1991),[10] who also comment on the lack of reporting of erotic transferences, describe – again in relation to seemingly heterosexual patients – possible sources of countertransference difficulties. They argue that a patient's erotic transference may elicit powerful and primitive defences in the analyst; these they describe in some detail. We have also become aware, through supervision and discussion, of the defences that therapists may employ when they are presented with sexual material by their lesbian clients – defences which, in various ways, block or diffuse the expression of eroticism by their clients, either within the transference or more generally.

In one example a patient, after several years of therapy, began to experience intense love feelings for her analyst which included many fantasies about the analyst's body, and about the two of them erotically engaged with each other, and experiencing mutual orgasm. The analyst, in a most untypical departure from her normal mode of working, suddenly found herself telling the patient about her husband and child. When the patient reacted to this intrusion of personal material, she was able to recognise the anxious nature of her response, the powerfully arousing nature for her of the patient's fantasies, and the fact that all this was so threatening that she was impelled to assert her unavailability and her heterosexuality to the patient. This illustrates what Welles and Wrye describe as defences against archaic, primitive and magical wishes concerning the bodies of both analyst and patient. The effect on the patient was to inhibit any further expression of her sexual feelings, and to leave her with a sense that her sexuality was too threatening and not acceptable, thus confirming her fears of rejection. Because of the analyst's openness to understanding her own responses, and because of an otherwise satisfactory therapeutic relationship, the situation was subsequently retrieved.

In a second example, with a patient who was very deprived, demanding and impulsive in seeking gratification, the therapist was aware of how frightened she felt of the patient's sexual longings for her, which were evident from early on in therapy. The patient herself felt that there was no difference between talking about sex and having it, and that the therapeutic relationship, with its constraints, constituted an unbearable rejection of her sexuality, since she couldn't act on it, and the therapist wouldn't sleep with her. The therapist felt that she had to fend off the patient's unmeetable desires; she felt overwhelmed by how she could never satisfy the patient, and guilty for apparently arousing so much longing, sexual and otherwise. She colluded with the patient's sense that to talk about sex was tantamount to having it, by only hesitatingly pointing out the silence in this area. This resembles the constellation that Welles and Wrye describe, in which the patient's longing to resist separation and fuse with the analyst is so threatening that it may be met by defensive refusals on the analyst's part, by over-enforcement of boundary and framework issues, or by too much intellectualisation of the patient's difficulties.

In this case, a therapeutic stalement ensued, in which the therapist could not let the patient fall in love with her, just as the patient's mother had apparently been unable to do. The therapist also felt ashamed that she was so frightened of the patient's sexual longings, so for a long time she was unable to discuss this in supervision. When her supervisor pointed out the patient's frustrated attempts at bringing her sexual feelings into the therapy relationship, she had great difficulty in accepting this, again feeling guilty that she could be the target of such homosexual longings. Although there were substantial improvements for the patient in many other aspects of her life through therapy, she did finally leave with her sexuality as a very unresolved area.

A third therapist, with a lesbian couple who were concerned about the low frequency of sex in their relationship, found himself attempting to reassure them that this did not matter too much – that in many long-term heterosexual relationships sexual intercourse often dwindled too – and questioning what sex was about anyhow. When he realised his difficulty in taking on board their concern about sex, and his wish not to talk about it, he could acknowledge that he felt at a loss at the thought of sex between two women; he could not imagine what it would be like, and felt that any interest or curiosity on his part would be intrusive, too male and heterosexual, and possibly vicarious. He also acknowledged how sex between two women made him feel redundant and unwanted, to which he reacted by withdrawing, whilst intellectually remaining supportive of the possibility of such relationships. All this inhibited his ability to be professionally available for the couple, and it replicated in the therapeutic situation many of their own difficulties in mobilising their sexual feelings and imaginatively exploring their sexuality. This example resembles Welles and Wrye's description of analysts who may too easily accept their patients' assertions of erotic disinterest – a defence they consider to be produced by insecurities on the analyst's part about sexual expression, and about containing the transference.

In a fourth example, a patient reported to her therapist a dream in a part of which she was intensely making love to her mother. The patient herself had felt very shocked by the intensity of her erotic expression and the vivid detail of her engagement with her mother; she was also taken aback by the degree of evident love towards her mother expressed in the dream, since she had a generally hostile relationship with her. When she told this dream to her therapist – along with the first part of the dream in which she had been tending to her mother, who had become ill with a migraine – the therapist found herself quite unable to deal with the erotic details of the patient kissing her mother orally and genitally. She directed the patient's attention solely to the first part of the dream – to the mother's apparent illness and the patient's desire to care lovingly for her – and when the patient protested that she was ignoring the worrying sexual part, she told the patient that it was just an instance of how she sexualised all close relationships, and that what was really involved was a dread of intimacy with her mother. This defensive reaction has parallels with Welles and Wrye's description of how analysts may unconsciously infantilise a patient in order to perpetuate a mother–baby fusion: avoiding conflict and separateness, relying too much on just the provision of a holding environment, and failing to notice patient development, especially sexuality. The therapist in this case was later able to acknowledge how difficult this material concerning the mother's body had been for her; but her reactions were all the more remarkable because with this particular patient she had been able to sustain and work through a complex erotic and idealising transference.

Finally, in consultation to a therapy organisation with considerable sensitivity to the issues facing lesbians in therapy, we became aware of how little erotic material there was in the various reports of therapist–client relationships with both heterosexual and lesbian patients, and women therapists. There was general agreement that very few erotic transferences were reported, and some feeling of being at a loss in knowing how to handle such material should it occur. Several therapists felt that they must have unconsciously inhibited such material. This echoes Welles and Wrye's descriptions of how some analysts may be unwilling or unable to participate in an erotically charged interaction, reacting to the erotic 'horror' that a patient may experience with their own erotic 'dread', and falling dull and silent as a result. Such defensive manoeuvres may underpin the relatively widespread silence in this area that we have already noted. An alternative defence against erotic material that Welles and Wrye describe is to raise the spectre of the forbidding oedipal father, becoming uncharacteristically authoritarian or making 'penetrating' interpretations, which perhaps finds some reverberations in Quinodoz's approach, described above.

All these considerations suggest how difficult it can be for therapists and analysts working with lesbian or other patients to be able to receive erotic material, either as indirectly reported or more directly in the transference, without unduly defensive reactions being mobilised. The capacity to do this should clearly be developed as part of professional training, but we doubt to what extent this happens – partly because of the theories of homosexuality that are most often taught, and partly because of the frequent avoidance of this area, especially in its countertransference manifestations. The examples we have given are not in themselves unusual, and may have parallels with other forms of erotic transference. They are striking only in a context of the virtual silence concerning lesbian sexuality, and an apparent lack of erotic material in the therapeutic encounter.

These examples also raise the question of why lesbian erotic material should arouse such difficulty, and what specific fears of homosexuality, as opposed to general difficulties in working with erotic transferences, are involved in this therapeutic defensiveness. As Fritz Morgenthaler (1988)[11] points out in relation to male homosexuality, stimulation of an analyst's own – possibly repressed – homosexual feelings has to be one consideration here. This is problematic where such feelings have not been sufficiently explored, analysed or integrated, as in McDougall's (1986) example considered above, and thus where their arousal is felt as acutely threatening. If this is so, it indicates a widespread shortcoming in the analyses of seemingly heterosexual practitioners – as, indeed, McDougall suggests was the case for her. It also indicates one possible avenue where progress could be made in relation to psychoanalytic work with lesbian patients.

These considerations about the ways in which therapists' theories and defensive reactions can contribute to silences about sexuality on the part of lesbian patients do not rule out independent sources of difficulty stemming from the patients themselves, from their individual histories as both female and lesbian in a culture that constructs female and lesbian sexuality in specific ways. Some patients may well experience degrees of shame and uncertainty about lesbian eroticism which inhibit articulation within the therapeutic or, indeed, any other situation; such shame and uncertainty can have both individual and social roots, in the taboo against homosexuality. Others may fear, perhaps unconsciously, that talking about sexual matters may lead to experiencing erotic feelings in the therapeutic situation. There may be many fears and fantasies of different kinds attached to this, and to how the therapist is imagined as responding, which make silence seem a safer option. Yet others, in response to adverse experiences of various kinds, may have developed ways of suppressing and cutting off their erotic sensibilities and spontaneity, so that erotic feelings are not easily mobilised, or are so only with the anticipation of great risk, pain or incomprehension. All these reasons, and many others, may explain why there are significant silences surrounding the erotic, why efforts may be made to desexualise the therapeutic encounter. The complex web of forces surrounding any one individual's experiences of lesbian eroticism needs a correspondingly wide range of understandings on the therapist's part.

Maternal eroticism and sameness of gender

Any attempt to understand lesbian eroticism psychoanalytically raises the question of who the 'other' is in lesbian relationships and whether, within a psychoanalytic framework, this should be seen in terms of the mother or various aspects of her – that is, whether we should seek to understand some manifestations of lesbian sexuality in terms that make reference to mother–daughter relationships. There are several questions involved here, both the way in which the mother is conceived, her invariable and exclusive presence, and about the concreteness this formulation gives to gender. One difficulty with this form of analysis lies in the assumption that all maternally directed sexuality is pre-oedipal in character. Recent psychoanalytic work, through a consideration of female–female erotic transferences, suggests how maternally directed sexuality could be reformulated within such a framework. Wrye and Welles (1989)[12] for example, note how maternal erotic transferences of all kinds have hitherto been seen as 'archaic', as precursors of oedipal genital eroticism. They argue instead that such transferences are erotic in their own right, as well as being oedipal precursors. Under 'erotic' they include tender, sensual, romantic wishes, as well as sadistic, aggressive and moralistic ones; and they take a broad view of the maternal erotic transference as including all manner of sensual wishes directed towards the analyst's body. This, they argue, is a 'goldmine' for the analysis rather than the 'minefield' that they claim others have seen it as. They maintain that the maternal erotic transference can express a sensuous relationship between baby and mother, with possible anal overtones; or dyadic and triadic issues; or an experience of the mother as a whole object. Since such maternally directed erotic expressions are often preverbal, they can be very difficult to recognise.

Eva Lester (1990)[13] puts forward a similar argument in an article on gender and identity issues, in which she maintains that erotic homosexual fantasies in female–female therapeutic dyads are not as uncommon as they are thought to be. She, like the authors considered above, describes possible countertransference reactions which may inhibit their expression. She also maintains that the nature of homosexual transference in heterosexual women is complex; in particular, that the sexuality which can be regarded as of pre-oedipal origin, with its concerns of fusion, merger and passivity, is combined with an active searching for the mother as a pleasure object, and an object of identification. She argues that generally the girl's continued active search for the mother should not be seen as a withdrawal from oedipal conflicts, a regression to the pre-oedipal mother, as it so often is; rather, such a 'negative' oedipal phase is normal for girls, and implies a degree of self–object differentiation between the daughter and mother, where the girl competes with the father for the mother's love. The early libidinal attachment to the mother, and positive identification with her, remain as part of and past the oedipal phase, along with other developments.

Lester does not consider lesbian sexuality, nor what the implications of her reconsideration of the possibilities in a daughter's relationship to her mother might be for lesbian relationships. However, both she and the authors considered above do argue for a form of eroticism towards the mother which is not only pre-oedipal but can have characteristics that are considered to be more mature – to involve a more developed differentiation of self and other, where the mother is viewed as a whole and separate object, as a source of both pleasure and identification. From a different perspective, Jessica Benjamin (1990)[14] also argues against a psychoanalytic conception of the mother which consigns her totally to the infantile, enmeshed and pre-oedipal, with the only sources of separation and sexual agency coming from the father – an argument which we consider further below (Chapter 10, p. 223).

These considerations are crucial for suggesting that where important aspects of the mother are re-enacted in a lesbian relationship, this does not invariably have to be only of the enmeshed pre-oedipal kind so often implied; other conceptions are possible. To hold open such a possibility is not in any way to deny that sometimes the participants in a lesbian relationship may experience or unconsciously construct their partners in a way that has features of the pre-oedipal mother. Nor is it to deny that some lesbian relationships may have powerfully symbiotic features, with all the attendant difficulties that this can entail. Our own clinical experience presents us, amongst other scenarios, with a range of manifestations of re-enactment of early maternal symbiosis, or wishes for this. Indeed, this could be thought of as one of the possible psychic dangers, as well as sometimes the felt attractions, of lesbian relationships, one of the ways in which a lesbian relationship is vulnerable to difficulties. From a different perspective, just such difficulties have been amply described (see Chapter 10, p. 232). This, however, ignores both those lesbian relationships where such symbiotic features are not marked, which are probably much less likely to be seen clinically, or those in which they are resolved or worked through in some way within a lesbian framework.

There are also several problems with the assumption of the mother as the invariable pre-oedipal figure, or with her alone as having this status and only this status. Such an approach too readily assumes that the mother is always the primary parent and the father a secondary one – indeed, that parents are universally heterosexually gendered, and that the second parent, who supposedly enforces separation from the primary one, is always male, not female. But there are many instances, as we illustrated in Chapter 6, where mothers, for some reason or other, are not primary pre-oedipal figures – where, for example, a child has a grandmother, a father, a nanny or a lesbian lover as a primary figure, and the mother is effectively a second parent; or where the two parents are less exclusively divided in this way.

Furthermore – leaving aside the issue of whether the mother is conceived of only in pre-oedipal terms – we are also presented with the question of why lesbian sexuality should be analysed in terms of mother–daughter relationships at all. To assume that because a woman desires another woman this other woman invariably represents aspects of her mother is to interpret gender and similarity of gender very concretely. To be so literal is to be quite markedly unpsychoanalytic; it is to take the manifest form at face value. Freud (1931)[15] pointed out how a woman often carries over aspects of her relationship with her mother into her adult sexual relationships with husbands or male lovers. It is now widely acknowledged (by, for example, Nancy Chodorow, 1978[16]) how women may look for aspects of maternal love in their male partners, as well as other qualities; that the possession of a male gender in a partner is not seen as precluding the search – however much this may be frustrated – for maternally founded qualities. With lesbian relationships, by contrast, such a cross-gender displacement does not seem to be conceived of by psychoanalytic writers, and the possibility that the female partner could represent aspects of the father is ignored. Although the importance of mothers in many women's lives perhaps makes it more likely that the mother will persist more strongly in adult relationships, none the less the female partner can also be endowed with features of the father, or come to represent the search for these. In working clinically with lesbian patients it is important not to exclude this possibility, and to be able to recognise elements of father–daughter eroticism that may be present in lesbian relationships, and may coexist (or not) with more maternally directed eroticism.

Perhaps the difficulty in recognising this is due not only to the way in which gender is taken too literally, but also to the restrictions gender divisions place on our thinking and feeling. For example, the considerable literature on the importance of the analyst's gender,[17] and its influence on the therapeutic relationship, underlines the salience of gender, and how it can preclude or make more difficult the emergence in the transference of cross-gender characteristics as perceived to belong to the analyst. In particular, with women analysts paternal transferences may be absent, or hard to recognise, and it may be particularly difficult for women analysts to see themselves as the focus of paternal transferences, whereas maternal identifications in male analysts appear to be more readily recognisable. This appears to illustrate a general difficulty in cross-gender identifications – something Benjamin (1990)[18] points to as an aspect of the polarised nature of the construction of gender difference. It may also illustrate a specific difficulty in seeing the lesbian love-object as anything other than an aspect of the maternal.

Another way in which gender can be interpreted too literally is that it becomes the defining feature of lesbian relationships. The charge that homosexual relationships 'deny difference' is a familiar one. Some psychoanalysts see the sameness of gender as in itself a barrier to 'real' sexual desire, as meaning that such relationships are inevitably narcissistic and deny difference, as we illustrated especially with respect to some of the writers considered in Chapter 5. Sameness of gender is treated as an unexplored given, as transparently and self-evidently betokening narcissism. Such a position assumes that all other features of a homosexual relationship pale into insignificance compared to the sameness of gender, including all other possibly important differences between the partners. It leaves unaddressed how the participants themselves actually experience their gender, the possible differences in this, and what significance this similarity does have for them. In other words, important aspects of psychic reality regarding gender are ignored in favour of what is assumed to be 'reality' in relation to gender. It cannot be assumed that just because two people are of the same gender, they therefore experience gender in similar ways. In practice many of the excitements, conflicts and pleasures of homosexual relationships may well concern differences in the way gender is experienced and lived out, including how, as a woman, desire for and from another woman is felt and expressed. In this way gender can be an issue of difference between two people of the same gender, either constructively or destructively, consciously or unconsciously, depending on the relationship in question. The notion of homosexuality as some kind of collapse into sameness, as inevitably narcissistic, attributes an over-concrete and over-simplified meaning to 'belonging to a gender' and in so doing runs counter to basic psychoanalytic principles.

10

Different Voices?
Sources of Dissent and Dialogue

MUCH OF THIS book testifies to the hegemony within psychoanalysis of certain views of homosexuality, and to the absence of any serious or extended dialogue about these various views. As we noted in the Introduction, this absence is remarkable. Several other authors have commented on it,[1] and we might well enquire to what this lack of debate and argument is due. It is an absence that applies both to the expression of ideas within a clinical and theoretical framework, and also to institutional practices concerning training. We might also wonder what strands of thought or theoretical positions within psychoanalysis are most likely to give rise to – or have given rise to – different views of homosexuality, or to critiques of prevailing views; and what their fate has been.

In pursuit of sources of dissent, we might most plausibly be drawn to those positions which provide radical critiques of psychoanalytic theory, seek to understand and locate its unspoken cultural and political assumptions as reflections of various aspects of the dominant social order. Feminist, socialist or anti-racist critiques and reformulations of psychoanalysis might well, it could be thought, provide the basis for a different view of homosexuality within psychoanalysis, or at least have that on their agenda. In this chapter we will consider what such positions have to say about homosexuality, but it is clear from the outset that their contribution, with the exception of a few rather specific feminist writings, is very limited, if not totally absent, for reasons which we shall examine. Instead, the most articulated opposition comes from what we might call a liberal scientific position within mainstream psychoanalytic practice. Such a position seeks to show the degree of evident prejudice in psychoanalytic writing about homosexuality, and its departures from the canons of 'objective' scientific modes of reasoning, and agreed psychoanalytic methods and aims. There has also been some critical discussion of psychoanalytic practice with homosexual patients from such a position within the profession.

—— *The liberal scientific tradition* ——

Freud, as we saw in Chapter 1, was emphatic that homosexuality existed in manifold and diverse forms, and that too simple or unified a picture of its nature and genesis should be eschewed. He also advocated caution in generalising from small numbers of clinical cases. As we have seen so far, and as Kenneth Lewes (1989)[2] amply demonstrates for male homosexuality, psychoanalysts in the main threw all such caution to the winds in their attempts to generalise about and explain homosexuality. As with male homosexuality, the depths of pseudo-objective generalisations about lesbians of a highly prejudicial nature were to be found in the psychodynamic writings of the 1950s and 1960s.[3] It is striking that these received almost no comment or review from within the psychoanalytic profession, despite their heavy reliance on psychoanalytic concepts. From the mid 1960s onward, however, Robert Stoller put forward arguments that homosexuality was not a diagnostic category, and that to view it as such, or to assume its necessary symptomatic status, was seriously misleading. He was one of very few psychoanalysts to argue for the deletion, in 1973, of ego-syntonic homosexuality from the American Psychiatric Association's list of mental disorders. Many others either held themselves aloof from this debate or argued in favour of its retention.[4]

Stoller's main arguments are that homosexuality does not constitute a syndrome (that is, a uniform constellation of signs and symptoms shared by a group of people), but is 'only a sexual preference'; that different people with this sexual preference have quite different psychodynamics underlying their sexual behaviour; and that there is no shared aetiology – quite different life experiences and family backgrounds can be associated with homosexual behaviour.[5] He further emphasises the huge variety of referents that the term 'homosexual' may have – covering conscious and unconscious homosexuality, lifelong or transient impulses, loving relationships or casual sex – so that there is considerable lack of clarity in its meaning. Accordingly he argues strongly against the term 'the homosexual' and also describes how, 'despite a rhetoric of science', it can be 'more insult than objectivity'.[6] Furthermore, his general approach to perversion is to exclude homosexuality *per se*, in that he considers perversion not a matter of object choice but, rather, of the unconscious fantasy that accompanies any given act. Perverse dynamics contain fantasies of hostility and revenge, attempts at retribution for past humiliations, in which 'trauma becomes triumph', acted out to different degrees and in different forms.[7] This leads him to consider not only the 'classical' perversions such as fetishism, transvestism, voyeurism etc., but also the use of pornography.

Stoller is not arguing from any generally anti-diagnostic position, but rather on the basis of his extensive experience with various forms of gender disorder, where many of his efforts have been directed towards differential diagnosis and developmental understandings. His standing in this field is well established and widely acknowledged, and if only for that reason it might be thought that his arguments against using homosexuality as a diagnostic category would carry considerable weight. This, however, seems not to be the case, and by 1985 Stoller is expressing his surprise that what seems so obvious to him is still obscured, and needs restating. He reiterates his argument that there is no such *thing* as homosexuality, and that there are as many different homosexualities as heterosexualities. On the basis of his work in the area of perversion and pornography, he also reports how he does not find heterosexuals any more normal than homosexuals – an idea which, he says, is not generally acceptable. He criticises the way that in so much work on homosexuality, heterosexuality – and particularly heterosexual happiness – is taken for granted. He underlines instead the way in which he feels that most people in the expression of sexual excitement, and regardless of preference, can be 'quite hostile, inept, fragmented, gratified at only considerable price, and deceptive with themselves and their partners'.[8] In other words, he questions whether the implicit comparisons with heterosexuality that are so often made are justified and, like other critics, argues that to generalise on the basis of specific clinical observations with patients who have come for treatment to all homosexuals or all homosexuality is absurd.

He also argues for great caution in saying anything about homosexuality, emphasising how little analysts know about it and criticising the over-use of many analytic concepts which, he says, give a misleading picture of homogeneity. He argues for a fresh start, and provides a case description of one homosexual woman where he tries to avoid falling into the traps he sees in other analytic work. In particular, he does not attempt to explain her homosexuality, or find causes for it, although he does discuss neurotic conflicts that played a part in her love relationships. Whilst he emphasises how all psychoanalytic descriptions are necessarily fictions, in that no 'true' picture is ever possible, he none the less strives to present a picture of his patient which allows her to come alive to the reader, to some extent in her own words, and permits us to see his lines of reasoning and argument in relation to her and the process of her therapeutic relationship with him. He is emphatic in his refusal to use his case history for any general or unified theory of homosexuality, and makes only minimal use of psychoanalytic concepts, although the whole process of his therapeutic work with his patient is psychoanalytically informed.

To some, Stoller's case description might seem rather a psychoanalytic non-event, the perhaps pedestrian analysis of a woman's neurosis, where the woman's homosexuality is seen only as a sexual preference, reflecting her neurotic conflicts, but not as an entity in itself. It is precisely this kind of ordinary case history that is so lacking in most of the literature, and makes what is a very ordinary presentation rather unusual. Stephen Mitchell (1981), in a review of treatment issues with homosexual patients, makes a similar point.[9] He suggests that psychoanalysts who work with their patients' homosexuality as they would with any other experiences, 'simply as material to be inquired into and analysed', rather than seeing it as a target for special explanation or even cure, are consequently less likely to write about their work. They are therefore underrepresented in the literature, because they do not see homosexuality as posing particularly distinctive features. One could add to this reason for the absence of such case presentations the difficulties felt in opposing more established or institutionalised views – something which Stoller, but very few other psychoanalysts or psychotherapists, appears able to confront.

Stoller (1968)[10] is also one of the few psychoanalytic writers to take up the issue of dread of homosexuality, citing Ralph Greenson's (1964) work with male patients.[11] This appears to show that such a dread, where it is extreme, contains a fear of turning into the opposite sex, of losing one's gender identity. Greenson describes how, when homosexual impulses or fantasies enter the clinical picture, this often produces panic, especially at the thought that it might mean the person in question 'is' a homosexual. He maintains that this panic arises because the patient feels as if he is losing part of himself when he is faced with his own homosexual feelings, the aspect in which his identity is construed in terms of his gender, whereby homosexual feelings make him feel 'less of a man'. It is, Greenson says, as if the gender of the sexual object determines the person's sense of his own gender. Indeed, he says it is true of both neurotic adults and so-called normal people that they appear to need some sense of heterosexual attraction to maintain their own gender identity, since this relies on a difference of gender between the love-object and oneself. By contrast, he sees many overt homosexuals and bisexuals as having much less anxiety of this kind about gender identity; this allows them to accept their homosexual feelings much more readily.

Greenson's work on this issue – which has not been taken up except by Stoller, and not developed any further – is important in several respects. It places the investigation of the fear of homosexuality within the psychoanalytic domain, and indicates how heterosexual gender identity may depend on a disavowal of homosexual feelings. Also it might make us question from another angle the recurrent psychoanalytic conflation of object choice and gender identity, and the apparent investment in this theoretical assumption. This is something which Stoller (1985) also notices and criticises, likening psychoanalysts to 'less educated' people in their confusion of object choice with issues of masculinity and femininity. He regards this as yet another clinical mess that could be resolved by 'better' – that is, less biased – clinical observations. However, Greenson's work, and also our own considerations about the absence of any acknowledgement of analytic countertransferences, strongly suggest that unconscious factors related to anxieties about homosexuality may also be involved. The frequent resort to notions of deviant gender identity, on the basis of often arguable clinical data, may reflect a displacement into theory and a projection on to homosexual patients of the kind of unconscious fears described by Greenson. Anxieties aroused by the stimulation of homosexual feelings that are normally held at bay or in repression may threaten the seemingly heterosexual practitioner's sense of his/her gender identity, and one way of dealing with this is to get rid of these unwelcome fears by perceiving them, in the form of theory, in the feared others, whose sexuality can trigger such feelings.

Stoller also raises – although he does not discuss in any detail – the question of the possible psychodynamic roots of psychoanalysts' problems in understanding homosexuality. He also suggests that such unconscious roots might underlie what he calls the 'by-laws' which prevent homosexuals being accepted as candidates for training, members of faculties, or as training analysts; whereas, as he points out, many heterosexuals with severe character defects are often accepted, to the detriment of others. He ends his arguments with a plea to his analytic colleagues:

> Nothing here is new, remarkable, subtle, hard to confirm, or
> beyond belief. At least half of you believe at least half of it.
> Yet hardly a twitch of recognition surfaces in the literature.
> . . . [Let] us then, regarding homosexuality, start afresh.[12]

Stoller is thus underlining the general analytic silence on this issue; despite his appeals to reason, logic and objectivity, his words have met with almost no response. Although he is respected for much of his earlier work, the overall impression created by the tone of his later writing is that he is increasingly sidelined and ignored.

Other writers have also argued that there is no 'scientific' foundation to the notion of homosexuality as a diagnosis, for the automatic ascription of symptomatic or pathological status to it, and have also been sharply critical of the attempt to generalise about all homosexuals from small clinical samples. Thus Fritz Morganthaler (1988), a Swiss analyst with an ethnographic interest which allows him to understand the differing social constructions of developmental issues, argues for the importance of differentiating between normal and neurotic male homosexuality, and against generalising from clinical samples.[13] He expounds his developmental theory of how normal homosexuality arises, via different developmental pathways which cannot be regarded as fixations or regressions, but are progressive, and illustrates his arguments with many clinical studies. Richard Friedman (1988) argues with painstaking detail that all the studies purporting to show associations between character pathology or disturbed family background and male homosexuality are methodologically vitiated or contradicted in some way; he does himself, however, consider male homosexuality in the perspective of earlier difficulties with gender identity.[14]

——— *Practice issues* ———

Stephen Mitchell's (1981) article is also an important contribution to the technical as well as the ethical issues involved in the analyst taking up any kind of directive, or other than neutral, position in relation to an analysand's homosexuality.[15] He examines the work of those analysts, such as Irving Bieber, Lionel Ovesy and Charles Socarides, who explicitly take a directive or suggestive approach, see homosexuality as necessarily pathological, and regard a change to heterosexual behaviour as a legitimate and important aim of treatment. Mitchell points out how the explicit aim of a heterosexual cure is a clear departure from the traditional analytic position of nondirective neutrality that is at least aimed for and held as a value, even if it cannot be achieved in an ideal form. The reasons for this attempted neutrality are the facilitation it provides to the psychoanalytic process, in the emergence of unconscious material, and the enhancement of the patient's own discovery of his/her wishes, of him/herself, of finding his/her own subjecthood and being able to speak it.

By examining the case reports of these various directive analysts, Mitchell graphically illustrates that the pursuit of an explicit treatment goal of change to heterosexuality induces in the patient either rebelliousness and resistance, with blocking or failure of the treatment, or compliance with the analyst. He shows how in many cases such compliance led either to some form of pseudo-heterosexuality, in which the patients manifested signs of feeling forced and interfered with, or, when it was not 'successful', to intense feelings of shame, failure. Mitchell's comments on these casualties of psychoanalytic attempts at curing homosexuality are ones that we share from our clinical experience with patients who have entered previous psychoanalytic treatment where 'cure' has been an explicit goal. The inability to change in this way can leave a patient feeling depressed and undermined, abandoned by the analyst, and locked into an asexual celibacy and inevitable loneliness, with no basis for exploring the many important conflicts that might arise in his/her love relationships.

Mitchell also shows how the transferential aspects of compliance by the analysand with the analyst's goals, the passive, submissive attitude the conforming patient takes up, and the way it may well be a re-enactment of previous compliant experiences, were not analysed and worked through as basic psychoanalytic principles require. Instead they were used by the analyst, in a way that does not help the patient to change fundamentally, but serves the analyst's goals and may also gratify the patient. Mitchell argues, with many examples, that in such cases an earlier symbiotic tie has simply been replaced by a submissive tie to the analyst, depriving the patient of any opportunity to work through his (or her) central difficulties. This is just one aspect of what, in the hands of such analysts, has been a gross – and largely unremarked – perversion of psychoanalytic principles.

Mitchell also criticises these approaches for their excessive reliance on behavioural criteria, where any manifestation of heterosexuality is seen as an improvement, and scant regard is paid to the meaning of such behaviour and what might motivate it – another departure from basic psychoanalytic canons. We are also aware of instances where any signs of heterosexuality – such as, in the case of a lesbian patient, fantasies about a man, or an actual sexual encounter – are seized upon by the analyst as signs of therapeutic progress, or even grounds for the termination of an analysis. Such over-interpretation not only runs the risk of increasing the patient's already existing confusion about her sexuality, but also deprives her of any effective analytic space in which to explore, non-defensively, her own conflicts about her sexuality.

Mitchell suggests that this tendency to block the full expression and working through of the transference that occurs with such directive or suggestive approaches also masks various countertransferential developments. He considers that the unwillingness to use the psychoanalytic interpretative framework for all aspects of a patient's transference is particularly marked with male homosexual patients and male analysts, and maintains that anxiety in the countertransference may well be a central factor. He does not, however, examine this possibility any further, but cites a review by Kwawer (1980)[16] which shows how there are very few descriptions of transferences with homosexual patients in the psychoanalytic literature and none of countertransferences, despite the growing acceptance of countertransference as an important consideration generally. It is as if there has been an exceptionally 'hands off' approach on the part of analysts to engaging with the transference and countertransference in homosexual patients – something we have already described in relation to lesbian sexuality.

Morganthaler is also very critical of analysts' aspirations to 'cure' homosexuality.[17] He points out how too often psychoanalysts have used different criteria in the treatment of homosexuals and other patients. In doing so they have departed from the psychoanalytic goal, as he sees it, of 'alleviating repressions that lead to symptoms'; instead they have allowed themselves to be seduced into a struggle against a symptom. He also argues that in general psychoanalysts can deal much more easily with transferences which have heterosexual overtones than with transferences which have homosexual ones, as we also discussed in Chapter 9. He considers, moreover, that in analysis with homosexuals, the analyst's countertransference is likely to be subject to particular stresses in which 'the susceptibility of the analyst's unconscious' to sexual material in the transference is increased, possibly involving an unconscious reactivation of their own homosexual wishes. Whilst he does not think that analyses of homosexuals necessitate any special techniques, he does advocate particular care in this area, and in not revealing any personal attitudes or opinions about homosexuality.

These critiques are directed against the practice of psychoanalysts whose goals are explicitly those of achieving a change to heterosexuality. Similar strictures apply to those who do not think it is either possible or advisable to aim for a cessation of homosexuality as a goal of treatment, but who none the less hold views about the more desirable status of heterosexuality which may be conveyed to the patient in various ways. McDougall, for example, quite explicitly eschews any change in sexuality as a legitimate goal for an analyst, but her reason is that the homosexual expression is necessary to sustain an extremely fragile sense of subjective identity.[18] Despite her apparent liberalism in not pursuing any change in sexual orientation, her views on homosexuality are clearly pejorative: at worst she calls it a perversion; at best she is patronising – it is not, she says, something anyone in this society would freely choose. Implicitly held views on the part of the analyst, despite a commitment to finding what is best for any individual patient, can still be transmitted, and affect the therapeutic relationship adversely. They may show, for example, in persistent ignorance about specifically lesbian issues, or in an exaggerated analytic response to any concerns involving men or children.

It would seem that all these critiques point in the direction of anxiety aroused in analysts by homosexual material, often leading to highly problematic countertransference reactions that have remained unacknowledged and unavailable for discussion or examination. Much of the writing that we have examined in earlier chapters concerning female homosexuality also points in the same direction.

Institutional issues

It is striking that so much of the dissenting material we have considered so far in this chapter is North American. The reasons for this greater degree of debate, such as it is, may lie in several cultural features of the United States as compared to Britain – for example, some of its more overtly democratic characteristics, especially as regards freedom of information. It may also lie in the much greater development of what is known as the cultural school of psychoanalysis, which – although it is generally regarded as revisionist and departing from classical psychoanalysis, and although it is put to quite conformist and reactionary uses – nonetheless does allow, in critical hands (such as those of Stoller, and also Clara Thompson – see below, p. 211), an understanding of the social dimensions of psychic conflicts. Furthermore, the publication of the Kinsey Report, with its findings regarding the widespread incidence of homosexual behaviour, and the public discussion around the official psychiatric categorisation of homosexuality as a mental illness, may also have facilitated what debate and criticism there has been within the North American psychoanalytic world.

The British psychoanalytic world, by contrast, has appeared even more closed and unresponsive to debate, and not until 1991 did a review article critical of prevailing psychoanalytic views and practices appear in a professional journal.[19] Even then the author, Rachel Cunningham, herself a psychotherapist, felt constrained to write under a pseudonym rather than identify herself publicly. This recourse to anonymity reflects the degree of fear and intimidation experienced in broaching any dissent from prevailing views, and also in being seen to be associated with homosexuality – something which those with no direct experience of these issues, and with generally liberal sentiments, often find hard to understand.

In her wide-ranging article Cunningham examines the criteria by which homosexuals are apparently deemed unsuitable for psychoanalytic training, and argues, as others have done, that there is no basis for assuming that there is any common factor in the personalities or aetiologies of male or female homosexuals that would exclude them *per se* from becoming psychoanalysts or psychotherapists. She criticises the psychoanalytic world for a failure 'to concede that anything truly good and valuable can arise from a homosexual disposition', despite overwhelming evidence from the worlds of art and creativity and in the ordinary lives of homosexuals. She is particularly concerned here with Janine Chasseguet-Smirgel's position on perversion and 'pseudo-creativity' (which does, in fact, run counter to Freud's many assertions of how male homosexuals have been amongst the most creative and socially responsible individuals). Cunningham perceives a form of splitting amongst many psychoanalysts and trainees, whereby homosexuality is not integrated as a constellation of qualities or forms of relating, but 'tends to remain raw and unprocessed. It seems almost to be, not a repressed entity or complex, but a disavowed one, projected or split off into the external world . . . where it can only be seen as threatening, pernicious'.[20] She is thus indicating the problem of analytic countertransference in this area – as it affects both work directly with patients, and also the kinds of theories and institutional practices that result. She argues that this prevents many analysts from seeing how some homosexual individuals are as able as some heterosexual ones to resolve basic conflicts, to bear pain in the process of change, to struggle with their biases, to form loving and enduring relationships, to be capable of depressive concerns, and therefore, according to these criteria, to be analysts.

Cunningham also puts forward a more specifically Kleinian criterion of psychological maturity – the ability to appreciate the 'beauty and creativity' of the notion of the heterosexual couple in reproductive sexual intercourse rather than wishing to attack or destroy it. She reiterates this criterion several times, in her attempts to prove that homosexuals as well as heterosexuals can recognise and accept this potency and fertility of 'the' parental couple. Whilst we recognise that in therapeutic work many individuals have to struggle with their difficulties in relation to their notions and experiences with their own parental couple (or variation on this), and that inability to acknowledge parental sexuality can create many difficulties, nonetheless we do not think that it is helpful to turn the heterosexual basis of reproduction into an essential ingredient of psychic maturity. Whilst unconscious fantasies of parental sexual intercourse, and conflicts surrounding this, may be important aspects of an individual's representation of their own sexuality or identity, this is very different from the Kleinian postulate, which fetishises a certain version of

parental intercourse by giving it a foundational and mytho-
logical status in the psychic lives of individuals. Once again –
and as with McDougall – it seems as though some aspects of
biology (heterosexual reproduction) are made into defining
criteria for mental health.

Cunningham's critique, and her adoption of a Kleinian
position, does raise the question of how far certain psychoanalytic theories can be modified, and in what ways, to incorporate the possibility of a normal, mature or healthy
homosexuality, as opposed to an inevitably pathological,
neurotic or immature one. Cunningham appears to bend
over backwards to prove that homosexuals can fit into the
Kleinian criteria for psychic health, without considering how
fundamentally biologistic and heterosexually construed these
are. The same question applies, in a different way, to another neo-Kleinian approach – the suggestion by Margot
Waddell and Gianna Williams (1991)[21] that the category of
perverse should simply be dropped from considerations
of object choice, and apply instead across all or any sexual
preferences to states of mind that are characterised by destructive, life-denying, cynical and false qualities. Whilst it
is constructive in some ways, this suggestion leaves unaddressed the question of what happens to the bulk of
Kleinian theory if its basic postulates (which we outlined
in Chapter 4) regarding the alignment of sexuality and gender
are simply abandoned.

Cunningham, like Stoller, ends her article with a plea for
dialogue, and it is just this difficulty of dialogue, and its institutional entrenchment, that is addressed in a study of some
psychoanalytic and psychotherapeutic organisations by Mary
Lynne Ellis (1993).[22] Her study developed from previously
frustrated efforts to elicit information from these organisations
about the training of lesbians and gay men – to go beyond the
many anecdotal reports gathered over the years from individuals who had approached these organisations for training, or
from those within them who felt unable to be open about their
sexuality. The aim was to clarify the situation for intending
trainees and also to initiate a debate. Her article is a vivid

testimony to psychoanalytic elusiveness and defensiveness on these matters.

One of the four organisations she approached, the British Association of Psychotherapists, reputed to be the most closed to lesbians and gay men, refused to grant her an interview with a member of the training committee, stating that her submitted questions were 'not relevant' to their selection policy. The other three organisations did respond positively to her requests for interviews. All the interviews were characterised by a sense of evasion and circumspection. In two cases a more liberal or open attitude could be detected, although it was ridden with contradictions, inconsistencies and unfortunate associations (such as homosexuality being spontaneously compared with kleptomania, transvestism, and heterosexual promiscuity) and a difficulty in acknowledging the effects of actual institutional practice as experienced by homosexual candidates and trainees. In these two cases the organisations appeared (just about) willing to admit that it might be possible for lesbians or gay men to be suitable candidates. The Institute of Psycho-Analysis, commonly regarded as dominant in the hierarchy of psychoanalytic and psychotherapy training organisations, responding in the person of its Chair of Admissions, was less equivocal, whilst stating (as did all organisations) that there was no specific policy. He expressed much more consistent doubts that someone of a homosexual orientation could be an adequate psychoanalyst, finally stating that a satisfactory sexual adjustment was more likely to be seen as coinciding with a heterosexual orientation. Such a position reflects the other reports Ellis gathered from individual encounters with various Institute psychoanalysts, all implying that homosexuals were not considered suitable candidates.

Ellis highlights the degree of defensiveness and evasion on the part of these organisational representatives, and the difficulty of having a more open, or, indeed, a theoretically informed, discussion. She views the evident lack of internal dissent as an aspect of the frequently noticed features of psychoanalytic institutions: the pressures of a conformist group intensified by the often dual roles of analyst and teacher, which make different or dissenting points of view very hard to sustain. To these pressures we may add the professional patronage that is available for dispensation, and the unwillingness of individuals to risk this or their future careers by raising uncomfortable issues.

Whatever the institutional features, group and individual dynamics, which contribute to this situation, it is perhaps the *silence* in this whole area that is most remarkable. This silence provoking, as it does, frustrated pleas for dialogue, mirrors, from the position of the enforcer, the silence that homosexuals have so often experienced: the silence of the closet, of (once again) the love that dares not speak its name. We do not doubt – indeed, we are reliably informed – that psychoanalytic institutions have knowingly or unknowingly contained many silent (that is, closeted) homosexual practitioners. 'Breaking the silence', as we know from both therapy and politics, is always painful, complex, disturbing, and never achieved without some kind of a struggle, but it is, as we also know, essential for any change.

Lewes (1989)[23] maintains that the absence of any homosexual psychoanalysts or psychoanalytic psychotherapists from the field of psychoanalysis, in the sense of those who could either identify themselves as such or be so identified, is a major factor in the lack of challenge to the dominant theories. He contrasts this state of affairs negatively to what he perceives women analysts to have achieved from within the profession in challenging prevailing male-orientated theory, and in raising different issues from a feminist or female perspective. This observation, which clearly has much historical validity, does, however, have recourse to the notion that it is probably only individuals or groups who have a direct personal stake in an issue who are likely to pursue it in opposition to a prevailing hierarchy.

It appears to be the psychoanalytic psychotherapy organisations which function most independently of the Institute of Psycho-Analysis that have been at the forefront in creating opportunities for lesbians and gay men to train and work; this independence consists of different theoretical stances, as well as – in some cases – political and feminist perspectives. This has created, perhaps for the first time, the possibility of lesbian and gay voices speaking from within rather than outside the field of psychoanalytic psychotherapy. The establishment of lesbian and gay psychodynamic counselling organisations, in England and in the United States, has also contributed to this process – in providing not only services specifically for gay men and lesbians but also a previously non-existent point of reference for gay and lesbian psychotherapists, and in furthering their professional development and influence. These changes have also brought other issues, not previously articulated, into focus; in particular, that of the identity of the therapist or analyst in relation to his or her sexuality, and its transference and countertransference implications; we discuss this further in Chapter 11.

The most notable absence, in terms of alternative voices, has been in those speaking from a broadly socialist position. Older socialist views, such as those of Wilhelm Reich and others influenced by him, have tended to take a liberationist view of sexuality, with a notion of the 'natural' that has been exclusively heterosexual. Reich himself regarded homosexuality as unnatural, neurotic and incapable of providing full sexual satisfaction.[24] He regarded it as a form of sexual inhibition, predisposing towards right-wing views, but did nonetheless argue against its criminalisation in Russia. Of all the various sexual liberationists, Herbert Marcuse perhaps comes closest to providing the most oppositional rendering of sexual perversion, arguing against the tyranny of procreational notions of sexuality, and seeing in perversion the triumph of the 'pleasure ego' over the 'reality ego'.[25] More modern socialist writers who have used psychoanalysis to understand the various ways in which personal attributes and unconscious conflicts are created by the formations and demands of capitalism do not consider the construction of heterosexuality as one aspect of this. Nor do they seek to understand why homosexuality is stigmatised and marginalised in various ways, and what the psychic reverberations of this might be. Works such as Joel Kovel (1981), Barry Richards (1984), Stephen Frosh (1987) and many others[26] – all concerned, in different ways, with the political location of psychoanalysis – do not consider its treatment of homosexuality at all.

Feminist voices

It might plausibly be thought that feminist psychoanalytic contributions to psychoanalysis would have opened up – or could open up – new avenues of thought and practice in relation to female homosexuality. From the 1920s onwards feminist psychoanalytic critiques have questioned ideas of femininity assumed in psychoanalytic theories, demonstrated various masculinist biases in accounts of development and constructions of women, and put forward other views of female conflicts and concerns, and of male–female relationships. This now amounts to a substantial body of still continuing work, which has not only had a considerable practical impact through the development of feminist therapy, but has raised many theoretical questions about the nature of psychoanalytic theory, the status of claims to objectivity, the intersections of psychoanalytic and political understandings, the different conceptualisations of the social and the individual, the various notions of 'sexual difference', 'women' and 'gender' in psychoanalytic theory. Feminist psychoanalytic thought about female homosexuality, however, has been extremely limited in both its extent and its ideas, and it is important for our purposes to examine why this is so, because it throws further light on some of the fundamental issues involved in a reconsideration of lesbianism and psychoanalysis.

Horney's[27] well-known criticism of Freud's view of female sexual development as distorted by 'masculine standards', and as ignoring other vital female experiences and male conflicts in relation to these, led her to reinstate heterosexuality as a natural and fundamental principle. Thus she describes the 'mutual attraction between the sexes' as a 'principle of nature', or a 'primal, biological' principle. This is part of her argument with Freud about the primacy of penis envy; whilst she in no way denies the existence of such a phenomenon in women – indeed, she has a great deal to say about it – she sees it as a secondary phenomenon based on the mortifications a girl may experience in relation to her gender, and also operating as a defensive flight against libidinal oedipal desires. Horney postulates as primary an 'attraction to the opposite sex, operating from a very early period, which draws the libidinal interest of the little girl to the penis'.[28] She also rejects Freud's account of the wish for motherhood in terms of penis substitution, putting forward instead an idea of it as a fundamental female capacity. Horney puts the basis of heterosexual attraction beyond the province of psychoanalysis – in nature. This flies in the face of Freud's undertaking to analyse all aspects of it, and his claim that as much needed to be explained about heterosexual attraction as homosexual. As Nancy Chodorow (1978) shows, Horney's adherence to a position of innate heterosexuality was to become influential in the writings of Jones and Klein.[29]

Horney's resort to biological principles – principles which are referred to superficially and briefly, with no examination of what constitutes them, but which play a key theoretical role – is in some ways surprising and not easy to understand. Her stated philosophical influence outside psychoanalysis at the time was that of a social philosopher, Georg Simmel, whose writings she quotes as showing the far-reaching effects of male presuppositions and points of view on our basic ideas of what is human or valuable, and how women are disadvantaged by this. Simmel raises the question of what the widespread dominance of men is due to – some 'essential nature of the sexes' or a 'preponderance of force in men' – but he appears mostly concerned to demonstrate the difficulties for women that this hegemonic appropriation creates, as Horney does. Horney's incredulity and indignation at Freud's account of female development are very great; perhaps these feelings underlie her resort to biological determinism and her concern to establish the distinctiveness of female development, and the importance of specifically female experiences and conflicts. This assertion of what is female, and valuably so, in the face of masculinist theories and practices is, of course, a vital feminist project, but it can create difficulties, which are now very familiar, in the attempt to specify what is held to be specifically or, indeed, essentially female, and how such differences come about. Horney's psychoanalytic accounts of the unconscious aspects of women's conflicts and the impact on women of male attitudes and social forces are still vivid and relevant today, but the biologism in her account of heterosexuality does create severe limitations in her understanding of female homosexuality (we have discussed some aspects of this in Chapter 2).

Horney's writings, although she does not present extended case histories, are scattered with references to homosexual women, to women with homosexual tendencies, and also to women whose dread of homosexuality makes them flee to men. Her overall analysis of homosexuality is in terms of a failure of heterosexuality. In her earlier writings (Horney, 1924), this is seen in terms of defences against the fears and terrors of heterosexual incestuous desires; in subsequent writings (Horney, 1934) in terms of a very early and far-reaching resignation in relation to men, and a receding from erotic rivalry with women.[30] She illustrates this latter position with several descriptions of women who, as girls, were in situations of greatly intensified rivalry with either their mothers or their sisters for their fathers' love, and as a result suffered what was felt to be acute defeat and hopelessness. She also sees homosexual love as an over-compensation for a destructive denied hostility towards other women. In all cases she posits a masculine identification and a rejection of female roles, but says that the dynamic primacy of this varies greatly. Homosexual love is thus seen only as a result of damaging earlier experiences in the pursuit of heterosexuality, experiences which cannot be surmounted, and which mean that the subsequent homosexual relationship is likely to be extremely ambivalent, unstable and prone to violent eruptions.

Clara Thompson – like Horney a feminist of the so-called

211

cultural school of psychoanalysis – presents what has been regarded as a relatively benign view of female homosexuality.[31] In her main consideration of the subject she starts by noting the force of cultural taboos on homosexuality, and raises the possibility that there are 'healthy' homosexual women.[32] These, however, she sees as being only those whose homosexuality derives from circumstantial difficulties, such as the shortage of available men. She distinguishes between these supposedly 'normal' homosexuals and those who have 'inner' difficulties that predispose them to homosexuality, whatever the circumstances. In these latter cases, she is firm that homosexuality is not a clinical entity but a symptom with different meanings for different personalities, and she compares its place in neuroses to that of a headache in various physical diseases. In her clinical experience she has found overt homosexuality to 'express' variously a fear of the opposite sex; fear of adult responsibility; a need to deny authority; an attempt to cope with hatred and rivalry towards the same sex; flight from reality; destructiveness towards self and other. Emphasising its lack of uniformity as a symptom, she maintains that there are as many types of homosexuality as heterosexuality, and that the 'interpersonal' problems of homosexuals are similar to those of heterosexuals. Noting the wide scope of these allegedly underlying problems, she then asks why homosexuality should be chosen as an attempted solution to these various difficulties, and what predisposing tendencies might arise in childhood.

She considers but dismisses the possible influence of parents for whom the child's sex was a disappointment, and maintains that in her view all possible personality combinations are to be found in the parents of homosexuals. Instead, she argues, various personality problems may find partial solutions in homosexual relationships, such as with those who are greatly intimidated and of low self-esteem, for whom the opposite sex would appear to make greater demands. She reiterates her position that nothing has been shown as specifically producing homosexuality, and argues that therapists have seen it as a more fundamentally significant symptom than it is. She considers that this bias arises from the influence of Freudian theory about the sexual origin of neuroses, and also from the strong cultural disapproval of homosexuality, which she sees therapists expressing in their theories (perhaps an indirect reference to the growing homophobia of American psycho-analytic work of that period). For Thompson, homosexuality is a problem which tends to disappear when general character problems are resolved. In her subsequent writing (Thompson, 1964)[33] she provides further details of factors which she considers predisposing but which, she is emphatic, do not specifically determine overt homosexuality. Some of her descriptions of parental backgrounds resemble those of McDougall; others, however, are quite different.

Thompson's position is interesting for its strong anti-diagnostic argument and its acknowledgement of the mean-ingfulness of diversity in relation to homosexuality, as well as for her appreciation of the significance of the cultural dis-approval of homosexuality. This understanding, however, is limited and does not enable her to advance with much con-viction the idea that there could be 'healthy' homosexuals. Further evidence of her uncertainty on this issue is her state-ment that homosexual marriages show all the characteristics of neurotic heterosexual marriages, at the same time as she states: 'The idea may be at least theoretically entertained that a homo-sexual adult love relationship can exist.'[34] She then says that whilst adult love is a rare experience in present-day culture, it would doubtless be even more so amongst homosexuals, because a person with the 'necessary degree of maturity' would probably prefer a heterosexual relationship, unless external circumstances made this impossible. She sees this presumed preference as arising not from any possible cultural or social demands, but because most people would prefer 'the biologically most satisfactory type of sexual gratification . . . that would prove to be found in the union of male and female genitals'. In other writings she also refers to hetero-sexual relationships as providing for women 'the most impor-tant intimacy in life, that with a man'.[35]

Thompson does not elaborate on why she considers

heterosexuality to lead to the biologically most satisfactory gratification, nor what this is. It is unclear whether she is referring to the reproductive possibilities of heterosexual sex or to the types of sexual experiences she thinks are possible, and whether this derives from the presence of a penis and vagina, or what. Her collapse into a form of biologism as a means of privileging heterosexuality is striking in view of her strongly cultural analyses of women's conflicts generally, and presents parallels with Horney's rather similar recourse to vague biological ideas of heterosexuality. In both cases an opposition is implicit between what is 'cultural', to which most attention is paid, and what is supposedly biological, which is invoked as a residual unexamined category. Whilst Thompson remarks on the difficulty of separating what is cultural and what is biological, she also maintains that '*biologically* a woman can only find her fulfillment *as a woman*'.[36] Again we are left not knowing what she means by this, given her radical critique of psychoanalytic and cultural norms of femininity. Just because of Thompson's much greater openness to the idea of a mature homosexual love, and her ultimate rejection of this as inferior to heterosexuality, it is apparent how central this appeal to vague 'biological' ideas is in the demotion of homosexuality, and how this in turn depends on a split or opposition between nature and culture – even, or perhaps particularly, for the most 'cultural' of feminists. For both Horney and Thompson 'biology' is where heterosexual attraction or satisfaction ultimately resides, despite their psychoanalytic understandings of its complex vicissitudes in individual lives.

This reliance on an unexamined opposition between what is biological and what is cultural recurs in much later feminist work, most often in the form of a sex/gender distinction, and also limits the usefulness of these analyses for an understanding of homosexuality; we explore this later (see Chapter 11). What is initially striking about the various modern feminist psychoanalytic writings, however, is the *absence* of lesbianism, the dearth of any extended attempts to understand sexual love between women, or to include this in the

214

suggested reformulations of female heterosexuality. This absence is particularly marked in Anglo-American writings, perhaps most glaringly so in the theoretically diverse works of Dorothy Dinnerstein, Juliet Mitchell, Nancy Chodorow and Jessica Benjamin, with some limited exceptions of other writers whom we consider below.

This complete marginalisation is all the more surprising because most of these authors are, from different perspectives, concerned to advance an understanding of female heterosexuality which does not resort to any kind of biological determinism or innate factors, and emphasises its contingent, precarious, complex and many-faceted formation, and the problematic and conflictful features of it that many women experience. Although there may be some specifically psychoanalytic sources of this heterosexual hegemony in feminist psychoanalytic writing, in particular the concern with sexual difference, it is a distancing that reflects the often ambivalent relationship of feminism generally to lesbianism. One commonly expressed fear is that feminism will be assimilated to lesbianism, seen in this perspective as the unacceptable face of feminism. Such an attitude represents an identification with the homophobia of society at large, equivalent to an identification with the aggressor.[37] It also, perhaps, betrays a fear that feminism could lead – as, indeed, it often has led – to lesbianism; so that the heterosexual distancing from lesbianism may constitute a defence against the very possibilities of sexual love between women brought closer through the concerns of feminism. A similarly problematic identification with Freud's linking of feminism and lesbianism, via the 'masculinity complex', may operate for feminists concerned to establish feminist psychoanalytic interests as predominantly heterosexual, and to deny or minimise any lesbian implications of their positions.

Another frequently noted feminist difficulty has been with the eroticism of lesbian relationships. Many writers have described the 'sexual silences' (Amber Hollibaugh and Cherrie Moraga, 1984) of feminists in relation to lesbian sexuality; the desexualised images of lesbianism (Wendy Clarke, 1982) projected by many feminists, including lesbians themselves, with the consequent denial of lesbian erotic dynamics.[38] These silences are to a large extent reflected in feminist psychoanalytic writings, which some critics, such as Elizabeth Wilson (1981), have seen as being used to justify heterosexual relationships for feminists.[39]

In many ways Juliet Mitchell's various accounts of psychoanalysis, and her attempt to produce a feminist Lacanian rereading of Freud and his ideas about women, do provide considerable promise of a less normative approach to homosexuality, although this is never spelled out in any specific way. Her repeated emphasis on Freud's arguments of the *Three Essays on the Theory of Sexuality*, against any notion of natural or innate goals of sexuality, against any idea of pre-given male or female entities which complete or satisfy each other, against any notion of gender identity based on biological phenomena – all these positions appear to situate homosexuality as an outcome comparable to heterosexuality, the assumed normality of which is seen as an 'ideal fiction' (Mitchell, 1982).[40] Furthermore, Mitchell has been concerned to show that Freud took a benign view of homosexuality – an enterprise which, as Wilson (1981) shows, involves her in somewhat over-selective quotation.[41] Mitchell (1974) emphasises how Freud did not see homosexuality as an illness but neglects to mention how, in the very same partially quoted sentence, he describes it as a developmental arrest.[42] And indeed, feminist and other psychoanalysts of this persuasion have often claimed to hold, or have been perceived as holding, more open, less normative views in practice. Despite all this, however, a fundamentally heterosexual frame is presupposed in the kind of foundational status Mitchell gives to sexual difference, and the difficulties of this position resemble some of the difficulties we have pointed out previously in relation to Lacan (see Chapter 7). Certain 'laws' of culture are seen as determining the structure and content of the unconscious:

> Understanding the laws of the unconscious thus amounts to
> a start in understanding how ideology functions, how we

216

acquire and live the ideas and laws within which we must
exist. A primary aspect of the law is that we live according to
our sexed identity, our ever imperfect 'masculinity' and
'femininity'.[43]

The fundamental nature of the distinction between the sexes
lies in the 'essential structure' (Mitchell, 1982) of society.
Sexual difference, she says:

> must exist because no human being can become a subject
> outside the division into two sexes. One must take up a
> position as either a man or a woman. Such a position is by no
> means identical with one's biological sexual characteristics,
> nor is it a position of which one can be very confident – as the
> psychoanalytical experience demonstrates.[44]

If we enquire about the nature of this 'must' – why one 'must'
take up a position as a man or a woman – the answer is not
(as many psychoanalysts would say) in order to avoid confusion of a psychotic order. Such an answer, were it given,
would invoke the idea that a stable sense of being either male
or female – of what is known as core gender identity – is
fundamental to the development of other important capacities
and functions. Rather, the answer implied by Mitchell is of
a different order:

> . . . because human subjectivity cannot ultimately exist
> outside a division into one of two sexes, then it is castration
> that finally comes to symbolise this split.[45]

Here, a universal necessary linkage is unequivocally made
between human biology and gender identity, in the form of
heterosexuality. In other writings she puts the answer in
more Lacanian terms, making reference to a 'division' of
which sexual difference is a consequence, a division in
language between the 'universal signifiers' of masculinity
and femininity, which signify only their relationship to each
other – that is, their difference. Here, as in Lacan generally,

there is constant slippage between language and society. There is a:

> structural distinction . . . Societies name the people on either side men and women and their attributes masculinity and femininity; these are not fixed qualities but the mark that distinguishes them means that each is the condition of the other and at no point can they occupy the same place.[46]

She continues:

> In all cases, the baby is born into a society that has already marked the distinction between the sexes, and has, as part of its essential structure, therefore, the signifying terms masculinity and femininity.[47]

There is a sense of paradox here: on the one hand, any universal specific content or any tie to biology of the distinction between male and female is contested; on the other, the absolute necessity of some distinction between the two is insisted on, in terms of their role in reproduction; as is their exclusive complementarity, and thus their binary nature. The claim seems to be not only that we cannot think of human beings except in terms of two genders, but that we cannot exist as human beings except in gendered terms, and that this is a universal and inescapable feature of human society. What constitutes these two genders for Mitchell is not in itself the facts of reproductive biology but the universal heterosexual and patriarchal meaning given to these facts.

What we are left with, therefore, is a form of social or cultural determinism which is at least as restrictive and unalterable as the kind of biologism that Mitchell is concerned to argue against, which lapses at times into a form of seamless functionalism, and sees human culture as resting on the gendered division of human beings, conceived of not as some kind of biological imperative but as a sociolinguistic one. As Janet Sayers (1986)[48] argues, it is very hard to see in such an account how women ever want or manage to become feminists, to struggle against the inscription of patriarchy in the unconscious; very little space is given to the contradictions of patriarchy as experienced by women. It is even harder, despite the anti-naturalism of this theory, to see how there is any place for lesbianism, because of the implicit heterosexualism of the complementary binary framework in which sexual difference is located – an issue which we discuss further in Chapter 11.

Nancy Chodorow (1978),[49] from a different theoretical perspective, is also concerned to argue against the introduction of any kind of biologism into psychoanalytic accounts, any kind of assumed natural or innate heterosexuality or femininity. As is argued elsewhere (Ryan, 1983),[50] Chodorow's omission of lesbian relationships is all the more striking because of her rich descriptions of the way adult female heterosexuality is very often built upon the primacy of emotional ties between women, and how often men are unsatisfactory emotional objects of love for women, despite being their erotic focus. Her emphasis is entirely on the possibilities for a reformed heterosexuality. Lesbianism is not seen as an erotic option of any significance: 'most women are heterosexual' and 'primary sexual bonds with other women [are] unlikely'.[51] Such statements effectively exclude lesbians from her category of women (as has often been argued, Chodorow falsely universalises notions of mothering, ignoring vital differences of class, race and culture). Lesbian sexuality, as one aspect of female sexuality, is not, as it is with Freud and the earlier psychoanalytic writers, even something to be thought about and understood, however imperfectly.

Chodorow's dismissal of lesbianism is also seen in her assumption – which she does acknowledge – that all mothers are straightforwardly heterosexual, and that therefore the erotic cathexis of early mother–infant relationships is likely to be much greater, more pronounced and enduring, with sons rather than daughters. Thus, the potential eroticism of mother–daughter relationships is minimised, and the daughter's bisexual oscillations are described as primarily emotional. Eroticism for the girl is seen as mainly 'coming from' the father, as entirely heterosexual in content, driven by the girl's need to separate from the mother and by the father's actual interest in and value to her. Lesbian relationships may, according to Chodorow, re-create mother–daughter emotions and connections, but the complexities of this for adult relationships between women are ignored, and the eroticism is simply left unaddressed. Instead we are left with the familiar picture of the mother as the site of merger, fusion and lack of differentiation, with no possibility of a mother–daughter relationship that could contain elements of autonomy, self–other recognition or eroticism, without the intervention of a father. For Chodorow, erotic as opposed to emotional bisexuality (which she amply documents) does not really exist. This makes her attribute to women what Judith Roof (1991) describes as a 'homogeneously heterosexual female identity',[52] which contrasts with the ability of Freudo–Lacanian accounts to accommodate non-heterosexual positions.

A feminist psychoanalytic account which is closely related to Chodorow's in its use of object-relations theory, but differs in other ways, is that of Luise Eichenbaum and Susie Orbach (1982),[53] who put forward a notion of 'women's psychology' based on their understanding of how women's status in society determines important aspects of mother–daughter relationships, and the formation of typical female propensities and conflicts. Much of their theorising is based on their practice as therapists, as the founders of the London Women's Therapy Centre, which provides psychoanalytic therapy for women; and the practice they advocate is one that is deliberately accepting and inclusive of lesbians. Unlike other feminist writers – and drawing on their understanding of the political locations of therapy – they do specifically address the position of lesbians in relation to therapy, and acknowledge the importance of the therapist's conscious and unconscious attitudes. They also include lesbian relationships in their discussion of work with couples. They point out the similarity between heterosexual and lesbian relationships in the presence of crucial emotional issues such as conflicts about intimacy, dependency, separateness; but they also emphasise how lesbian relationships exist in a much more hostile and undermining cultural context than do heterosexual ones. Furthermore, they consider the specific issues that they see arising when a relationship involves two women rather than a man and a woman, for which they draw on their wider considerations of 'women's psychology', emphasising especially issues of caring and neediness. They see lesbian relationships as involving the crossing from one partner to another of mother–daughter dynamics, with the potential for reciprocal nurturance and also difficult identifications:

> There are two 'little girls' as well as two potential 'mothers'
> . . . both women are simultaneously attempting to curb their
> own neediness at the same time as the needs of their lover
> stimulate their own.[54]

Eichenbaum and Orbach see issues of envy, betrayal and competition, which are difficult to handle in female friendships, as being intensified within a sexual relationship. Whilst they do not address the sexuality in lesbian relationships they do acknowledge the potential eroticism of the mother–daughter relationship, and its usual fate:

> Mothers both relate physically and erotically to their young
> daughters at the same time as they hold back, cut off or
> contain that aspect . . . mothers express difficulty with the
> erotic feelings they have towards their infants.[55]

They also hold open the possibility of sexual development as homosexual, whilst acknowledging the forces that militate against this.

Despite this relatively unusual inclusion of lesbians, the main emphasis and subsequent development of their work is almost exclusively heterosexual, and no further thought is given to specifically lesbian concerns beyond these initial suggestions. The focus of much of their theory and case material is women in relation to men, or women as each other's friends but not sexual partners. Later writings from the Women's

Therapy Centre do not remedy this lack, even though as an organisation it has given considerable attention to the position of lesbians, as both clients and therapists, and has been concerned with the issue of training.

Apart from any strategic or personal concerns that may contribute to this relative absence of lesbianism in such feminist psychoanalytic writing, we can also see how the notion of gender difference on which much of this work is premised has itself an underlying heterosexual structure. A great deal of this work depends on the implicit highlighting of gender differences – of what is special to women, and different from men. Much of the plausibility of the theory, and of the generalisations about women, depends on an appeal to women's experience but also on an implied comparison with men – sometimes, as with Chodorow, explicitly made; sometimes not. Such a comparison depends on a sense of men as other and different, as always there for women to be different from, so that women, despite the exclusive focus on them, are always ultimately only women in relation to and in distinction from men. The binary framework appears to be a necessary, albeit implied, part of this approach.

Sameness of gender is taken for granted – not just as an important political strategy but as a psychological category that bears much explanatory weight, as in the notion that daughters and mothers identify with each other because of their similarity of gender. Difference and diversity between women become hard to recognise and acknowledge, both in theory and in practice, as do any similarities and identifications with men. Thus the qualities of which men are deemed to have the monopoly (such as autonomy, sexual agency) become almost impossible to discern in (some) women.

This difficulty with difference and diversity amongst women relates to several important categories of difference, of which sexuality is only one, but it has meant that the specificity of lesbian experience and sexuality has tended to be submerged. It has also meant that the body of feminist theory, written from heterosexual perspectives, with concerns to understand the structures of heterosexuality that women

222

experience and reproduce, has itself done just this: reproduced heterosexuality and given little credence to those women who precisely do not do this, or to the possible processes by which this happens. It is as if the fascination with the dominant structures of heterosexuality involves an acceptance of its dominance, even whilst this is also challenged.

The omission of any consideration of lesbianism from Jessica Benjamin's (1986, 1990)[56] reformulation of psychoanalytic theory is even more surprising, because her critique of notions of gender in psychoanalytic theory is in some ways much more far-reaching than that of other feminist writers. Despite this silence, her work provides useful pointers in evolving a different understanding of lesbianism because it questions the conceptions of sexual difference within psychoanalytic theory; and it shows how a particular formulation of sexual difference underlies the oedipal model of heterosexual development. Benjamin's position is one of attempting to incorporate understandings from intersubjective theory into psychoanalysis, and her particular concern is with problematic aspects of 'normal' femininity, such as female masochism. Like other feminist writers she argues that the main cultural representations of sexual agency tend to be cast in phallic terms, with no equivalent symbol to suggest female desire, agency or potency. Rather, the sexual woman is most often represented as the object rather than the subject of sexual desire, and her desire is known as a function of her ability to attract and be desirable.

Benjamin sees psychoanalytic theory as echoing many of these cultural limitations: the question of women's desire is largely unresolved, and mothers in particular are articulated largely in terms which deny sexuality – from what, Benjamin argues, is akin to the child's wishful view, in which the excitement, independent subjectivity and selfishness of the mother's passion are excluded. Fathers are seen as having the monopoly of sexual agency and desire, and Benjamin argues that within psychoanalysis girls' fathers are seen too exclusively in terms of relationship to the phallus and as love-objects, and not enough as important sources of identification and identificatory love. She shows how, in developmental descriptions, girls' phases of identification with their fathers, of activity and strivings for independence, are often overlooked or minimised. She sees women, in practice, as often experiencing difficulties in finding sources of identification for sexual agency; as often caught within the tension of identifying with and separating from a desexualised mother; and wishing to, but being unable to, identify with a father who stands for desire and agency.

Benjamin is thus partly arguing that the state of affairs which psychoanalysis describes for the development of femininity, which often leads to difficulties for women, is a reflection of the cultural structures of heterosexuality, where fathers are seen as supplying the missing excitement of the mother–child relationship, as a way out of the maternal dyad; and mothers' own subjectivity, agency and sexuality are largely denied, so that they cannot be figures of separation for either boys or girls. She maintains that there is very little scope within psychoanalytic theory for other outcomes for women, and that conflicts with femininity are too often seen pathologically. Although she does not draw this implication, her comments on the lack of possibilities for women to be seen as identifying with their fathers, with the crucial emphasis on fathers as mainly sexual objects for girls, are of relevance to our critiques of the psychoanalytic rendering of lesbianism. Here the desire to identify with the father is seen only pathologically as an oedipal failure, and as a repudiation of femininity and heterosexuality, and seldom in terms of a girl's aspirations for agency and independence, or in terms of the limitations of accepted notions of femininity or the constraints of gendered roles.

In questioning the psychoanalytic split between the 'mother of attachment' and the 'father of liberation', Benjamin is also questioning the way identification and love are split along gender lines within classic oedipal theory. This is a split that we have noticed several times (see, for example, Chapter 2 and 6) in the various formulations of homosexuality. This split places severe limitations on the way homosexuality is viewed – namely, that desiring someone of the same sex has to mean an identification with someone of the opposite sex, which is then seen as problematic. She also criticises what she calls the 'deep structure of gender complementarity', which she sees as underlying the oedipal model, and the inherent theory of difference associated with this. Masculinity and femininity are defined in opposition to each other, 'and gender is organised as polarity'. Gender identity is typically seen as involving repudiation of the other sex and the qualities associated with this, and is at its most stark in the masculine repudiation of femininity. For both sexes the oedipal demand is the same: identify with the same-sex parent.

Benjamin argues that the idea of the formation of gender identity through repudiation is an unacknowledged contradiction of the oedipal model, since repudiation precludes real differentiation. As we saw in Chapter 1, what is repudiated remains part of the repudiator: Benjamin sees this as repudiation leaving primitive identifications intact. This means that a gender identity based on repudiation needs rigid enforcement and defence. We might well feel that this is reflected in the various psychoanalytic insistences on recognition of gender difference as the basis for being human, as constituting sexual truth, and the virulence of attack on those who are deemed not to acknowledge this difference sufficiently. Benjamin maintains that where, through repudiation, identification with the opposite sex is blocked, no real appreciation of difference is possible; instead, an excluding defensive difference is created. On this model, identification only confirms likeness or sameness. It does not serve as an entry into the experience of an other; therefore, it hinders real recognition of difference. Benjamin maintains: 'The two central elements of recognition – being like and being distinct – are split apart. Instead of recognising the other who is different, the boy either identifies or disidentifies';[57] and a hardening of the opposition between male and female individuality results.

Benjamin argues, rather, for a formulation of gender identity that is based much more on recognition of the other sex, on incorporation of cross-gender identifications, on a less defensive split between conceptions of masculinity and femininity.

This perspective, combined with her arguments for the possibility of a mother–daughter eroticism (that is not just fused, symbiotic and regressive), which contains elements of differentiation, self–other recognition, rivalry with the father, triadic structures,[58] would, it might be thought, lead to some formulation of lesbian desire that does not repeat the usual psychoanalytic formulas. However, lesbian sexuality and lesbian relationships receive no mention. Instead, feminism is ultimately seen as opening up new possibilities of recognition between men and women; its aim is a reinstatement of a reformed heterosexuality. The fact that feminism has also opened up new possibilities of women recognising other women, and continues to do so, is sidelined. Perhaps this illustrates again the domination of sexual difference (binary) modes of thinking, however this difference is formulated; it leaves us again with what Diane Hamer (1990)[59] calls the 'frustrating unevenness' in feminist psychoanalytic theory – although the status quo has been problematised, existing alternatives are largely unaddressed and untheorised.

Hamer is amongst the few feminist writers who have attempted to theorise lesbianism psychoanalytically; she argues for the relevance of psychoanalysis for understanding lesbianism, and points to the gaps in feminist psychoanalytic accounts. She describes how, despite her anger at some of McDougall's accounts, she also found herself identifying with important aspects of these case histories. In particular McDougall's emphasis on how her patients felt they were different from other women, how disinclined they were to identify with the 'genital mother', how much activity seemed to be the province of the male rather than the female, with women being 'nothing' – Hamer identified with all these aspects from her own history and experience as a girl. In particular she describes the many ways in which she tried to be like a boy and denied the signs of womanhood at puberty. She comments that in the absence of any critique of patriarchy, McDougall's account is very problematic, since it renders women's different identifications and disavowals as only symptoms of individual pathology; but she also argues that from a different feminist perspective McDougall can be seen (whatever her intentions) as providing a description of the internalised experience of patriarchy – how as individual women we 'take in', often in multiple and contradictory ways, patriarchal structures.[60]

This leads her to propose, from an understanding of the psychic costs of femininity, that 'lesbianism, sometimes, for some women is a psychic repudiation of the category "woman" '. She observes how the category 'woman' is not a category based on any biological necessity but a cultural fiction, a social construction which demands, whatever the content, that woman should be what 'man' is not. She emphasises that this is a contradiction which all women must live out, and outlines the many different ways in which the psychic costs of femininity may be experienced and responded to – how various anxiety states and symptoms can be seen as unconscious forms of resistance to femininity – resistance which, because of her particular adherence to a Freud–Mitchell–Rose position, she deems 'masculine'. She draws a contrast between feminism and lesbianism, seeing feminism as a political movement that contests the 'truth' of men's superiority to women, and lesbianism as a psychic, often unconscious, contestation of the 'truth' of women's castration (the acceptance of which guarantees women a place in the dominant heterosexual order). She then argues that there are reasons for supposing that lesbianism is:

> the one identity that brings closest to consciousness a recog-
> nition of contradictions that women are forced to live out.
> As such it may be an extremely healthy response to the
> contradictory positioning of women in our culture. This is not
> to suggest that lesbianism is without psychic costs, however,
> and one of these must be the production of anxiety states in
> individual women attendant upon the challenge a lesbian
> identification offers to patriarchal authority.[61]

Hamer's suggestion strikingly echoes much of Riviere's (1927) article (see Chapter 2), in which she describes the psychic costs of femininity for women who are professional and ambitious, and the anxiety experienced about appearing to challenge men. Riviere asks how homosexual women – who in her view most overtly challenge men – appear to manifest less anxiety than heterosexual women. Like these later formulations, Riviere's analysis of homosexuality is one which foregrounds the refusal of conventional womanhood as a motive for lesbianism, rather than giving a primacy to desire.

Hamer goes on to argue that it is not right to ascribe a singular and unified psychic identity to all lesbians (hence the importance of her careful qualification, above, that what she is suggesting may apply only to some lesbians, sometimes). It also seems to us problematic to analyse lesbianism entirely in terms of refusal, unconscious or otherwise, of aspects of female gender identity, despite the considerable political or subjective appeal this may have. To do so is to leave the question of desire and sexuality sidestepped, to assume that desire just follows from these various identifications; this, in fact, is Hamer's position, as exemplified in her claim that psychic identifications are constitutive of desire. To adopt this position is in fact very similar to conflating gender identity and sexual object choice, to seeing the latter as stemming from the former, as do the mainstream psychoanalytic positions that we have criticised, even though Hamer's perspective on this reverses the implicit evaluation.

In her descriptive conflation of the young tomboy with the adult lesbian Hamer is assuming the same form and direction of developmental causality as McDougall's theories contain. What is omitted is any consideration of how the construction of lesbian desire, in its various conscious and unconscious forms, may create or produce particular gender-identity conflicts, where these are deemed to exist. Clearly the interconnections between desire and gender identity are very complex, as we try to spell out further in Chapter 11; we have to be able to hold open the diversity of these interconnections as well as retain an understanding of how psychoanalytic discourse constructs one particular version of these interconnections, in its attribution of primacy to identification.

Hamer, however, does consider the diversity of lesbian psychic identifications and emphasises how lesbian sexual desires cannot be encompassed by the forms of desire possible within psychoanalytic accounts, because of the way desire is construed in terms of the binary opposition between masculine and feminine identities. She approaches the question of how to understand desire between lesbians in terms of relations of difference, erotic partnerships which involve a relation between two positions, a negotiation between two desiring partners. The relation of difference round which lesbian desire turns may take the form – for some women, or at some points – of different masculine or feminine identities, or versions of butch and femme, but Hamer emphasises how this is only one expression of possible difference. Rather, for her, lesbian desire transgresses such binarisms – not because lesbians stand entirely outside these, but because 'oscillation, fluidity, movement' are much more possible within such relationships; lesbians are able to take up different positions in relation to the desire of another, simultaneously or at different moments. These claims for the mobility of lesbian desire were foreshadowed in Deutsch's descriptions of lesbian lovemaking – that what made it so 'happy' was the possibility of playing both active and passive parts, being sometimes the child and sometimes the mother. Charlotte Wolff (1971)[62] also claims that one major feature differentiating homosexual sex from heterosexual sex was the ease and flexibility that her interviewees describe in moving between 'male' and 'female' sexual reactions, 'from sexual aggressiveness to feminine surrender'.

Such mobility of desire is also claimed by Parveen Adams (1989),[63] another feminist who attempts to theorise the relationship between psychoanalysis and lesbianism. She concerns herself with one particular group of lesbians, those she calls lesbian sadomasochists. The issue of lesbian sadomasochism has aroused strong and complex feelings in lesbian discussions, and has often seemed to split apart lesbian organisations or groups concerned with sexuality. It has undoubtedly put severe strains on the ability of lesbian communities to encompass diversity. Writing at times almost teasingly, so that it is hard to assess the seriousness of her project, Adams tries to show that within the terms of Freudo–Lacanian accounts of sexual development and difference, lesbian sadomasochism, whilst it is technically perverse, is not pathological. She distinguishes it from the masochism of the clinical heterosexual male masochist, whom she sees as remaining within an oedipal framework whilst actively having to deny the relation between the sexes. Lesbian sadomasochism she regards as perverse because of the elements of fetishism and bondage, the way fantasy and suspense are used. She also regards the 'disavowal of the truth of sexual difference' underlying the construction of fetishes as applicable here, although this is not spelled out, and we would question whether it is actually involved, except as it is deemed to be by the choice of a female partner.

Adams does not regard this form of sexuality as pathological, because there is no marked element of compulsion, no especial rigidity or repetitiveness, and no flight from genitality. Here she is appealing to criteria similar to those Freud set out in the *Three Essays on the Theory of Sexuality* in relation to perversion: those of fixation and exclusiveness. Instead, Adams claims, there is:

> choice and mobility . . . there is the construction of a sexuality
> between women; there is genital satisfaction as one among
> many pleasures of the body . . . there is an erotic plasticity
> and movement: she constructs fetishes and substitutes them,
> one for another, she multiplies fantasies . . . All this is done
> quite explicitly as an incitement of the senses, a proliferation
> of bodily pleasures, a transgressive excitement; a play with
> identity and a play with genitality.[64]

Adams further claims that the lesbian sadomasochist has organised her sexuality outside the phallic field, has 'refused to operate within the space of masculine and feminine choices'. She contrasts this to the 'traditional' homosexual woman, where she accepts the applicability of the Freudo–Lacanian analysis in terms of a masculine identification, the offering of 'that which she does not have'. Adams sees this operation outside the phallic field as meaning that the lesbian sadomasochist has effectively divorced the question of sexuality from that of gender.

Adams's differentiation of lesbian sadomasochism from clinical masochism is important, but it would seem that she is claiming for this specific group of lesbians features which may also apply to other manifestations of lesbian sexuality, without the particular sadomasochistic content. Thus her emphasis on mobility of desires, and a loosening of the ties between gender and sexuality, are important features of other accounts of lesbian desire, as we have shown above. Her exclusive concentration on lesbian sadomasochism, and the rather rigid distinction she draws between this and lesbianism more generally, obscure the possible wider applicability of her analysis, and also the way in which lesbianism as a general phenomenon does expose the limitations of existing psychoanalytic theories.

The feminist writers who have begun to theorise lesbianism in psychoanalytic terms do not, for the most part, concern themselves with clinical material or issues of psychotherapeutic practice. For this we have to turn to the somewhat different literature arising from clinical experience that is especially focused on lesbian issues.

——— *Lesbian 'psychologies'* ———

A considerable – mainly American – literature now exists, of a broadly psychodynamic character, written by lesbian psychotherapists and counsellors about recurring issues in lesbian relationships, and common lesbian experiences and conflicts. This body of work takes as its starting point the assumption that the 'choice' to be lesbian is not in itself pathological. It also assumes that the homophobic context within which lesbians live and form relationships will have far-reaching effects both on individuals and on relationships, and in part seeks to understand this in the various forms of distress that present clinically.[65] Various theoretical models are used, but few of them are explicitly psychoanalytic, and for this reason our consideration of such work will be quite brief and selective. Many of the ideas advanced, however, do owe an indirect debt to psychoanalytic concepts, and this is particularly true of the work that makes use of Chodorow's ideas about the psychology of women.

A recurring concern has been with difficulties in lesbian relationships, particularly those that involve issues of intimacy and sexuality. Frequently notions of 'fusion' and 'merger' are invoked in relation to difficulties such as anxiety over separateness, conflicts over differences, loss of sexual desire. On the one hand it is noted how the lack of social support for lesbian relationships, the hostility and invisibility that lesbian couples often experience, create many problems in defining the boundaries of relationships (e.g. Jo-Ann Krestan and Claudia Bepko, 1980).[66] This can, as one consequence, result in particularly rigid boundaries against the rest of the world, the couple operating in a relatively closed and cut-off system, with the intensity of fusion between partners likely to increase. The importance of these social dynamics cannot be doubted, with their tendency to push couples into isolated, imploded and defensive modes of operation, or even into fragmentation. This underlines the often vital role of lesbian communities and networks in providing a framework for lesbian couples in which such pressures do not operate with such virulence.

Additionally, however, it is also argued (e.g. Joyce Lindenbaum 1985; Dianne Elise 1986, Beverley Burch, 1987)[67] that the very fact that there are two women in a relationship is likely to produce greater possibilities of fusion because of the way in which such relationships re-create early mother–daughter intimacy, and because of certain features of women's psychology that are held to stem from female mothering. Lesbian relationships are seen as having the potential to re-create primal intimacy for women much more readily than heterosexual ones, just because of the presence of two women; as offering the possibility of bodily and psychic oneness, and also stimulating the fears and earlier disappointments associated with this, the particular difficulties of what are seen as the female pre-oedipal period, in relation to separation/individuation issues. Many difficulties in relationships are seen in terms of the dilemma for each woman of the desire to merge and the terror this arouses. This terror is in turn seen as involving a loss of self that too great a closeness can bring, a loss that is uniquely threatening and cannot be borne. Also identified are problems in tolerating either the self or the partner as autonomous, and difficulty in moving between more merged and more differentiated positions. Often in lesbian couple relationships these dilemmas tend to become split and polarised between each member of the couple, with one apparently wanting greater closeness and one greater distance. Although this is a common conflict in all kinds of relationships (and in heterosexual ones may operate along gender lines), there may be specific manifestations of it in lesbian relationships, where the inability to resolve these conflicts may take particular forms. Thus the often observed loss of sexual desire in long-term relationships, or 'sacrifice of sex' (Lindenbaum, 1985), is seen in terms of an attempt to deal with the various terrors of merging, since sex is often the site of most acute primal anxieties, with intimacy being maintained in other less threatening ways. It is as if what is felt for many women to be the appeal of lesbian relationships, the intensity and depth of psychic and bodily closeness, is also the source of subsequent difficulties.

A brief description such as this does not do justice to the range of thought and practice on these and other issues, nor to the undoubted importance that this kind of work has in practice for many lesbian clients who would not otherwise find appropriate therapeutic help. The shortcomings of such an approach derive from features of its main theoretical base, in particular the tendency to over-generalise and homogenise the lesbian subject, with the resulting impression of sameness in lesbian relationships, and a suppression of lesbian diversity and difference. Also, the key concepts such as 'merger' and 'fusion', whilst they have wide applicability, are too simplistically rendered; as a result, important distinctions between different forms and extents of merger and fusion are not made – something that a psychoanalytic, as opposed to a psychodynamic, approach does achieve. Furthermore, all lesbianism is viewed as an aspect of the maternal, a re-enactment of actual or longed-for mother–daughter relationships; the possible ways in which aspects of father–daughter relationships may be reproduced in adult lesbian relationships is ignored, as are possible paternal identifications that daughters may have.

Additionally, we would argue that the concept of a lesbian psychology, even where this is pluralised to lesbian psychologies, is inappropriate and based on a misleading model. The notion of lesbian psychology implies that lesbians have something in common psychologically by virtue of being lesbian, something which can be ascertained and generalised about. In the mainstream literature these common features are seen in terms of typical personality characteristics or developmental histories; in the literature under consideration they tend to be seen in terms of lesbians' status as women, and hence women's psychology, combined with what lesbians share as the experience and effects of lesbian oppression. Whilst it is undeniable – and we discuss this further in Chapter 11 – that lesbians share a great deal in terms of commonality of experience and recurrent issues in relation to becoming and leading a life as lesbian in a homophobic world, and whilst this can set up common dilemmas and conflicts (such as the problems of 'coming out'), this does not necessarily mean that lesbians have essential features in common. The fact that lesbians have reasons to group together, forge a common political or strategic identity for certain purposes, or request lesbian-only space for therapy (see Ryan and Trevithick, 1988)[68] does not in itself create a descriptive or ontological category. It is, of course, fruitful to ask how far, or in what ways, structures of oppression, which may be shared by many lesbians, do constitute or contribute to the forms of expression of lesbian desire, but this is very different from perceiving inherent features of such desire.

This work has, however, opened up whole new fields for

thought and consideration; as have the changes we described above, in relation to the training of lesbian and gay psycho-analysts and psychotherapists. These have foregrounded the identity and position of lesbian therapists with lesbian clients, and provoked many discussions of transference, boundaries and professional ethics, some of which we consider further below.

In this chapter we have shown how fundamentally political is the question of lesbianism in relation to psychoanalysis. Whilst clinical matters do have a specificity and autonomy of their own, they are also at the same time embedded in a system of thought and practice that has a distinct location in the social and political world. This is perhaps most vividly illustrated by the various silences we have described, particu-larly on the part of those practitioners who do not adhere to the kinds of positions that have dominated the literature and the various professional trainings. We have also illus-trated how very hard it is to think differently about lesbianism within a psychoanalytic framework, even for those who might be most motivated to do so. The next chapter considers some consequences of trying to do so.

—————————— 11 ——————————

Identities:

Mistaken, Assumed, Revealed or Concealed?

W E SHALL NOW address some recurrent questions that arise regarding the notion of 'lesbian identity' in relation to psychoanalytic theory and practice. To talk thus is not to make any ontological assumptions about the nature of such identity, nor is it to enter into any of the contestations about the range or limits of such a term – issues which are illuminatingly discussed by Biddy Martin (1992).[1] Rather, it is to indicate a range of issues which arise when we consider psychoanalysis in relation to lesbianism, issues that importantly turn around various questions of identity and identification, and how these are theorised. As we have repeatedly seen, lesbians are specified in many psychoanalytic theories as having made the 'wrong' parental identifications, with ensuing 'deviant' identities, especially gender ones.

The silence of psychoanalysis on the historical relativity of its own discourse is striking, in this respect as in many others. Foucault (1981)[2] provides an account of the position of psychoanalysis in relation to conceptions of sexuality. He argues that psychoanalysis allied itself to the search for truth in terms of a challenge to taboos, notably the incest taboo. By focusing on sexuality in terms of repression, psychoanalysis operates with a substantive notion of the human; with a notion of a 'true' underlying sexuality. This leads to a linking of notions of identity and sexuality. We, like many other writers, would argue against any conception of a 'true' lesbian sexuality (or identity) that can be uncovered or discovered. This does not contradict the salience, as we see it, of various issues of being out as lesbian, or of experiences of conflict and resolution in relation to identity as lesbian. In particular contexts these issues have a crucial significance which we try to illuminate further in relation to psychoanalytic concerns.

These questions of theory have vital practical implications. This is illustrated graphically by the dire warnings issued by some psychoanalysts:

> The symbolic equation (in Freud's sense of the phrase) of self with parental genital is one of the regular identifications made in childhood. Perhaps the difficulty in making such an identification should be a strong reason against the bringing up of a child by a lesbian couple. (John Padel, 1986)[3]

Such statements, like a similar one by Segal (see p. 89), are made with utter certainty, on the basis of no clinical evidence whatsoever, and ignoring all relevant research and experience. The implications of such theories are also seen in the too frequent misunderstandings of lesbian experience as presented in the consulting room, and in the complex position of those psychotherapists and psychoanalysts who do identify as lesbian (or gay); we consider both these questions further below. First, however, we look at the way in which these attributions of 'wrong' identifications rest not just on an unreflectingly normative position but also on a specific developmental theory of identification and identity within psychoanalysis. This we consider both in terms of its internal structure, in how desire is seen as constituted by identifications, and also in terms of the kind of theory that is posited, and its epistemological basis.

Identification and identity
—————— *in psychoanalysis* ——————

The concept of identification plays a crucial role in psycho-analytic theory, particularly in the elaboration of ego develop-ment, and in the development of gender identity and sexual identity. Laplanche and Pontalis define identification as the

> psychological process whereby the subject assimilates an aspect, property, or attribute of the other and is transformed, wholly or partially, after the model the other provides. It is by means of a series of identifications that the personality is constituted and specified.[4]

In most psychoanalytic accounts this is an unconscious mechanism, with many different developmental aspects. Whereas 'identification' is a central psychoanalytic concept, 'identity' is not, and it only appears peripherally in Laplanche and Pontalis's dictionary of psychoanalytic terms. The notion of identity has tended to be associated with American ego-psychology, and has frequently been criticised from a Lacanian position as implying the fictional possibility of a fixed, unified and stable identity. Such a polarisation of the debate about identity as a concept tends to obscure the unconscious dimensions of important social categories, and also other considerations about personal identity.

Leon Grinberg (1990)[5] provides an extensive mapping of psychoanalytic concepts in this area, within the tradition of a two-person psychology. The intricacies of different forms of identification – primitive and more mature, partial or total, projective and introjective – are often a central part of much psychoanalytic work, variously theorised. Important for pre-sent purposes, however, is the way in which, at the basis of psychoanalytic theory, certain kinds of identification are seen as constituting desire.

Freud (1921)[6] put forward a specific account of the devel-opment of identification, in which he claims that it is the 'original form' or 'earliest expression of an emotional tie with another person'. Identification derives from the oral phase, which Freud compares in its assimilative and annihilating aspects, to eating. Counterposed to identification in this account is 'true' object-cathexis which, according to Freud, develops at the same time or a little later. Freud's formula (which, he says, is easy to state) for this distinction between identification and object choice is that between what one would like to *be*, and what one would like to *have*. The distinction, Freud says, depends on whether the tie 'attaches to the subject or to the object of the ego', the former being possible before any sexual object choice is made – that is to say, developmentally earlier. Having made this categorical and apparently fundamental distinction, Freud then goes on to admit that it is much more difficult to give it a 'clear metapsychological representation'. Such a warning, we might well feel, has not been sufficiently heeded.

Much of subsequent psychoanalytic theory, especially as it pertains to the formulation of the Oedipus complex and its 'normal' resolution, depends upon this dualism of being and having in relation to objects. Within such a dualism, the possibility of one depends on the exclusion of the other. As John Fletcher (1989)[7] describes it, and as we saw most starkly in connection with McDougall's writings, the polarity at the heart of the oedipal injunction is 'You cannot *be* what you desire, you cannot *desire* what you wish to be'. Identification with and desire for an object are counterposed, only to re-emerge together in cases of neurosis or disappointment in love – where, as Freud claims, object choice has 'regressed' to identification.[8]

As Diana Fuss (1993)[9] points out, the very notion of identification is gendered for Freud, modelled on a masculine subject in relation to the father of identification. It is also fundamentally heterosexual; the boy, in Freud's account, progresses from identification with the father to a 'true' cathexis towards his mother. Desire, in the sense of 'true' object-love, is made heterosexual at the outset, and heterosexually gendered objects are made the basis of the distinction between desire and identification. Furthermore, identification not only antici- pates desire developmentally, it constitutes it. Identification – the position from which the desiring is done, rather than any other considerations pertaining to sources of desire – deter- mines desire. Thus, the structurings of these earlier identifi- cations also structure desire. Prime amongst these structurings is the distinction between the sexes. The kind of identifica- tion Freud describes assumes a perception of the difference between the sexes and an alignment with one. As Fuss argues, primary identification is thus itself a social process, already presupposing a prior knowledge of some kind of sexual differ- ence and its meanings: 'Preoedipality is firmly entrenched in the social order.'[10] Thus the desires that are held to flow from these various identifications already have gender and gender difference inscribed in them. Desires, such as homosexual ones, which do not fit with these supposed same-gender iden- tifications are read as heterosexual desires stemming from the 'wrong' identifications, so that the binary opposition of desire and identification, and the heterosexual rendering of desire, is preserved at all costs.

It is one thing to acknowledge in a clinical context that when desire does collapse into identification of an enmeshed or total kind, difficulties of various kinds may ensue. It is quite another to base a theory of desire on a total and prohibitive disjunction between the objects of desire and identification. To do so leaves little room for forms of identification with love-objects which are not of the primitive kind, which are more partial or com- bined with apprehension of difference and dissimilarity. As many critics have pointed out, it is also to value disaffiliation and difference over affiliation and likeness, and to tie desire and identification so tightly together in opposition to each other that other sources of desire and other forms of identifi- cation other than gender-based ones recede into oblivion. Psychoanalytic theory appears to assume that similarity of gender in homosexual relations betokens only primitive identi- fication of the kind Freud describes in advancing his theory of identification, and that other kinds are not possible between two people of the same gender who also desire each other.

240

We might also wonder whether the 'clear' distinction Freud draws between 'having' and 'being' is really as clear as all that, and certainly whether it can carry the theoretical weight ascribed to it. Freud's own example of primitive identification, likening it to eating, itself muddies the distinction, because in this case the incorporative identification could amount to a form of having.

Furthermore, Freud's theorising of this distinction assumes the unquestioned division between subject and object, and ignores all the philosophical objections to such a division. This is where our further critique of the metapsychological under-pinnings of psychoanalytic theory is relevant. The 'identifica-tions' of psychoanalytic theory, conceived of in terms of psychic mechanisms which are outside language, are postu-lated as causal and determinative. (As we saw in Chapter 7, Lacan is a notable exception to this mechanistic theorising.) Such causal and mechanistic theories of development have serious consequences for the elaboration of the complexities and variations of gender identities and sexual identities.

Phenomenological emphasis on descriptions can counter psychoanalytic claims to explain the developmental 'failures' which 'cause' homosexuality. Maurice Merleau-Ponty (1964)[11] provides an important perspective on the relationship be-tween childhood and adulthood. He argues against develop-mental theories which reduce existence to the notion of the natural, or to 'pure' knowledge. For Merleau-Ponty there is a crucial link between the acquisition of language and the child's place in the family. He argues that it is not that the child first 'knows' rules, patterns and words, and then moves to use them, but that from the start the child's relation to others, to the environment, is within a world of language.[12] This emphasis on development, relations with others as linguistically constituted, challenges the causal mechanism of psychoanalysis and its characterisation of lesbian identity as pathological:

> The linguistic usage achieved by the child depends strictly on the 'position' (in psychoanalytic terms) that is taken by the

child at every moment in the play of forces in his family and his human environment . . . it is not a question of saying that the linguistic progress is explained by the affective progress, in the sense in which expansion is explained by heat.[13]

Merleau-Ponty's arguments find much resonance in the post-modern emphasis on language as constructing meaning, rather than as the vehicle for expression of extra-linguistic entities.[14] Such a position, we would argue, is vital for any attempt to view homosexuality in a less restrictive way within psychoanalysis.

Judith Butler (1990) also criticises psychoanalysis for claiming to account for development in terms that are outside discourse, outside language. She poses a crucial question to psychoanalytic metapsychology:

Is psychoanalysis an antifoundationalist inquiry that affirms the kind of sexual complexity that effectively deregulates rigid and hierarchical sexual codes, or does it maintain an unacknowledged set of assumptions about the foundations of identity that work in favour of those very hierarchies?[15]

Butler argues that the masculine/feminine binary frame is maintained by the psychoanalytic positing of sexual duality in the realm of the pre-discursive, outside language. Like our earlier considerations, this indicates the foundational status given to a particular rendering of sexual difference that is seen unequivocally as 'reality'. Since this is basic to the attribution of 'deviant' identities to homosexuals, we must pursue the psychoanalytic production of these categories further.

———— *'Male' and 'female'* ————

Psychoanalysis importantly opened up the recognition that masculinity and femininity are not present from birth in boys and girls, but are evolved as a complex process of development. It also showed how these are not just attributes of men and women but can be found in either sex, repressed or otherwise, and are therefore important constituents of adult personality. However, despite the psychoanalytic insistence on this cross-gender assimilation, the concepts of masculinity and femininity always and inevitably contain a referencing to biological sex, as we saw in our earlier discussion of gender identity (Chapter 6). This is problematic from any critical perspective, because the notion of 'biological sex' is left untheorised, apparently obvious and given, and contrasted with the supposedly more social categories of gender identity, masculinity and femininity, which are seen as highly variable and culturally specific.

Butler describes this status of 'biological sex' as 'prediscursive', because the question of the way this category is itself constructed, what is included and excluded or implied by the notion of biological sex, is left unexamined. She argues that this pre-discursive frame is one in which the duality of the sexes is taken as natural, inevitable – as 'reality'. This fundamental binarism has important consequences in how other linked terms, such as femininity and masculinity, and sexual desire, are constructed. Butler maintains that gender identity, as the supposedly cultural meaning or expression of biological sex, is not as radically independent of this as is often supposed (especially by some feminist writers). Rather, as a presumption of the binary framework, gender identity 'mimics' biological sex. Furthermore, the designation of gender identity as carrying the cultural meaning of biological sex is in itself part of the way in which this latter term is established as prediscursive, natural and given.

Butler's analysis of the binary framework in which thought about gender and sexual desire is located has especial relevance to psychoanalytic theories, and also to lesbian self-understandings. Fundamental to the category of biological sex, to the notions of male and female, is the notion that there are only two sexes, and that a person can be of only one kind (unless, exceptionally, things have gone 'wrong'). This binary exclusive framework, together with any content that may be assigned to it, has far-reaching implications for our linked categories of thought pertaining to sexuality and gender identity. Thus, Butler argues, one is one's gender to the extent that one is not the other – a restriction imposed by the binary framework. Although masculinity and femininity are not exclusive terms in the sense that one person can have attributes of either, they are exclusive in the sense that they are linearly related: for a woman, to be masculine is to lack femininity; to have more of one is to have less of the other. (Indeed, psychological tests for masculinity/femininity reflect this linear exclusivity.)

One example of the operation of this binary framework is to be found in the common psychoanalytic notion that men and women *complement* each other, and that full psychic maturity is to be found only in such a complementary union. Frequently, some reference to biological sex differences is made to justify this notion of complementarity. Thus John Sklar (1989),[16] in a contribution to a psychoanalytic symposium on gender identity maintains: 'Nature has made the sexes essentially different.' This is used as the basis for his psychoanalytic thinking:

> The description is one in terms of the other. As there is no
> such thing then as men without women and vice versa *as a*
> *baseline for being human*, then it is the castration that symbol-
> ises the psychological split of the division of one sex from the
> other.[17] [emphasis added]

Here, the dualism of male and female is elevated to an overriding status, that of the criterion for being human. The naive essentialism of this appeal to 'nature' is obvious, but none the less surprising in its crudity. The further limitations of this form of thought are apparent in Sklar's rendering of this 'essential' difference in genital and heterosexual terms. Having a penis is seen as 'not having a vagina' (whereas it could mean all kinds of other things), and therefore requiring one: 'phallic potency and maternity are complementary parts of the whole'.

This is a particularly transparent example of how the binary construction of male and female is made part of the conception of heterosexuality, which is also adduced as a normative principle. The implications for homosexuality are stark. For Sklar, homosexuality is a refusal to acknowledge the 'essential' complementarity of men and women: lesbians deny sexual difference, and emasculate men by claiming to be able to do everything without them, including having babies.

The idea of complementarity in relation to gender appears to exert a strong hold on the psychoanalytic imagination, and is found in many psychoanalytic writings. It is in effect a version of popular naturalism: that men and women are made for each other. At the basis of many psychoanalytic ideas about homosexuality appears to be the conviction that male and female are required for a 'real' sexual relationship to take place, as a baseline for being human.

To show, as Butler does, the constructed nature of all our concepts relating to sex, gender and desire is not, as is sometimes mistakenly thought, to deny or minimise sexual difference. Rather, it is to underline how the binary exclusive complementary framework of this discourse inevitably produces homosexuality as a failed or deviant development; how the various notions of sex/gender identity/desire follow from each other; how the internal coherence of notions of gender and gender identity require an oppositional heterosexuality. It becomes clear that a psychoanalytic theory or practice that has such strong notions of gender complementarity, even if they are not expressed in such crudely biological terms, is not able to encompass different notions of homosexuality. It would appear that different constructions of gender and desire are needed, but many questions arise about how to situate a psychoanalytic practice within such an understanding.

If we follow Butler in her deconstructive efforts, we can see how the construction of heterosexuality and gender identity in terms of basic binarism needs to be thrown open so that desire is not held to follow from gender identity, and gender identity does not have to follow from biological sex. What this might mean, in effect, is that in order to provide room within psychoanalytic discourse for forms of homosexuality that are not always or necessarily pathological, deviant or immature, heterosexuality is not seen as tied so tightly to the development or maintenance of 'appropriate' gender identities, and homosexuality is therefore conceived of as possible without indicating a 'disturbance' of gender identity. It may also mean – and this would probably require a greater shift in thinking – that the ties between biological sex and the expression of femininity/masculinity are loosened; that much more variation and diversity in the expression of gender identity are envisaged; that the extent of the construction of these concepts is understood; and that gender divisions can be conceived of in a less sharply polarised and exclusive way. It would mean eschewing all forms of naturalism in psychoanalytic thinking, but to do so does not involve denying or ignoring the significance in any one individual's life of their biological sex as they see and experience it.

Butler sees lesbians at the site of contestation of various meanings about gender and desire and also, at the same time, inevitably within the binarism of these discourses. The different arguments surrounding the understanding of 'butch' and 'femme' in lesbian self-constructions illustrate the difficulties in representing a marginalised experience in terms of the dominant discourse, and the barriers to conceiving of or hearing other meanings. 'Butch' and 'femme' as ways of describing different lesbian sexual positions appear to adopt an exclusive binarism akin to the heterosexual male and female roles they are so often seen as representing. Many writers – from Deutsch within a psychoanalytic framework to Joan Nestle (1987)[18] from a particular lesbian perspective – have pointed out what a common misunderstanding this is, in that 'butch', for example, does not necessarily imply any wish to be a man or male. Rather, Nestle argues, in a much-quoted passage, 'butch' may signify the courage to desire another woman sexually and to pursue this desire, rather than any aspirations to be a man or masculine. Such an interpretation underlines the otherwise invisible status of lesbian sexuality, the lack of any other cultural means of expression. Although butch/femme may appear to mimic the binarism of dominant heterosexuality, many writers (e.g. Butler, 1990; Martin, 1992)[19] have pointed out how they are also a play and a subversion of these categories: the seeming 'man' is also a woman, and this may be part of her attraction to another woman; two butches, or two femmes, may desire each other; a butch may become a femme, and vice versa, within different erotic partnerships.

Despite the appositeness of these understandings and ascriptions to many facets of lesbian experience, we would hesitate to make the notion of butch/femme as pivotal to lesbian sexuality as these and other writers do. It is often observed that many lesbians do not see themselves in these terms. In our clinical practices we are struck by how little these terms are used; their use appears to us, within our remits, to be more exceptional than usual. This poses the questions of whether there is something inherent in the therapy situation that discourages their use; whether the kinds of experience to which they customarily apply are articulated in different ways within therapy; or whether those individuals most likely to cast themselves or their partners in these terms do not come to therapy. Whatever the reasons, we are once again presented with a significant gap in relation to language and lesbian sexuality.

Judith Roof (1991)[20] also emphasises the impossibility that lesbian sexuality presents to thought shaped by a two-gender heterosexual framework. She emphasises the diversity of meanings that butch/femme configurations may contain, and how this diversity can be an attempted resolution of the inconceivability of lesbian sexuality, recuperating that inconceivability by the imposition of a heterosexually gendered model. She sees butch/femme as necessarily contradictory: it challenges the seemingly given connections between sexuality and gender identity; it forces an awareness of the constructedness of gender identities; it also, at the same time, reaffirms heterosexuality. She also points out, in a way that has considerable relevance for psychoanalytic theorising, how lesbians are faced with a situation of having to express a desire in terms that are not its own:

> If lesbian sexuality is 'inconceivable' in a phallocentric
> imaginary, then the best approximation of lesbian sexuality
> that can be achieved is an approximation whose significance
> lies in the ways in which representation fails to account
> for it.[21]

We can suggest that what Roof calls this 'transliteration' underlies some of the difficulties lesbians have in articulating their sexuality, and in being heard in a psychoanalytic setting. It puts especial demands on the skill, sensitivity and imagination of the practitioner in enabling a therapeutic relationship wherein some mutual understanding concerning sexuality may be communicated.

Lesbian identities

We might turn the normal psychoanalytic question round somewhat, and consider: not how do supposedly deviant or wrong identifications explain or lead to lesbianism, but rather on what basis do lesbians experience and build their identities; what is needed for, and what contributes to, a viable sense of identity as lesbian? Or, as it is often expressed: 'Who, as a lesbian, am I?' and 'How, as a woman, can I or do I desire another woman?' Such questions might be asked or addressed within a different framework, in which there was the possibility for desire between women as not only or invariably pathological. Asking them, we are able to see why identity often becomes such a salient issue for lesbians.

For many, the realisation of same-sex eroticism and desire is experienced in part as a question of identity, often in a threatening or disruptive way, as Ralph Greenson's work on male homosexuality also suggests (see p. 196).[22] 'Does this mean I'm not a real woman?' is one question that often accompanies the attempt to assimilate and integrate the implications of same-sex attraction – an indication not just of the possible fears and anxieties involved, but also of the problematics of identity that are thrown up. Given the context in which lesbian attraction is situated, it is almost inevitable that such questions of identity should arise; this does not mean, however, that lesbians actually do have the 'wrong' identifications, or that lesbianism is caused by these; rather, that the experience of lesbian love and sexuality is constituted by the discourse of which it is part, and to which it is marginal.

We can see how such questions of identity arise by considering that in a context of assumed heterosexuality, lesbians and gay men *discover* that they are homosexual, and that they are not heterosexual. It is seldom said of heterosexual people that they *discover* that they are heterosexual and not homosexual in quite the same way. Heterosexuality as such does not provoke or require issues of identity in relation to sexual orientation because it is the assumed, expected and given form of sexuality from which many other attributes follow; homosexuality has to be discovered or revealed, and this can throw into question many other seeming certainties about gender and identity.

Such considerations also underline why 'coming out' is of such concern to lesbians (and gay men). Coming out involves both acknowledgement and disclosure. In relation to both self and others, important unconscious conflicts may be involved, and also issues of identity. The unconscious dimensions of such common lesbian dilemmas are largely uncharted, and their ever-present complexity is largely unacknowledged except in lesbian writings. Coming out to oneself may be experienced as a relief, a cessation of attempts to be something one feels unable to be, the opening up of the possibilities for love and relationships. It may also involve enormous fears about the unacceptability of oneself as lesbian, about rejection, abnormality, freakishness, isolation. It seems to us very rare for someone to be lesbian in this society without some degree of accompanying self-hatred or self-doubt, irrespective of the certainty with which a lesbian identity may be adopted. We are certainly aware that the exploration of such feelings is an important clinical need of lesbians in therapy, and not necessarily one which is readily met. The resistance to uncovering and exploring these feelings of self-hatred aroused by lesbian attraction may be very great; in part because of the unpleasant and disturbing nature of the feelings themselves, and also because they can be experienced as threatening to a hard-won identity or way of life, as representing too great an identification with the hostile outside world. We have learned, however, how necessary such an exploration often is in therapy to achieve a less conflictful and more satisfying sexuality of whatever kind, and it is in this respect that the perceived attitudes or theories of the therapist may be particularly important in either a facilitative or an inhibiting way.

Coming out as lesbian may thus represent the attempted resolution of a range of fears and anxieties. Not the least of these anxieties and fears are those created by the taboo against homosexuality, and it is in this area that we might expect psychoanalysis to be of use in understanding the individual inscriptions of this taboo, its inhibiting and disabling effects on the capacity for same-sex love. It might also enable us to understand the personal resources needed to overcome this, the psychic work that needs to take place to achieve a viable identity as lesbian, to preserve what is precious and valuable in the face of a highly stigmatising world.

Coming out to others may also involve a variety of unconscious conflicts, for the most part uncharted, as well as the better-recognised dilemmas of any one individual's material and social circumstances.[23] The unconscious dimensions of such a decision about how open to be, and to whom, may involve issues other than sexuality. For example, a basic degree of trust in others and in oneself may be involved, a belief in the benignness or otherwise of the world around. Unarticulated fears about loss, rejection and separation, which may be felt to be not survivable, can be present, perhaps particularly in relation to significant parental figures. There may be degrees of shame and self-disgust; desires for or pleasure in secrecy and concealment; desires for acceptance, honesty, and inclusion. Or else masochistic over-exposure may be involved, prompted by naivety, denial, or a search for self-punishment. There may be underlying degrees of fragmentation which either require a falsely assumed and over-asserted identity, or make the sustaining of any such identity seem quite impossible. Coming out in all its aspects thus demands of the therapist an ability to understand both the individual, possibly unconscious, dimensions and also the social location and construction of such conflicts, if they are not to be misinterpreted.

Lesbians are also likely to be faced with their relationship to heterosexuality much more acutely than most heterosexual women are with their possible homosexuality. This is so even if it is only to feel that they have no choice, they could never envisage any heterosexual feeling or expression, as is sometimes the case. Heterosexuality pervades homosexuality in a multiplicity of ways, and the latter is therefore likely to be a much more difficult identity to establish with any sense of security and consistency. It is one which is especially vulnerable to question and doubt, to disruption, to possible heterosexual arousal, wishes and fantasies. Indeed, it is often reported[24] that many more lesbians have heterosexual experiences, desires or fantasies than heterosexual women have homosexual ones. As Kinsey also found, there are proportionately many more exclusive heterosexuals than there are exclusive homosexuals.

For lesbians, as for any woman – or, indeed, for any man – there are many possibilities for maternal identifications, both conscious and unconscious, but these may be entwined with an often painful and confusing sense of difference in relation to femininity, sexuality and their implications. It may emerge in therapy that having an adult sexuality so different from that of the mother requires being able to negotiate the enormous difference involved, the separateness, the possible losses and disappointments, as well as the gains. The not uncommon resistance to these painful differences may underlie what is sometimes expressed as a sense of childishness, and also some of the difficulties that may be experienced in creating or sustaining an adult lesbian sexuality. Pulls towards maternal identification may make the development of an adult lesbian sexuality especially difficult.

Martin (1992),[25] in her essay on conceptions of lesbian identity and sexuality, notes how the concept of lesbians as women-identified-women, which challenged the masculinisation of lesbians, and their supposed male identifications, also challenged the split on which this is based: between desire and identification. The emphasis of this whole concept was very much on lesbians' identification with each other as women; much less was said about desire, and particularly the multiplicity of lesbian desires. It was as if the notion of lesbians as women-identified-women had, as Martin says, 'erased desire in favour of identification'. The common understanding of this was that sexuality was sacrificed to political correctness, and that the requirements of sameness and identity obliterated erotic tension and desire, as well as diversity. Elizabeth Wilson (1983)[26] refers to the Freudian perception of desire requiring a barrier or hindrance: where these are removed, excitement lessens.

We might suppose that these issues of identification and desire, although they are played out in a public and political domain, also relate to important points of difficulty that may face some lesbians in their efforts to create and sustain erotic partnerships. An identification with the mother, or later representatives, which is incorporative and symbiotic, which cannot allow for much difference or conflict, is very likely to inhibit the capacity for sexuality. This applies as much to the capacity for lesbian sexuality as to heterosexuality, and underlines how the achievement of an adult lesbian sexuality may involve the negotiation of sufficient differentiation from the mother, as well as the preservation of forms of identification.

Symbiotic desexualised relationships may be one form of difficulty to which lesbianism is vulnerable, but to point this out is no different from the description of various forms of pathology to which heterosexual relationships are vulnerable. Just as heterosexuality can be allowed its various and multiple pathologies without these being seen as the cause of heterosexuality or as meaning that it is itself necessarily and always pathological, so psychoanalysis could provide helpful descriptions of the various and diverse hurdles that have to be negotiated in the achievement of a viable lesbian sexuality, and the possible attendant psychic dangers or forms of pathology.

Also, it cannot necessarily be assumed, as McDougall assumes, that lesbians never identify with the (heterosexual) mother, in her genital capacity. Such an assumption attributes an undue concreteness and literalness to gender which, as we have already pointed out, is most unpsychoanalytic. Just because a (heterosexual) mother's love-object is male, this does not therefore mean that the lesbian daughter cannot identify with her mother's capacity, such as it is, for sexual love and enjoyment. Indeed, conscious and unconscious messages about sex are often transmitted in such a way as to construct the felt possibilities for lesbian sexuality. For example, one patient, who saw her mother as having a rich and satisfying, if complex, sexual life with her father, felt that her mother conveyed to her the importance of sexual enjoyment, and her entitlement to it. Although she was deeply ambivalent about identifying herself as lesbian, she nonetheless found great scope for both sexual pleasure and intimacy in her relationships with women. Another – apparently less ambivalent – patient, who had always seen herself as a lifelong lesbian, and to whom this identification was very important, experienced only very restricted scope for sexual expression and pleasure. Her mother had conveyed to her a depressed, inhibited and dutiful picture of sex, with little sense of enjoyment and a fear of anything very spontaneous, and this was replicated in the daughter's lesbian relationships.

'Identity' can also be a vital point of difference, as well as identification, between lesbians, and this is sometimes apparent in the various tensions or conflicts thrown up by lesbian relationships. Part of what may be at issue between two partners in a relationship may concern, or be focused on, questions of identity as lesbian, and this can be a point of attraction and excitement, or of conflict and distrust. Each woman will bring to the relationship a specific sense of herself as lesbian, of lesbian identity as she sees it (which may indeed involve not construing herself in these terms). This experience of identity as lesbian can involve radically different histories, different experiences of becoming and being lesbian and of heterosexuality; different self-conceptions as lesbian; and different expectations, feelings and attitudes about lesbian sexuality – different degrees of openness or concealment. Sometimes, conflict between partners may focus on these felt differences: one partner may feel much more established in her lesbianism and lesbian identity than the other, who may be more preoccupied either with a heterosexual past or with her possible heterosexuality, or with the felt disadvantages of being lesbian. The first partner may feel more confident about living as a lesbian, but be undermined and made insecure by her partner's much greater ambivalence. As in any enduring relationship, such differences can become polarised between the two, so that all the ambivalence is carried by one partner, and the seemingly less ambivalent partner's doubts are suppressed or denied. What this example brings out, however, is how important issues of lesbian identity may be entangled with all the other factors that contribute to the capacity for love and intimacy in a relationship; and that the notion of a homogenised lesbian subject, or of lesbians as in important respects the same as each other, obscures the understanding of these often vital differences, and the psychic meaning they may carry.

The centrality of issues of identity for lesbians is also brought out by the frequent experience of a limbo concerning identity for those lesbians who are also mothers, especially for those who conceive and give birth as lesbians, rather than having children within a heterosexual partnership of some kind. For many – especially, perhaps, older lesbians – it has been virtually inconceivable that one could be both a lesbian and a mother – the two identities have seemed almost to exclude each other, so closely has motherhood been tied to heterosexuality. Clearly important cultural shifts have taken place in that this is now much more of a felt and actual possibility, albeit one which attracts especial hostility and anxiety both inside and outside the psychoanalytic community. For the individual in question these different identifications, lesbian and maternal, have to be reconciled or integrated in some way, and this can be extremely difficult. As Jill Brown (1983) describes it:

> Lesbian pregnancy felt like a contradiction in itself and I experienced depths of isolation . . . a distinct sense of separation from other lesbians in my life . . . I had sensations of being fragmented and torn in several directions at once . . . part of me desperate to connect to other lesbians, to say I was still the same, and part of me needing to connect through my pregnancy to heterosexual women.[27]

Brown also describes the disturbances in her close relationships that her pregnancy and motherhood provoked – conflicts which are not unlike those often experienced in heterosexual relationships around the birth of a child. These recurring issues of exclusion, jealousy, envy and different desires for sexual engagement can take on further significances in lesbian relationships. The intensity of envy towards the one who gives birth can be especially great, since this is a capacity that both partners may feel they have, but which perhaps only one has succeeded in realising at that point in time. Not only do all the adjustments to parenthood have to be negotiated, but the partners' respective roles and identities in relation to the baby have to be worked out, and this is relatively new and unformulated territory, with many and various outcomes. These outcomes raise further issues of identity – most obviously for the non-biological parent, who must somehow pick her way through all the possible identifications available to her with the functions of parents as represented by mothers and fathers, to find a coherent and viable identity for herself as a lesbian parent.

–'Out' psychotherapists and analysts–

We observed in Chapter 10 how the development of lesbian and gay psychotherapy and counselling organisations, the opening up of possibilities for lesbians and gay men to train as psychotherapists, and feminist work on lesbian concerns have brought many new questions into focus. Amongst these is the question of the sexual identity of the therapist, whether and how this is known, and the implications for the therapeutic relationship. It is striking that this is an issue which tends to raise great professional anxiety; whilst some of this is understandable, it also betrays the extent to which the issue of the identity of the presumptively heterosexual therapist has not been thought through. This is, perhaps, a further aspect of how psychoanalysis tends not to acknowledge or reflect on its basic assumptions, nor on the historical relativity of its own discourse and institutions.

It is perhaps in relation to the question of being out as a lesbian or gay psychotherapist or psychoanalyst that the gulf between a heterosexual psychoanalytic understanding and lesbian and gay experience is at its widest. Being out as a therapist would appear to flout one of the most basic canons of psychoanalytic work – namely, that the therapist discloses as little as possible to the patient about him- or herself, especially details of personal and private life. The reasons for this are well established: non-disclosure facilitates the psychoanalytic process through the development of transference and fantasy; it protects the patient from being burdened or gratified and hence hindered in his/her therapeutic process; and it preserves professional boundaries for the benefit of both patient and therapist. Being out as a therapist does, then, appear to present conflicts of interest between professional and political or personal concerns. However, the situation is perhaps not as stark as our description would imply, nor as necessarily detrimental.

Being out or being known about is not necessarily the same as disclosure, either practically or in terms of its therapeutic import, although it is often assumed to be. A patient may know something about a therapist or an analyst from extra-sessional sources of information, chance occurrences or coincidences beyond the therapist's control, from public writings or appearances by the therapist, transactions around the arranging of sessions or their physical setting, and so on. Most therapists would never consider giving their patients such information as that they are married, have children, support the Labour Party, take *The Times*; yet sometimes patients have – or assume that they have – such information, through various avenues. Equally, most therapists become adept at working with these intrusions of extra-sessional sources of information, and understanding their possible significance for the patient in the context of the therapeutic relationship and the transference.

The situation is not essentially different where the therapist's sexual identity is concerned; the therapist's public activities, organisational affiliations, published writings or information passed around social networks, or chance encounters, may all lead to a patient assuming that his or her therapist is lesbian or gay, either in advance of starting therapy or during the process of therapy. What is of crucial importance to any psychoanalytic perspective is that the perceived, assumed or discovered homosexuality of the therapist has to be available for analysis in its implications within the transference and for the overall therapeutic relationship, as we illustrate below. This is no different in principle from the ways in which the perceived sexual characteristics of an assumedly heterosexual therapist are likely to be part of the transference material, although there may be particular difficulties connected to the homosexual issues involved. For a patient to know, imagine or acquire such information about his or her therapist is very different from the kind of disclosure in which a therapist directly informs a patient about his or her sexual identity within the therapeutic relationship – something which we would consider inappropriate. How requests for this information are understood and responded to is, however, important, but it does not demand anything other than usual therapeutic skills, combined with an ability to appreciate the probable roots of such a question in all its dimensions.

This issue of the therapist's sexual identity has been especially brought into focus by the persistent demand voiced by many intending lesbian patients for lesbian therapists – a demand that raises many complex questions of politics and professional practice. We see this demand as rooted in a largely accurate perception of the position of psychoanalysis in relation to homosexuality, often backed up by actual experiences with mental health professionals of various kinds. Such perceptions and experiences, added to the generally homophobic nature of much of the social world, can create enormous fear in an intending patient as to how their sexuality will be seen. This may manifest itself in various forms of defensiveness, which are often misunderstood and mishandled – as, for example, when analysts react to initial demands on a patient's part that she does not want her sexuality questioned by an insistence that the patient must be open to this, failing to see the fear and longing behind this defensive position, and being unable to treat it like any other defensiveness. It is hardly surprising that the search for a seemingly safe situation in which to start the always difficult process of therapy often leads to requests for lesbian therapists who, it is assumed, will have a much greater capacity for productive understanding of lesbian sexuality.

These fears and assumptions can be reality-based, although they may be more or less appropriate with different practitioners; or they may have other, perhaps unconscious, dimensions – for example, the search for the perfect union, and for a relationship without conflict, or an attempt to control immense unconscious hostility. Furthermore, the request for a lesbian therapist is only one voice amongst many; other lesbians may feel that they definitely do not want a lesbian therapist – again from a whole variety of conscious and unconscious motives. However, these widespread fears of analytic attitudes have kept countless lesbians and gay men away from psychoanalytic therapy; so that one obvious benefit of the advent of openly lesbian and gay therapists has been the greatly increased access to professional help of this kind for lesbians and gay men, who have felt able to go to these therapists. It does, however, produce a situation with its own complexities.

The apparent benefits to a homosexual patient of having a seemingly homosexual therapist include the presumption of a less homophobic attitude on the therapist's part. They also include the expectation that the therapist will know more about what it is like to be lesbian or gay, about the kinds of experiences and issues faced by someone who so identifies themselves, and will be familiar with the language and mores of various subcultures, and not necessarily see any of this from a heterosexual viewpoint. There is a presumption of a shared understanding that comes at least partly from experience, in relation to the position of lesbians or gay men in this society, and the impact of this on any one individual.

These benefits are undoubtedly very real in many cases, but several other considerations come into play in the therapeutic relationship which greatly complicate the situation, some of which involve disadvantages. It is certainly not always true that a homosexual therapist will be relatively free of homophobic attitudes and feelings, especially in their more unconscious and unanalysed aspects, which can lead, for example, to collusions with the destructive or self-hating aspects of a patient's personality. An intending patient is in no position to assess this, just as discriminating between those presumptively heterosexual therapists who are good enough for homosexual patients and those who are not is also extremely difficult, especially in an initial consultation.

Most crucially, however, the question of what it means to the patient to know, or assume that she knows, that she has something of this kind in common with the therapist has to be kept alive and understood in its various dimensions. A seeming sameness of sexual identity may facilitate the entry into therapy, an initial positive transference, and an ability on the patient's part to reflect on aspects of her sexuality that have heretofore been defensively denied. That is, the therapist may be experienced as unproblematically lesbian, and may be felt as having many good things to offer such as safe holding, inspirational ways of being, and facilitative understanding. But there are many other possible developments within the transference that we, as therapists, are aware of.

One patient who had very actively sought out a lesbian therapist came to experience the sameness of sexual identity as restrictive, so that any sexual fantasies or actual experiences involving men were construed as a betrayal of the therapist, who was seen as requiring faithfulness to women, and to herself. This fear of being disloyal echoed both the experience this woman had had with a group of lesbian friends who demanded strong identificatory adherence, and also her own longings to adhere to a maternal figure. The strength and persistence of this patient's conviction that her (lesbian) therapist could not tolerate her having any sexual involvement with men was very great, despite all the therapist's efforts at comment and interpretation, and indicated a degree of merged fusion with the image of the therapist that could barely tolerate any difference, in any sphere.

In another example, the patient who perceived the therapist as lesbian was initially inhibited from expressing how bad she felt about her own sexuality, how second-rate she felt being a lesbian was, because if that was how she thought about it, that must be how any other lesbian, including her therapist, really felt, even if they seemed to behave otherwise. In her view the therapist's lesbianism made her a second-rate therapist, and they were locked together in this inferiority with no chance of her therapist having anything good to offer her – all good things lay outside the situation, in other people's heterosexual lives which neither she nor the therapist could enter. Several dreams of the therapist in heterosexual encounters presaged the feeling that there might be something good and alive about the therapist after all, and allowed the experiencing of the terrors contained in this possibility. In this case the therapist had to be able to sustain a highly negative denigrating and despising bombardment, especially in the area of her sexuality, whilst retaining her own belief in her analytic skill, which required her to be able to deal with any of her own negative attitudes and feelings about her sexuality that may have been touched upon by the patient's attacks. In principle, of course, this is no different from attacking negative transferences which take other forms, but it illustrates the specific demands that the similarity in sexual identity may set up.

In both these examples what was assumed, because of the

similarity of sexual identity, to be outside the therapeutic relationship – namely, heterosexuality – was defensively split off: in the first case as something terrifying and seemingly forbidden by the therapist; in the second as longed for and unavailable to or from the therapist. In a third example, a patient who idealised her therapist in many different ways, felt that the therapist embodied all the secrets of how to be a 'good' lesbian, have successful relationships, be confident and straightforward about her sexuality, and not hate herself for being lesbian. The extent of her idealisation was such that for a long time she could perceive herself only by contrast as a 'bad' lesbian, as unsuccessful in her relationships, and as too ambivalent and unassertive about being lesbian. She could only imagine her therapist condemning her for this, as she condemned herself. In this instance, the assumed similarity of sexual identity became the main – although not the only – focus for some powerful projections, in which the assertion of apparently huge differences between patient and therapist overlaid desperate attempts at symbiotic fusion with the therapist, between the image of the therapist and the severely judgemental superego parts of the patient. The idealisation of the therapist also hid and blocked any expression of conflict and hostility, which were instead directed against the self.

We have given these examples not as part of any argument against the identity of lesbian therapists being generally known, nor against therapeutic pairs where similarity of sexual identity does exist, but to point out the various complexities that may arise and have to be handled within the therapeutic framework. Our examples are far from exhaustive, nor do they include the situation of a presumptively heterosexual patient, of either gender, and a lesbian therapist, where the presumed homosexuality of the therapist will again take on various meanings. None of the underlying issues that arise around the sexual identity of the therapist, however, is outside the psychoanalytic understandings of transference and countertransference, although they may require particular analytic skill to negotiate. What our considerations add up to is that whilst we would not advocate direct disclosure of

lesbianism or homosexuality – or of other personal information – within the therapeutic relationship, we do argue that the
need and demand for this information has to be understood
within the context of what it means to be lesbian or gay in
this society. We have pointed out the various complexities
that may arise when a therapist is out in relation to her sexual
identity, and the patient may know about this, but we do not
consider these in any way beyond a psychoanalytic understanding.

Finally, we must underline the difficulty facing therapists
who are also lesbian, in relation to professional colleagues
rather than patients. Historically, lesbians have been able to be
therapists only by completely concealing their sexuality, or by
being, as one psychoanalyst at the Institute of Psycho-Analysis
put it, 'very discreet'.[28] There appears to be a psychoanalytic
suspicion that to be open means to flaunt one's sexuality in
an inappropriate way – a suspicion that seems to be based
mostly on ignorance about the issues involved. The arguments
for a degree of openness are very basic, but should perhaps be
reiterated in this context. It is well understood that nothing
can change for lesbians and gay men whilst deception and
cover-up prevail. It is also well understood that having to be
silent about or deny one's sexuality can hinder self-acceptance
and the creation of a satisfying life.

Being in the closet, in whatever situation, entails a degree of
isolation, deception, fear of discovery, and dissimulation that
leaves the person without an effective voice, and in important
ways split, particularly in relation to public and private life.
It is not conducive to what we may loosely call mental health
to be in the closet in substantial areas of one's life, although the
degree of effective choice about this varies enormously,
depending on one's particular social and personal situation.
There are, of course, many situations where it is necessary or
prudent to avoid revealing one's sexuality; where it would be
masochistic, self-defeating or dangerous to do so – this is the
kind of judgement that lesbians have to make as a matter of
course. To have to conceal one's sexual identity totally in an
ongoing training or professional situation, most particularly

one so centrally concerned with mental health, creates enormous stresses. The testimony of those lesbians and gay men in these organisations who have not felt able to be open bears witness to this. Such experiences do not convey a very positive message about how a psychoanalytic framework can help to facilitate the overcoming of difficulties.

Those lesbian and gay psychotherapists who have, for a combination of personal and historical reasons, been able to be open about their sexuality are thus flying in the face of the weight of psychoanalytic history. As with any situation involving homosexual identity, they are likely to find themselves caught between either silence and total invisibility, or a too prominent and visible definition of their identity. The latter can bring its own complexities and disadvantages, resulting in the therapist being seen only in terms of this identity, and not in terms of his or her other characteristics as a therapist. In practical terms, this can be quite ghettoising. A different approach to homosexuality by the psychoanalytic organisations would contribute to making this a more normal, less remarkable identity for a therapist.

Postscript

WE HAVE LOOKED at the various psychoanalytic discourses in which questions of lesbianism and lesbian sexuality arise, and we have tried to show the diverse and multiple aspects of these discourses, their continuities and discontinuities, their location within a complex body of psychoanalytic thought on gender and sexuality. We have focused on what is said and seemingly required by the various theories, the ways in which such discourses can act as 'practices that systematically form the objects of which they speak'.[1] We have also focused on what is not said, what is seemingly excluded from being spoken of, thought or theorised about. We have paid particular attention to the gaps and the silences, the displacements and the various resistances; and considered their possible sources, both in terms of personal anxieties that lesbian sexuality can arouse, and in terms of the structures of the various theories which produce these phenomena. We have raised the question of who does the speaking 'about', as opposed to the speaking of symptoms and suffering, and from what position. We have noted that one fundamental feature of existing psychoanalytic discourse, an aspect of its discursive practice, is that the lesbian is always the patient and never the analyst, and that the analyst speaks from a position of implicit heterosexuality. Whilst this situation is beginning to change, as the very writing of this book indicates, nonetheless the articulated voice of theory is dominantly heterosexual: a heavy silence surrounds other views – which do exist – within mainstream psychoanalytic practice, and attempts to engage in debate and discussion are greeted with evasiveness.

Examining what cannot be said, or is not encompassed by the theories, and also the parallel exclusionary practices of psychoanalytic institutions, brings into question some fundamental aspects of psychoanalytic theory, and also the operation of power within the psychoanalytic world, particularly as power relates to knowledge and theory, as well as professional ambition. In this Postscript, we consider the ways in which we think that allowing for something other than inevitable pathology concerning lesbian relationships and sexuality would require psychoanalytic theory to change. We consider what is called into question by a less exclusively normative view of homosexuality and heterosexuality, and a greater ability to encompass the social location of homosexuality, and reflect upon the position of psychoanalysis in relation to it. We do this by addressing various issues that have arisen in the course of this book.

We said at the outset that we were not concerned to elaborate an alternative or reformed theory of lesbian development, and we gave several reasons for this: the inappropriate level of generalisation that this enterprise requires, and the suppression of significant diversity; the problems with universalising psychoanalytic concepts; the over-reductiveness of seeing a whole range of phenomena in terms of one, or even several, original factors or probable causes. We have been concerned to understand the discursive practices which lead to the particular psychoanalytic accounts of lesbian development, and their claims to 'truth', rather than to attempt to establish any alternative truth. Such a project does, however, also generate other perspectives.

This approach stems from our strongly held view that complexity and ambiguity are not merely to be overcome and discarded. Rather, they open the development of questioning and thoughtful reflection. Limitations of psychoanalytic theories of the subject, or the analysand, are in many cases limitations of the ontological, philosophical tradition to which Freud was heir, although this remains unacknowledged by many psychoanalysts who persist in presenting a theory of the psyche which is claimed to be outside history. Psychoanalysis cannot genuinely allow for a theory of separation, of differences, as long as it remains within an ontological framework. In other words, it fails to recognise the element of irreducible uniqueness in the relationship of speaking subjects. Who the analysand is cannot be reduced to what she is.

Derrida's work shows us that to begin as if the meaning of difference were already established is to have no further problem, because it is to assume that it is derived, controlled, ordered, and known from the start.

It might well be objected that it is inconsistent to maintain any notion of lesbian identity while criticising psychoanalytic accounts of gender and sexuality. Throughout this book our strategy has been to examine the psychoanalytic tradition by engaging with it, thus beginning a nuanced conversation in order to elucidate the shifting themes that intersect to produce the discourse of psychoanalysis and lesbianism. This is to stress the contingency of the term 'lesbian' without reifying it into an eternal truth of the psyche.

It could be further objected that the implication of our critique is therefore that we are not psychoanalytic, that we are not providing a developmental account of 'the lesbian' in terms of the interaction between conscious and unconscious mechanisms. We have stressed the centrality of language: children develop in relationships with others, and these relationships occur within the world of language. We do not interpret development in terms of subjects in opposition to objects, as mechanistic views of development do. Thus we do acknowledge the centrality of development in our psycho-

therapeutic practices, but again, we do not see it as determin-
atively causal.

As we have shown, mother–daughter relationships have
been a crucial cornerstone of psychoanalytic interpretations of
lesbian sexuality. Analysis of mother–daughter relationships
within a linguistic framework acknowledges their complexity
and variability: there is no paradigmatic mother–daughter
relationship. By holding open questions such as Who is the
mother? Who is the daughter? we can acknowledge the history of their relationship within psychoanalytic concepts such
as identification, anxiety, splitting, defence. These concepts are
descriptively useful, and their use does not necessarily imply
an ontological causal mechanism.

Merleau-Ponty succinctly expresses such an open-ended
descriptive approach:

> I am not the outcome . . . of numerous causal agencies which
> determine my bodily or psychological make-up. I cannot
> conceive myself as nothing but a bit of the world, a mere
> object of biological, psychological, or sociological investig-
> ation . . . My existence does not stem from my antecedents,
> from my physical and social environment; instead it moves
> out towards them and sustains them . . . [2]

We have considered the question of analysing any given lesbian relationship in terms of a re-enactment of infantile pre-
oedipal relations to the mother, with symbiotic features that
suggest a lack of separation, a merger between self and other,
an inability to recognise or allow otherness. We have pointed
out how this may well be a major dimension of some lesbian
relationships, although we have also insisted on keeping alive
and prominent the possibility that quite different lines of
analysis may – and do – apply to others; we think this possibility needs constant re-emphasis. But what such an understanding also raises, crucially, is the question of the resolution
of such symbiosis, in its adult manifestations, in the instances
where such a notion can be fruitfully applied – how a lesbian
relationship that was not fraught with such difficulties would

be understood. Would a resolution, perhaps achieved through therapy or analysis, mean an inevitable heterosexual outcome, or could symbiotic difficulties be resolved from a lesbian position? That is, is the only alternative to maternal symbiosis a heterosexual 'turning-away' from the mother, or is a non-symbiotic erotic relationship, as realised in aspects of the female partner, a possibility?

This is clearly an important issue in relation to therapy with lesbians in terms of what outcomes are conceived of by the therapist, or seen as satisfactory, and even what is implicitly encouraged or discouraged. It also – importantly – holds open the possibility that there are resolutions of symbiotic difficulties other than heterosexual ones which lesbians might wish, or could be helped, to pursue; and that the prospect of therapy does not, therefore, have to contain quite such fears as it can for some lesbians. But this also raises further questions of theoretical importance, because if a non-symbiotic resolution to a lesbian's conflicts which allows her to remain as a lesbian is held to be possible, what then becomes of the classical Oedipus conflict as the required passport to sexual maturity, the breaking of the maternal dyad by the intervention of the paternal figure, and the gendered split that is supposed to be achieved between who is identified with (same-sex) and who is desired (different sex)?

It appears, therefore, that a psychoanalytic position which allows for different and more diverse views of homosexuality would involve a rethinking of the status of the Oedipus complex within that theory. On general grounds we are critical of the Oedipus complex as a universal principle of all development, because of the imperialism of such attempts at abstract universality. It is striking that hitherto the main challenges to the universality of the Oedipus complex have come either from a cross-cultural perspective, or from those speaking from a position of exclusion and marginality and not included within the mainstream of psychoanalytic positions. Thus Frantz Fanon (1967)[3] argues that the prevailing psychoanalytic conception of the Oedipus complex cannot be applied to the position of the black male in a colonised society subjected to the forces of racism. The father's position in a black family, and his relation to structures of the state and patriarchy, is utterly different from his position and relation in white society; this means that probable black male identifications will not be those of the classic father of psychoanalytic theory, but will involve a very different image and relationship between father and son. So also have some feminist theorists challenged the universality of the classic Oedipus complex as it applies to women, on the grounds of different understandings of mother–daughter relationships.

It seems to us that in relation to homosexuality the necessary rethinking applies most particularly to the universalised aspect of the Oedipus complex which instates gendered identities in relation to desire, and supposedly results in individuals who identify with the same-sex parent and desire the parent of the opposite sex. That is, it is the gendered split between desire and identification that is most called into question as a universal principle of mature development. We do not think that the aspect of the Oedipus complex that involves exclusion from parental sexuality, the taboo on incest, is so called into question by different views of homosexuality, nor do we think it should be, on either theoretical or clinical grounds.

The gendered split between desire and identification which typifies the classical Oedipus complex appears to us to rest on a prior assumption that the complementary necessity for each other of male and female constitutes the source of 'real' desire. In Chapter 11 we tried to describe the location of this notion of fundamental complementarity within a framework of binarism. It does appear that any such complementarity, whether it rests on naturalistic or biologistic notions or not, is called into question by any commitment to a more diverse, less totally pathologising account of homosexuality. The possibility of an adult same-sex relationship which can be regarded, psychoanalytically speaking, as non-pathological, as not overly defensive, rigid, split, which is satisfying to both individuals – such a possibility does require that gender difference, as exemplified in real male and female persons, is not regarded as a *necessary* organising principle of desire for all individuals. In many ways homosexuality involves not so much a denial of gender difference, as is so often said, as a different construction of its role in relation to desire. Sometimes this construction involves a de-emphasis on gender difference as the main source of desire, sometimes a translation of gender difference into different forms that are not represented concretely by male and female individuals. Or, as Butler (1992)[4] expresses it: 'the psyche is not a grid through which a pre-given body appears; that formulation would figure the body as an ontological in-itself . . .'.

In showing how one fundamental aspect of the Oedipus complex is challenged by a commitment to different possibilities for homosexuality within psychoanalysis, we are also raising the question of lesbian identifications. This seems to us to be ground for fruitful clinical explorations, with the different psychoanalytic questions we posed in Chapter 11, always bearing in mind the immense diversity that is involved. It also seems to us to raise questions about the primacy of identification in relation to desire, the assumption that desire follows from or is constituted by identification – that primitive identification precedes object choice. It seems to us that lesbian desire often presents issues of identity and identification just because it is not always experienced as following from assumed identifications, and that it indeed calls into question such identifications, or requires others. This is very different from seeing such desire as following from such identifications.

It would seem that new theorisations are needed. A different approach to homosexuality would require much greater openness to lesbian identifications. Again we stress the contingency of identifications, and we are not arguing for the inevitability or primacy of identification in sexual development. We would include the possibility, as one amongst many, of diverse male or masculine identifications as sources of positive identification, coexisting with other identifications, without these being seen negatively as some kind of 'deviation' in gender identity. Indeed, Benjamin argues (1990)[5] that just such a possibility is needed within psychoanalytic theory for all women. This does involve tying gender identity much less closely to biological sex – indeed, problematising the whole notion of gender identity, of the status of 'as a woman' as a theoretical construction (as opposed to an aspect of individual experience or political engagement), and also the language of 'male' and 'female'. New theorisations are also needed of the possibilities within mother–daughter relationships – indeed, of the whole conception of the mother, as Benjamin has also argued. Like Irigaray, we are challenging the premise that the relationship with the mother is always and inevitably something to be avoided and only grown away from, rather than explored and changed in various adult forms. We are holding open the possibility that lesbian relationships are not necessarily a collapse into a stuck symbiosis but an erotic partnership in which the more infantile and adult positions can be taken interchangeably and flexibly, and new positions evolved.

Perhaps what is partly at issue here is the degree of openness of psychoanalytic theory to new formulations: whether accepted formulations are regarded as cast in stone, true for all time, utterly determinative of what may be thought; or whether psychoanalytic theory can encompass the theoretical changes that are required by new and different possibilities. The history of psychoanalysis does not encourage confidence in its ability to change and adapt, except by fissure and expulsion, but perhaps the pluralism that is now demanded and evident in so many other areas of thought and theory could extend to psychoanalysis.

Our eschewal of a competing developmental theory also makes reference to the degree of generalisation inherent in most such attempts, in their use of both supposedly general clinical observations and universalising concepts. This does, however, raise the question of whether we are prepared to say anything general 'about' lesbians from within a psychoanalytic perspective. In the current context of gross overgeneralisation, the emphasis on diversity is clearly of immense strategic and corrective importance – the huge variety of ways

271

of becoming and being lesbian can begin to be apprehended. To this extent it is an admonition not to hide behind stereotyping and appropriative theory, not to 'make sense' too readily of material which may be strange, disturbing or unfamiliar by imposing well-worn constructions on a patient's experience. Given all this, however, do we not still think there are some common developmental pathways or features which are more likely to lead to lesbianism than to heterosexuality – or, in a reduced version, which typify at least some lesbians to varying extents or in different ways?

We do not dispute that the discerned clinical patterns which we have described may have a relevance to some individuals; nor that such accounts can contribute to a therapist's understanding of a lesbian patient. But to make this into a generalised developmental theory is a step we would not take, because to do so is to endorse too many other assumptions and premises, which this book has attempted to reveal. Whilst the developmental question is always posed within the framework of a heterosexual normativity and a denial of the social structure of heterosexuality, inevitably the developmental question is of the order of 'What went wrong?' rather than 'What went right?' for someone to have become lesbian.

If we ask – or at least hold open the possibility of – 'What went right?', as well as 'What went wrong?' then, as we tried to show in Chapter 11, our attention might be focused differently: towards the hurdles that have to be overcome, the psychic work that is necessitated, to achieve a viable lesbian identity, style of life, or relationship, however these are construed. Such a question, if we are concerned with generality, also points us in the direction of what we do see lesbians as having in common – lesbian oppression, or the social construction of lesbianism, rather than lesbian psychology or psychopathology. This can appear to, and often does, create a commonality, whether of identity, interests, or recurrent conflicts. Whilst this commonality is real and important, it is also seriously misleading if it is interpreted in terms of an underlying similarity in the psyches of all or even some lesbians. We have tried to spell out some of the implications of what we see as the impact of lesbian oppression, of the self-constructions which reflect the problematics of heterosexual normativity, particularly as we are aware of this clinically: in the manifold fears, doubts and anxieties that can be connected with – or even construe – lesbian desire, in its many individual expressions.

We have also noted throughout this book the frequent difficulties in the area of analytic countertransference. We have described the many accounts of broken-off, difficult or failed analyses with lesbian patients, and the lack of any understanding of this except in terms of the patients' perceived resistance or other defects. There has been an astounding absence of any considerations of analytic countertransference that might contribute to these difficulties in the therapeutic encounters, yet all the signs of trouble in the countertransference are there, as we have described.

With a subject such as homosexuality, which can arouse so much personal and social anxiety, it is especially likely that difficult countertransference reactions will be involved. Any commitment to a less rigid, more diverse view of homosexuality, therefore, puts especial demands on practitioners not to defend themselves from such anxieties as may be aroused by rigid, attacking and inappropriate theorising. It requires much greater opportunity in training courses and training analyses for the examination of attitudes, both conscious and unconscious, towards homosexuality and homosexual material as this presents itself clinically, in a way that is facilitative rather than censorious. The enabling of such reflective self-examination would be a major step – not just in the provision of more fruitful and helpful psychotherapy for lesbians and gay men by practitioners who do not identify as such, but also in advancing our psychoanalytic understanding. What is suggested here is hardly contentious as an aspect of good psychotherapeutic training and practice, but it does require the will and commitment to such a project, and we have to ask where this might come from.

It is perhaps in posing this question that we encounter the irretrievably moral aspects of psychoanalysis. Our reading of psychoanalytic texts has shown the interweaving of three questions: that of psychic health and pathology; that of human happiness; and that of right and wrong. In many versions of psychoanalytic theory, these questions are conflated. In particular, questions of ethics or morality are reduced to or rendered as purely 'scientific' questions within the terms of psychoanalytic metapsychology, so that the moral basis of psychoanalysis is left obscured and untheorised, inherent in the nature of its concepts and sometimes revealed in the casual remarks or the slips and aberrations of its less disciplined practitioners. Homosexuality presents a particular challenge to this obscuring of the moral in psychoanalysis – not in the guise of any greater claims to an ideal neutrality, but in the ability of psychoanalytic theory and practice to deal explicitly with its own moral and political positions, with the moral issues involved in designating one kind of sexuality the 'wrong' kind.

Our position, reiterated throughout this book, is to raise questions, to point to closures in psychoanalytic theory. Our hope is that such a strategy will avoid the splitting off of lesbians from psychoanalysis, and will hold the tension of complexity and ambiguity in order to enhance the lives of people who seek to engage in psychoanalytic psychotherapy.

Notes

Introduction

1. A phenomenological approach is concerned with the descriptive elucidation of people's lives and experiences. A problem with many phenomenological writers, such as Husserl, is that they remain focused on the irreducibility of meaning, thereby postulating a foundation outside language. Post-phenomenologists have criticised such foundationalism and argued for an approach that acknowledges the inevitably linguistic character of human interaction. Maurice Merleau-Ponty, in *The Phenomenology of Perception*, Routledge & Kegan Paul, London, 1962, and *The Primacy of Perception*, Northwestern University Press, U.S.A. 1964a, has attempted to bring phenomenological and psychoanalytic approaches into relation with each other. So too have many of the writers in Robin Cooper *et al.* (eds), *Thresholds between Philosophy and Psychoanalysis*, Free Association Books, London, 1989, who also pursue an anti-foundationalist approach.

2. C. Oakley, 'Introducing an Incomplete Project', in Cooper *et al.* (eds), *Thresholds between Philosophy and Psychoanalysis*, p. 5.

3. K. Lewes, *The Psychoanalytic Theory of Male Homosexuality*, Quartet, London, 1989.

4. J. Derrida, *Of Grammatology*, transl. G. C. Spivak, Johns Hopkins University Press, Baltimore, MD, 1976.

5. G. C. Spivak, *The Post-Colonial Critic: Interviews, Strategies, Dialogues*, (ed.), Sarah Harasym, Routledge, London, 1990, p. 104.

275

6. Derrida, *Of Grammatology*.

7. For example, Jeffrey Weeks, *Sex, Politics and Society*, Longman, London, 1981; Mary McIntosh, 'The Homosexual Role', in K. Plummer (ed.), *The Making of the Modern Homosexual*, Hutchinson, London, 1981.

8. M. Foucault, *The History of Sexuality, Volume 1*, Penguin, Harmondsworth, 1981.

9. J. Butler, *Gender Trouble: Feminism and the Subversion of Identity*, Routledge, London, 1990.

10. In James Strachey (ed.), *The Standard Edition of the Complete Psychological Works of Sigmund Freud*, 24 vols, Hogarth, London, 1953–73, vol. 18 (1955), pp. 145–72.

11. E. Jones, 'The Early Development of Female Sexuality', *International Journal of Psycho-analysis*, 8, 1927, pp. 457–72; H. Deutsch, 'Homosexuality in Women', *International Journal of Psycho-Analysis*, 14, 1933, pp. 34–56; M. Khan,'The Role of Infantile Sexuality in Early Object Relations in Female Homosexuality', in I. Rosen (ed.), *The Pathology and Treatment of Sexual Perversions*, Oxford University Press, Oxford, 1962; J. McDougall, 'The Homosexual Dilemma', in I. Rosen (ed.), *Sexual Deviation*, Oxford University Press, Oxford, 1979, and 'The Dead Father', *International Journal of Psycho-Analysis*, 70, 1989a, pp. 205–19.

12. L. Faderman, *Odd Girls and Twilight Lovers: A History of Lesbian Life in Twentieth-Century America*, Penguin, Harmondsworth, 1992.

13. K. Lewes, *The Psychoanalytic Theory of Male Homosexuality*.

14. A.E. Bergin and S.L. Garfield, *Handbook of Psychotherapy and Behaviour Change: An Empirical Analysis*, Wiley, New York, 1971.

15. J. McDougall, *Theatres of the Body*, Free Association Books, London, 1989b.

16. P. Casement, *On Learning from the Patient*, Tavistock, London, 1985.

Chapter 1
Freud: Disappointment and Repudiation

1. *Standard Edition*, vol. 8, pp. 145–72. Freud's first case study, the Dora case, published in 1905, is in one sense also about female homosexuality, most particularly Freud's blindness to Dora's homosexual desire. Its relevance to the present study lies in this overlooking, later acknowledged by Freud, and its

countertransference implications. This case is thoroughly explored in Charles Bernheimer and Claire Kahane (eds), *In Dora's Case*, Virago, London, 1985.

2. *Standard Edition*, vol. 7, pp. 123–245.

3. Some of Freud's contemporaries, such as Karen Horney, Jeanne Lampl de Groot and Helene Deutsch, make passing references to 'Psychogenesis' but there is no extended discussion, and Jones, in his own article on female homosexuality (see Chapter 2), written in 1927, does not refer to it at all. Some modern clinical writers, such as Charles Socarides and Joyce McDougall, provide brief paraphrases. Jacques Lacan (see Chapter 8) in his reassessment of the debates on female sexuality and on transference, does give 'Psychogenesis' more prominence, and usefully compares it to the earlier Dora case, as do both Suzanne Gerheart and Jacqueline Rose in Bernheimer and Kahane (eds), *In Dora's Case*. Mandy Merck, 'The Train of Thought in Freud's "Case of Homosexuality in a Woman" ' *m/f*, 11/12, 1986, pp. 35–46, reprinted in M. Merck, *Perversions: Deviant Readings*, Virago, London, 1993, provides the most extended discussion to date, with a critical analysis of some of the underlying theoretical issues, and of Freud's countertransference difficulties. This has recently been added to by Diana Fuss, 'Freud's Fallen Women: Identification, Desire, and "A Case of Homosexuality in a Woman" ', *Social Text*, forthcoming, 1993; and by Mary Jacobus, 'Russian Tactics: Freud's "Case of Homosexuality in a Woman" ', in M. Jacobus, *First Things: Literature, Psychoanalysis and Reproduction*, Routledge, London, forthcoming, 1994.

4. K. Lewes, *The Psychoanalytic Theory of Male Homosexuality*, Quartet, London, 1989.

5. Freud, *Leonardo da Vinci and a Memory of his Childhood*, *Standard Edition*, vol. 11, pp. 59–138.

6. Freud, *Three Essays on the Theory of Sexuality*, p. 145 (footnote, 1915).

7. Freud, 'On Narcissism: an Introduction', *Standard Edition*, vol. 14, pp. 67–102. This description also occurs in the earlier *Three Essays*.

8. Freud. Letter published in *American Journal of Psychiatry*, 107, 1951, p. 786.

9. Robert Stoller, *Perversion: The Erotic Form of Hatred*, Delta, New York, 1975.

10. So great has been the tendency to see all homosexuality as a form of perversion that Socarides, one leading proponent of this

view, even describes Freud as having classified homosexuality as perversion. This falsified reading stands uncorrected in several places, e.g. C. W. Socarides, *The Overt Homosexual*, Grune & Stratton, New York, 1968; and 'The Psychoanalytic Theory of Homosexuality with Special Reference to Therapy', in I. Rosen (ed.), *Sexual Deviation*, Oxford University Press, Oxford, 1979.

11. For example, J. Chasseguet-Smirgel, *Creativity and Perversion*, Free Association Books, London, 1984.

12. J. Roof, *The Lure of Knowledge: Lesbian Sexuality and Theory*, Columbia University Press, New York, 1991.

13. O. Rank, 'Perversion and Neurosis', *International Journal of Psycho-Analysis*, 4, 1923, pp. 270–292.

14. K. Lewes, 'The Psychoanalytic Theory of Male Homosexuality'.

15. C. Thompson, 'Changing Concepts of Homosexuality in Psychoanalysis', *Psychiatry*, 10, 1947, pp. 183–9.

16. Freud, *Three Essays on the Theory of Sexuality*, p. 144.

17. ibid., p. 145.

18. Freud, 'Psychogenesis of a Case of Female Homosexuality', p. 154.

19. Freud, 'On Narcissism'.

20. Freud (1910), 'A Special Type of Choice of Object made by Men', *Standard Edition* vol. 11, pp. 163–75.

21 J. Lacan, 'Guiding Remarks for a Congress on Female Sexuality', in J. Mitchell and J. Rose (eds), *Feminine Sexuality: Jacques Lacan and the Ecole Freudienne*, London, Macmillan, 1982.

22. Freud, 'Psychogenesis', p. 158.

23. M. Merck, 'The Train of Thought in Freud's "Case of Homosexuality in a Woman" '.

24. R. Bowlby, 'Still Crazy after All These Years', in Teresa Brennan (ed.), *Between Feminism and Psychoanalysis*, Routledge, London, 1989.

25. ibid., p. 51.

26. Lacan, 'Of the Subject of Certainty', in J. Lacan, *The Four Fundamental Concepts of Psycho-Analysis*, Penguin, Harmondsworth, 1979.

27. *Standard Edition*, vol. 21, pp. 221–43.

28. Freud, 'Psychogenesis', p. 164.

29. Lacan, 'Of the Subject of Certainty'.

30. Merck, 'The Train of Thought in Freud's "Case of Homosexuality in a Woman"'.

31. J. S. Kwawer, 'Transference and Countertransference in Homo-

sexuality: Changing Psychoanalytic Views', *American Journal of Psychotherapy*, 34, 1980, pp. 72–80; Lewes, 'The Psychoanalytic Theory of Male Homosexuality'.

Chapter 2
The Masculine Woman

1. E. Jones, 'The Early Development of Female Sexuality', *International Journal of Psycho-Analysis*, 8, 1927, pp. 457–72.
2. H. Deutsch, 'Homosexuality in Women', *International Journal of Psycho-Analysis*, 14, 1933, pp. 34–56.
3. K. Horney, 'On the Genesis of the Castration Complex in Women', *International Journal of Psycho-Analysis*, 5, 1924, pp. 50–65.
4. ibid., p. 61.
5. Jones, 'The Early Development of Female Sexuality'.
6. C. W. Socarides, *The Overt Homosexual*, Grune & Stratton, New York, 1968.
7. O. Rank, 'Perversion and Neurosis', *International Journal of Psycho-Analysis*, 4, 1923, pp. 270–92.
8. J. Lacan, 'Guiding Remarks for a Congress on Female Sexuality', in J. Mitchell and J. Rose (eds), *Feminine Sexuality: Jacques Lacan and the Ecole Freudienne*, London, Macmillan, 1982.
9. S. Freud, (1905), *Three Essays on the Theory of Sexuality*, *Standard Edition*, vol. 7, p. 146.
10. J. Lampl de Groot, 'The Evolution of the Oedipal Complex in Women', *International Journal of Psycho-Analysis*, 9, 1928, pp. 332–45.
11. J. Riviere, 'Womanliness as a Masquerade', *International Journal of Psycho-Analysis*, 10, 1929, pp. 303–13.
12. J. Lacan, 'The Meaning of the Phallus', in *Feminine Sexuality*. For an interesting discussion of Riviere's article, and Riviere in relation to Jones and Freud, see Stephen Heath, 'Joan Riviere and the Masquerade', in V. Burgin, J. Donald, and C. Kaplan (eds), *Formations of Fantasy*, Methuen, London, 1986; Judith Butler, *Gender Trouble: Feminism and the Subversion of Identity*, Routledge, London, 1991.
13. Riviere was analysed by Jones, on whose 1927 typology she bases her description of her patient, although her clinical writing and theoretical concerns are much more detailed and sophisticated than his. Her analysis with Jones had a seemingly unresolved transference long after its termination. Jones sent her

to Freud, and his letters of exchange reveal the accepted opposition between erotic attractiveness and intelligence in women as objects of men's interest.

14. C. Wolff, *Love Between Women*, Duckworth, London, 1971. This was an unusual attempt to look at the lives of lesbians from a psychodynamic point of view – unusual in that it did not revert to the sensationalised pathologising of much other work, but sought to understand the constraints on lesbian relationships. Its rather eccentric medico-scientific framework, and ready acceptance of psychoanalytic notions of masculinity/femininity, make it of limited usefulness, but it is an important testimony to lesbian lives and experiences of that era.

15. M. Klein, 'Early Stages of the Oedipus Conflict', *International Journal of Psycho-Analysis*, 9, 1928, pp. 167–80.

Chapter 3
The Child and the Mother

1. H. Deutsch, 'Homosexuality in Women', *International Journal of Psycho-Analysis*, 14, 1933, pp. 34–56; *The Psychology of Women*, Grune & Stratton, New York, 1944.
2. Deutsch, 'Homosexuality in Women', p. 40.
3. P. Roazen, *Helene Deutsch: A Psychoanalyst's Life*, Meridian, New York, 1985, p. 267.
4. Deutsch, *The Psychology of Women*, p. 334.
5. Deutsch, 'Homosexuality in Women', p. 48.
6. ibid., p. 53.
7. ibid., p. 40.

Chapter 4
Klein: The Phantasy that
Anatomy is Destiny

1. L. Eichenbaum and S. Orbach, *Outside In . . . Inside Out*, Penguin, Harmondsworth, 1982, p. 111.
2. D. Dinnerstein, *The Rocking of the Cradle and the Ruling of the World*, Souvenir Press, London, 1978, p. 100.
3. T. Brennan (ed.), *Between Feminism and Psychoanalysis*, Routledge, London, 1989, p. 19.

4. M. Klein, 'On the Criteria for the Termination of a Psycho-Analysis', in *Envy and Gratitude and Other Works 1946–1963*, Hogarth, London, 1984, p. 45.

5. Klein, 'Early Stages of the Oedipus Conflict', in *Contributions to Psycho-Analysis 1921–1945*, Hogarth, London, 1984, p. 202.

6. Klein, 'Our Adult World and Its Roots in Infancy', in *Envy and Gratitude*, p. 252.

7. Klein, 'The Development of Mental Functioning', in ibid., p. 245.

8. Klein, 'The Oedipus Complex in the Light of Early Anxieties', in *Contributions to Psycho-Analysis*, p. 378.

9. Klein, *Envy and Gratitude*, p. 191.

10. Klein, 'The Emotional Life of the Infant', in *Envy and Gratitude*, p. 67.

11. Klein, 'The Origins of Transference', in ibid., p. 54.

12. Klein, 'The Oedipus Complex in the Light of Early Anxieties', p. 379.

13. Klein, *The Psycho-Analysis of Children*, Virago, London, 1989, p. 196.

14. Klein, 'Early Stages of the Oedipus Conflict', p. 208.

15. Klein, *The Psycho-Analysis of Children*, p. 235.

16. Klein, *Envy and Gratitude*, pp. 191–201.

17. ibid., p. 199.

18. Klein, *The Psycho-Analysis of Children*, p. 216.

19. Klein, *Envy and Gratitude*, p. 200.

20. ibid.

21. ibid.

22. N. O'Connor, 'Is Melanie Klein the One Who Knows Who You Really Are?', *Women: A Cultural Review*, vol. 1, no. 2, Oxford University Press, Oxford, Summer 1990b, p. 188.

23. C. Barrett and L. Wittgenstein (eds), *Lectures and Conversations on Aesthetics, Psychology and Religious Belief*, Basil Blackwell, Oxford, 1978, pp. 41–3.

24. O'Connor, 'Is Melanie Klein the One . . .?', p. 180.

Chapter 5
Spoiling the Perverse Gratification

1. M. Khan (ed.), *Alienation in Perversion*, Hogarth, London, 1979, p. 62.

2. ibid., p. 64.

3. ibid., p. 73.

4. ibid., p. 68.
5. ibid.
6. ibid., pp. 85–6.
7. ibid., p. 213.
8. A. Limentani, 'Clinical Types of Homosexuality', in *Between Freud and Klein*: *The Psychoanalytic Quest for Knowledge and Truth*, Free Association Books, London, 1989, p. 103.
9. ibid., p. 109.
10. ibid., p. 105.
11. ibid.
12. J. Rose, 'Hanna Segal Interview', *Women: A Cultural Review*, vol. 1, no. 2, Oxford University Press, Oxford, November 1990, p. 209.
13. E. H. Baruch and L. J. Serrano (eds), *Women Analyze Women*, New York University Press, New York and London, 1988, p. 250.
14. H. Segal, *The Work of Hanna Segal*, Free Association Books, London, 1986, p. 220.
15. Rose, 'Hanna Segal Interview', p. 212.
16. ibid., p. 207.
17. Baruch and Serrano (eds), *Women Analyze Women*, p. 250.
18. Rose, 'Hanna Segal Interview', pp. 210–11.
19. Segal, *The Works of Hanna Segal*, p. 217.
20. H. Guntrip, *Schizoid Phenomena, Object Relations and the Self*, Hogarth, London, 1983, p. 303.
21. I. Rosen, 'The General Psychoanalytical Theory of Perversion: A Critical and Clinical View', in I. Rosen (ed.), *Sexual Deviation*, Oxford University Press, Oxford, 1979, p. 34.
22. D. Meltzer, *Sexual States of Mind*, Clunie, Perthshire, Scotland, 1979a, p. 66.
23. ibid.
24. ibid., p. 84.
25. D. Meltzer, *The Psycho-Analytical Process*, Clunie, Perthshire, Scotland, 1979b, p. xi.
26. ibid.
27. ibid., p. xii.
28. C. W. Socarides, 'The Psychoanalytic Theory of Homosexuality with Special Reference to Therapy', in I. Rosen (ed.), *Sexual Deviation*, p. 244.
29. ibid., p. 244.
30. ibid., p. 254.
31. ibid., p. 263.
32. ibid., p. 261.
33. E. V. Siegal, 'The Search for the Vagina in Homosexual Women',

in C. W. Socarides and V. D. Volkan (eds), *The Homosexualities and the Therapeutic Process*, International Universities Press, Madison, WI, 1991, pp. 47–73.

34. E. V. Siegal, *Female Homosexuality: Choice Without Volition*, Analytic Press, Hillsdale, NJ, 1988, p. 6.
35. Siegal, *The Search for the Vagina*, p. 51.
36. Siegal, *Female Homosexuality*, p. 205.
37. ibid., p. 206.
38. F. Roustang, *Dire Mastery*, transl. Ned Lukacher, Johns Hopkins University Press, Baltimore, MD and London, 1982, p. 136.

Chapter 6
'Truth' and 'Reality'

1. J. McDougall, 'The Homosexual Dilemma: a clinical and theoretical study of female homosexuality', in I. Rosen (ed.), *Sexual Deviation*, Oxford University Press, Oxford, 1979. A shorter version of the same material is in J. McDougall, *Plea for a Measure of Abnormality*, International Universities Press, New York, 1980, Chapter 3.
2. J. McDougall, 'The Dead Father: on early psychic trauma and its relation to disturbance in sexual identity and in creative activity', *International Journal of Psycho-Analysis*, 70, 1989a, 206.
3. J. McDougall, 'Identifications, Neoneeds and Neosexualities', *International Journal of Psycho-Analysis*, 67, 1986a, 19–31.
4. McDougall, 'The Homosexual Dilemma', p. 209.
5. ibid., p. 209.
6. R. C. Friedman, *Male Homosexuality; A Contemporary Psychoanalytic Perspective*, Yale University Press, New Haven, CT, 1988.
7. McDougall, 'The Homosexual Dilemma', p. 206.
8. McDougall, *Plea for a Measure of Abnormality*.
9. ibid., p. 73.
10. J. McDougall, 'The Homosexual Dilemma', p. 211.
11. Ursula Owen (ed.), *Fathers: Reflections by Daughters*, Virago, London, 1983.
12. McDougall, 'The Homosexual Dilemma', p. 213; original emphasis.
13. ibid., p. 214.
14. ibid., p. 218; emphasis added.
15. ibid., p. 219.
16. ibid., p. 221.

17. ibid., p. 223.
18. ibid., p. 224.
19. McDougall, 'The Dead Father'.
20. R. Stoller, *Sex and Gender: On the Development of Masculinity and Femininity*, Hogarth, London, 1968; *Perversion: The Erotic Form of Hatred*, Delta, New York, 1975.
21. McDougall, 'The Dead Father', pp. 205–6.
22. ibid., p. 206.
23. J. Butler, *Gender Trouble: Feminism and the Subversion of Identity*, Routledge, London, 1990, p. 17.
24. J. Laplanche and J.-B. Pontalis, *The Language of Psychoanalysis*, Hogarth, London, 1973.
25. S. Freud, 'Psychogenesis of a Case of Female Homosexuality', *Standard Edition*, vol. 7, pp. 123–245.
26. McDougall, 'The Dead Father', p. 206.
27. E. Balint, 'Technical Problems Found in the Analysis of Women by a Woman Analyst: a contribution to the question "What does a woman want?" ' in G. Kohon (ed.), *The British School of Psychoanalysis: The Independent Tradition*, Free Association Books, London, 1986.
28. T. H. Ogden, 'The Transitional Oedipal Development in Female Development', *International Journal of Psycho-Analysis*, 65, 1987, 485–98.
29. I. Blackman and K. Perry, 'Skirting the Issue: Lesbian Fashion for the 1990s', *Feminist Review*, 34, 1990, 67–78.
30. McDougall, 'The Homosexual Dilemma', p. 237.

Chapter 7
Promises and Contradictions

1. F. Roustang, *Dire Mastery*, transl. N. Lukacher, Johns Hopkins University Press, Baltimore, MD and London, 1982, p. 23.
2. E. Grosz, *Jacques Lacan: A Feminist Introduction*, Routledge, London, 1990a, pp. 148–9.
3. J. Mitchell, Introduction–I in J. Mitchell and J. Rose (eds), *Feminine Sexuality: Jacques Lacan and the Ecole Freudienne*, Macmillan, London and Basingstoke, 1982, p. 4.
4. See S. Schneiderman (ed.), *Returning to Freud: Clinical Psychoanalysis in the School of Lacan*, Yale University Press, New Haven, CT and London, 1980.

5. B. Benvenuto and R. Kennedy, *The Works of Jacques Lacan*, Free Association Books, London, 1986, p. 92.
6. J.-A. Miller (ed.), *The Seminar of Jacques Lacan, Book II*, Cambridge University Press, Cambridge, 1988b, p. 255.
7. J. Lacan, *Ecrits*, transl. A Sheridan, Tavistock, London, 1982, p. 251.
8. M. Borch-Jacobsen, *Lacan, The Absolute Master*, transl. D. Brick, Stanford University Press, Stanford, CA, 1991, pp. 182–7.
9. Benvenuto and Kennedy, *The Works of Jacques Lacan*, pp. 118–19.
10. J.-A. Miller (ed.), *The Seminar of Jacques Lacan, Book I*, Cambridge University Press, Cambridge, 1988a, p. 107.
11. Lacan, *Seminar, Book II*, ed. Miller, pp. 228–9.
12. Lacan, *Seminar, Book I*, ed. Miller, p. 244.
13. The imaginary originates at the mirror stage when, at between six and eighteen months old, the baby recognises him/herself in the mirror. The baby jubilantly assumes an image of him/herself as an ideal unity, whilst he/she is still unable to co-ordinate his/her own body movements. There is, therefore, a fundamental alienation in this action. Lacan claims that the formation of the ego commences at this stage.
14. Lacan, *Seminar, Book II*, ed. Miller, p. 306.
15. Lacan, *Seminar, Book I*, ed. Miller, p. 277.
16. Lacan, *Seminar, Book II*, ed. Miller, p. 246.
17. S. Schneiderman, 'Lacan's Early Contributions to Psychoanalysis', in *Returning to Freud*, p. 618.
18. Rose, 'Introduction–II' in J. Mitchell and J. Rose (eds), *Feminine Sexuality*, p. 50, note 15.
19. Lacan, *Seminar, Book II*, ed. Miller, p. 262.
20. The 'objet petit *a*' – Stuart Schneiderman explains this concept succinctly:

    > We can distinguish the object *a* from the imaginary phallus attributed to the mother. The object *a* is not the representation of the denial of a lack; it indicates the place of the lack and its irreducibility. The object *a* is a trace, a leftover, a remainder. We can summarize its concept by saying that it leaves something to be desired . . . there is no such thing as the perfect sexual act, the act that is totally satisfying. (*Returning to Freud*, p. 7)

21. Rose, 'Introduction–II' in J. Mitchell and J. Rose, 'The Meaning of the Phallus', p. 42.
22. Lacan, 'The Meaning of the Phallus', in J. Mitchell and J. Rose, p. 82.

23. Lacan, 'Intervention on Transference', ibid., p. 69.
24. ibid., p. 68.
25. Lacan, 'Guiding Remarks for a Conference on Feminine Sexuality', ibid., p. 96.
26. ibid. This position is taken up and developed by Parveen Adams in 'Of Female Bondage', in T. Brennan (ed.), *Between Feminism and Psychoanalysis*, Routledge, London, 1989, p. 263.
27. Lacan, 'A Love Letter', in Mitchell and Rose, pp. 155–6.
28. J. Butler, *Gender Trouble: Feminism and the Subversion of Identity*, Routledge, New York and London, 1990, p. 49.
29. J.-P. Sartre, *Being and Nothingness*, transl. Hazel E. Barnes, Routledge, London and New York, 1989, pp. 371–2.
30. Lacan, *Seminar, Book I*, ed. Miller, p. 222. Cf. J. Clavreul, 'The Perverse Couple', in Schneiderman (ed.), *Returning to Freud*, p. 219.
31. L. Irigaray, 'The Gesture in Psychoanalysis', transl. E. Guild, in Brennan (ed.), *Between Feminism and Psychoanalysis*, pp. 127–37.
32. L. Irigaray, 'The Poverty of Psychoanalysis', in M. Whitford (ed.), *The Irigaray Reader*, Basil Blackwell, Oxford, 1991, p. 83.
33. ibid., p. 126.
34. Cf. L. Irigaray, *Speculum of the Other Woman*, transl. G. C. Gill, Cornell University Press, New York, 1985a.
35. Cf. L. Irigaray, 'When Our Lips Speak Together', in *This Sex Which Is Not One*, Cornell University Press, New York, 1985b, pp. 205–18.
36. ibid., pp. 207–9.
37. ibid., p. 209.
38. ibid., pp. 209–10.
39. ibid., p. 218.
40. L. Irigaray, 'The Power of Discourse', in Whitford (ed.), *The Irigaray Reader*, p. 78.
41. L. Irigaray, 'Women – Mothers, the Silent Substratum of the Social Order', in ibid., p. 52.
42. L. Irigaray, 'Psychoanalytic Theory: Another Look', in *Speculum of the Other Woman*, p. 37.
43. L. Irigaray, 'The Bodily Encounter with the Mother', in Whitford (ed.), *The Irigaray Reader*, p. 35.
44. ibid., p. 39.
45. E. Grosz, *Irigaray and the Divine*, Occasional Paper 9, Local Consumption, Sydney, Australia, 1986, p. 9.
46. M. Whitford, *Luce Irigaray: Philosophy in the Feminine*, Routledge, London, 1991, p. 53.

47. L. Irigaray, 'The Limits of the Transference', in Whitford (ed.), *The Irigaray Reader*, p. 116.
48. ibid., p. 115.
49. N. O'Connor, 'The Anarche of Psychotherapy', in J. Fletcher and A. Benjamin (eds), *Abjection, Melancholia and Love: The Work of Julia Kristeva*, Routledge, London, 1990, pp. 42–5.
50. J. Kristeva, *The Powers of Horror*, Columbia University Press, New York, 1982, p. 5.
51. ibid., p. 15.
52. J. Kristeva, *Revolution in Poetic Language*, Columbia University Press, New York, 1984, pp. 28–9.
53. T. Moi, 'Introduction', in T. Moi (ed.), *The Kristeva Reader*, Basil Blackwell, Oxford, 1986, p. 13.
54. J. Kristeva, 'Freud and Love: Treatment and Its Discontents', in Moi (ed.), *The Kristeva Reader*, p. 262.
55. ibid., p. 258.
56. J. Butler, 'The Body Politic of Julia Kristeva', in N. Fraser and S. L. Bartky (eds), *Revaluing French Feminism*, Indiana University Press, Bloomington, 1992a, p. 170.
57. E. Grosz, 'The Body of Signification', in J. Fletcher and A. Benjamin (eds), *Abjection, Melancholia and Love*, p. 97.

Chapter 8
Jung: The Waters and the Wild

1. C. G. Jung, 'The Love Problem of a Student,' in *Aspects of the Feminine*, transl. R. F. C. Hull, Routledge & Kegan Paul, London, 1982, p. 36.
2. C. G. Jung, Foreword to Jolande Jacobi, *The Psychology of C. G. Jung*, Routledge & Kegan Paul, London, 1968, p. ix.
3. A. Samuels (ed.), *Psychopathology: Contemporary Jungian Perspectives*, Karnac, London, 1989, p. 17.
4. C. G. Jung, 'Psychological Aspects of the Mother Archetype', in *Aspects of the Feminine*, p. 103.
5. ibid., p. 105.
6. C. G. Jung, in Robert H. Hopcke, *Jung, Jungians, and Homosexuality*, Shambhala Publications, Boston, MA and Shaftesbury, 1989, p. 36.
7. Hopcke, *Jung, Jungians, and Homosexuality*, p. 126.
8. Jung, in ibid., p. 16.
9. ibid., p. 15.

10. Hopcke, *Jung, Jungians, and Homosexuality*, p. 55.
11. Jung, in ibid., p. 19.
12. ibid.
13. ibid., p. 20.
14. ibid., pp. 23–4.
15. ibid., p. 24.
16. In contrast to Hopcke's stress on the intrapsychic relationship between masculinity and femininity, Michael Fordham, a contemporary Jungian analyst, presents a particularly biologistic reading regarding animus and anima identification in relation to perversion:

    > Thinking of the functioning of the archetypes . . . helps us to recognize some of the roots of the process of identification with the opposite sex in both men and women, and how, if excessive, it can lead to lesbianism and homosexuality . . . it is the dynamic energy in animus or anima identifications which may result in a man experiencing himself as a woman or a woman as a man. This state can lead to the perverse use of physical organs by making them simulate the normal form of intercourse.

    M. Fordham, 'The Androgyne', in Samuels (ed.), *Psychopathology: Contemporary Jungian Perspectives*, p. 278.
17. Jung, in Hopcke, *Jung, Jungians, and Homosexuality*, p. 34.
18. ibid., p. 37.
19. Hopcke, *Jung, Jungians, and Homosexuality*, p. 43.
20. N. Hall, *The Moon and the Virgin*, The Women's Press, London, 1980, p. 33.
21. ibid.
22. N. Chodorow, *The Reproduction of Mothering: Psychoanalysis and the Sociology of Gender*, University of California Press, Berkeley and Los Angeles, 1978; and L. Eichenbaum and S. Orbach, *Outside In . . . Inside Out*, Penguin, Harmondsworth, 1982.
23. D.S. Wehr, *Jung and Feminism: Liberating Archetypes*, Routledge & Kegan Paul, London, 1988, p. 115.
24. ibid., p. 71.
25. ibid., p. 75.
26. Hall, *The Moon and The Virgin*, p. 109.
27. ibid., pp. 127–30.
28. ibid., p. 130.
29. ibid.
30. S. B. Perera, *Descent to the Goddess*, Inner City Books, Toronto, 1981.

31. ibid., pp. 13–15.
32. ibid., p. 46.
33. J. Singer, *Androgyny*, Routledge & Kegan Paul, London, 1976, p. 292.
34. ibid., p. 327.
35. ibid.
36. Hopcke, *Jung, Jungians, and Homosexuality*, p. 187.

Chapter 9
Eroticism and Countertransference

1. H. Deutsch, 'Homosexuality in Women', *International Journal of Psycho-Analysis*, 14, 1933, pp. 34–56.
2. J. Roof, *The Lure of Knowledge: Lesbian Sexuality and Theory*, Columbia University Press, New York, 1991.
3. J.-M. Quinodoz, 'Female Homosexual Patients in Psychoanalysis', *International Journal of Psycho-Analysis*, 70, 1989, pp. 55–63.
4. ibid., p. 58.
5. E. Jones, 'The Early Development of Female Sexuality', *International Journal of Psycho-Analysis*, 8, 1927, pp. 457–72.
6. J. S. Kwawer, 'Transference and Countertransference in Homosexuality: Changing Psychoanalytic Views', *American Journal of Psychotherapy*, 34, 1980, 34, pp. 72–80.
7. R. Schafer, *The Analytic Attitude*, Hogarth, London, 1983.
8. E. S. Person, 'Women in Therapy: Therapist Gender as a Variable', *International Review of Psycho-Analysis*, 10, 1983, pp. 193–204.
9. J. McDougall, 'Eve's Reflection: On the Homosexual Components of Female Sexuality', in H. C. Meyers (ed.), *Between Analyst and Patient*, Analytic Press, Hillsdale, N.J., 1986b.
10. J. K. Welles and H. K. Wrye, 'The Maternal Erotic Countertransference', *International Journal of Psycho-Analysis*, 72, 1991, pp. 93–106.
11. F. Morganthaler, *Homosexuality, Heterosexuality, Perversion*, Analytic Press, Hillsdale. NJ, 1988.
12. H. K. Wrye and J. K. Welles, 'The Maternal Erotic Transference', *International Journal of Psycho-Analysis*, 70, 1989, pp. 673–84.
13. E. P. Lester, 'Gender and Identity Issues in the Analytic Process', *International Journal of Psycho-Analysis*, 71, 1990, pp. 435–44.
14. J. Benjamin, *The Bonds of Love*, Virago, London, 1990.

15. S. Freud (1931) 'Female Sexuality', *Standard Edition*, vol. 21., pp. 221–43.

16. N. Chodorow, *The Reproduction of Mothering: Psychoanalysis and the Sociology of Gender*, University of California Press, Berkeley, 1978.

17. For example, N.M. Kulish, 'The Effect of the Sex of the Analyst on Transference, *Bulletin of the Menninger Clinic*, 48, 1984, pp. 95–110; E. P. Lester, 'The Female Analyst and the Eroticised Transference', *International Journal of Psycho-Analysis*, 66, 1985, pp. 283–93.

18. Benjamin, *The Bonds of Love*.

Chapter 10
Different Voices?

1. S. A. Mitchell, 'The Psychoanalytic Treatment of Homosexuality: Some Technical Considerations', *International Review of Psycho-Analysis*, 8, 1981, pp. 63–80, describes the absence from the psychoanalytic literature of differing points of view in relation to goals of treatment. R. Cunningham, 'When is a Pervert not a Pervert?', *British Journal of Psychotherapy*, 8, 1991, pp. 48–70; and M. L. Ellis, 'Lesbians, Gay Men and Psychoanalytic Training', *Free Associations*, forthcoming, 1993, both underline the lack of open dialogue in relation to issues of training.

2. K. Lewes, *The Psychoanalytic Theory of Male Homosexuality*, Quartet, London, 1989.

3. For example, F.S. Caprio, *Female Homosexuality: A Psychodynamic Study of Lesbianism*, Peter Owen, London, 1955; C. Wilbur, 'Clinical Aspects of Female Homosexuality', in J. Marmor (ed.), *Sexual Inversion: The Multiple Roots of Homosexuality*, Basic Books, New York, 1965; C. W. Socarides, *The Overt Homosexual*, Grune & Stratton, New York, 1968.

4. Lewes, *The Psychoanalytic Theory of Male Homosexuality*, provides a detailed description of this debate, and records Marmor joining Stoller in favour of deletion, and psychoanalysts such as Bieber, Socarides, Gershman and Kardiner as voting against.

5. R. J. Stoller, *Perversion: The Erotic Form of Hatred*, Delta, New York, 1975.

6. R. J. Stoller, *Observing the Erotic Imagination*, Yale University Press, New Haven, CT, 1985.

7. Stoller, *Perversion*.
8. Stoller, *Observing the Erotic Imagination*, p. 97.
9. Mitchell, 'The Psychoanalytic Treatment of Homosexuality'.
10. R. J. Stoller, *Sex and Gender: On the Development of Masculinity and Femininity*, Hogarth, London, 1968.
11. R. Greenson, 'On Homosexuality and Gender Identity', *International Journal of Psycho-Analysis*, 45, 1964, pp. 217–19.
12. Stoller, *Observing the Erotic Imagination*, p. 183.
13. F. Morganthaler, *Homosexuality, Heterosexuality, Perversion*, Analytic Press, Hillsdale, N.J., 1988.
14. R. C. Friedman, *Male Homosexuality: A Contemporary Psychoanalytic Perspective*, Yale University Press, New Haven, CT, 1988.
15. Mitchell, 'The Psychoanalytic Treatment of Homosexuality'.
16. J. S. Kwawer, 'Transference and Countertransference in Homosexuality: Changing Psychoanalytic Views, *American Journal of Psychotherapy*, 34, 1980, pp. 72–80.
17. Morganthaler, *Homosexuality, Heterosexuality, Perversion*.
18. J. McDougall, 'The Homosexual Dilemma', in I. Rosen (ed.), *Sexual Deviation*, Oxford University Press, Oxford, 1979.
19. Cunningham, 'When is a Pervert not a Pervert?'.
20. ibid., p. 50.
21. M. Waddell and G. Williams, 'Reflections on Perverse States of Mind', *Free Associations*, 22, 1991, pp. 203–13.
22. Ellis, 'Lesbians, Gay Men and Psychoanalytic Training', *Free Associations*, forthcoming, 1994.
23. Lewes, *The Psychoanalytic Theory of Male Homosexuality*.
24. W. Reich, *The Sexual Revolution*, Farrar, Straus & Giroux, New York, 1935.
25. H. Marcuse, *Eros and Civilisation: A Philosophical Enquiry into Freud*, Beacon Press, Boston, MA, 1955; J. Dollimore, *Sexual Dissidence*, Clarendon, Oxford, 1991, provides an interesting account, amongst other things, of the political import of various literary and psychoanalytic ideas about male homosexuality and perversion, ranging over a large time span.
26. J. Kovel, *The Age of Desire: Reflections of a Radical Psychoanalyst*, Pantheon, New York, 1981; B. Richards (ed.), *Capitalism and Infancy: Essays on Psychoanalysis and Politics*, Free Association Books, London, 1984; S. Frosh, *The Politics of Psychoanalysis: An Introduction to Freudian and Post-Freudian Theory*, Macmillan, London, 1987. The omission of any consideration of homosexuality is perhaps most glaring in the last case, because Frosh is explicitly concerned to establish the 'politics inherent in

psychoanalytic theories', and considers a wide range of issues, including feminist concerns with subjectivity and sexuality. Understanding why homosexuality is such an ignored subject on the left is beyond the scope of this book, but an acknowledgement of this as a problem from those concerned to achieve a broad understanding of the political dimensions of psychoanalysis would be an encouraging start.

27. K. Horney, 'The Flight from Womanhood', *International Journal of Psycho-Analysis*, 7, 1926, 324–39.

28. ibid., p. 336.

29. N. Chodorow, *The Reproduction of Mothering: Psychoanalysis and the Sociology of Gender*, University of California Press, Berkeley and Los Angeles, 1978.

30. K. Horney, 'On the Genesis of the Castration Complex in Women', *International Journal of Psycho-Analysis*, 5, 1924, 50–65; 'The Overvaluation of Love', *Psychoanalytic Quarterly*, 3, 1934, 605–38.

31. By Lewes, in *The Psychoanalytic Theory of Male Homosexuality*.

32. C. Thompson, 'Changing Concepts of Homosexuality in Psychoanalysis', *Psychiatry*, 10, 1947, 183–9.

33. C. Thompson, 'Problems of Womanhood: Relations with her own Sex', in M.R. Green (ed.), *Interpersonal Psychoanalysis: Selected Papers of Clara Thompson*, Basic Books, New York, 1964.

34. Thompson, 'Changing Concepts', p. 188.

35. C. Thompson, 'Cultural Pressures in the Psychology of Women', *Psychiatry*, 5, 1942, 331–9.

36. ibid., p. 338; emphasis added.

37. For a useful list of homophobic attitudes and their underlying defence mechanisms, see L. Margolies, M. Becker and K. Jackson-Brewer, 'Internalised Homophobia', in Boston Lesbian Psychologies Collective (eds), *Lesbian Psychologies: Explorations and Challenges*, University of Illinois Press, Urbana, 1987.

38. A. Hollibaugh and C. Moraga, 'What We're Rollin' Around in Bed With: Sexual Silences in Feminism', in A. Snitow, C. Stansell and S. Thompson (eds), *Desire: The Politics of Sexuality*, Virago, London, 1984; W. Clarke, 'The Dyke, the Feminist and the Devil', *Feminist Review* 11, 1982, 30–39. These themes have been developed further by J. Nestle, *A Restricted Country*, Sheba, London, 1987.

39. E. Wilson, 'Psychoanalysis: Psychic Law and Order?', *Feminist Review*. 8, 1981, 63–78.

40. J. Mitchell, 'Introduction I', in J. Mitchell and J. Rose (eds),

Feminine Sexuality: Jacques Lacan and the Ecole Freudienne, Macmillan, London and Basingstoke, 1982.

41. Wilson, 'Psychoanalysis'.
42. J. Mitchell, *Psychoanalysis and Feminism*, Allen Lane, London, 1974, p. 11.
43. ibid., p. 403.
44. Mitchell, 'Introduction I', in J. Mitchell and J. Rose (eds), *Feminine Sexuality: Jacques Lacan and the Ecole Freudienne*.
45. J. Mitchell, 'The Question of Femininity and the Theory of Psychoanalysis', *Women: The Longest Revolution, Essays in Feminism, Literature and Psychoanalysis*, Virago, London, 1984, p. 307.
46. J. Mitchell, 'Psychoanalysis: A Humanist Humanity or a Linguistic Science?', ibid., p. 242.
47. ibid., p. 242.
48. J. Sayers, *Sexual Contradictions: Psychology, Psychoanalysis and Feminism*, Tavistock, London, 1986.
49. N. Chodorow, *The Reproduction of Mothering*.
50. J. Ryan, 'Psychoanalysis and Women Loving Women', in S. Cartledge and J. Ryan (eds), *Sex and Love: New Thoughts on Old Contradictions*, The Women's Press, London, 1983.
51. Chodorow, *The Reproduction of Mothering*, p. 200.
52. J. Roof, *The Lure of Knowledge: Lesbian Sexuality and Theory*, Columbia University Press, New York, 1991.
53. L. Eichenbaum and S. Orbach, *Outside In . . . Inside Out*, Penguin, Harmondsworth, 1982.
54. ibid., pp. 96–7.
55. ibid., p. 40.
56. J. Benjamin, 'The Alienation of Desire: Women's Masochism and Ideal Love', in J. L. Alpert (ed.), *Psychoanalysis and Women: Contemporary Reappraisals*, Analytic Press, Hillsdale, NJ, 1986; J. Benjamin, *The Bonds of Love*, Virago, London, 1990.
57. Benjamin, *The Bonds of Love*, p. 170.
58. Benjamin's argument for a different conception of mother–daughter eroticism is similar to the views of writers such as Lester, and Welles and Wrye, described in Chapter 9, based on more purely clinical considerations.
59. D. Hamer, 'Significant Others: Lesbians and Psychoanalytic Theory', *Feminist Review*, 31, 1990, 134–51.
60. In this respect Hamer is making an argument that has a very similar logic to that of Juliet Mitchell, in *Psychoanalysis and Feminism*, that psychoanalysis is effectively describing the laws

of patriarchy, as realised in the unconscious.

61. Hamer, 'Significant Others', p. 144.
62. C. Wolff, *Love Between Women*, Duckworth, London, 1971.
63. P. Adams, 'Of Female Bondage', in T. Brennan (ed.), *Between Feminism and Psychoanalysis*, Routledge, London, 1989.
64. ibid., p. 262.
65. The extensive work described in Boston Lesbian Psychologies Collective (eds), *Lesbian Psychologies* takes up many aspects of these starting points, developed in relation to various issues and problems of concern to lesbians.
66. J. Krestan and C. Bepko, 'The Problem of Fusion in the Lesbian Relationship', *Family Process*, 19, 1980, 277–81.
67. J. Lindenbaum, 'The Shattering of an Illusion: The Problem of Competition in Lesbian Relationships', *Feminist Studies*, 11, 1985, 85–103; D. Elise, 'Lesbian Couples: The Implications of Sex Differences in Separation–Individuation', *Psychotherapy*, 23, 1986, 305–10; B. Burch, 'Barriers to Intimacy: Conflicts over Power, Dependency and Nurturing in Lesbian Relationships', in *Lesbian Psychologies*.
68. J. Ryan and P. Trevithick, 'Lesbian Workshop', in S. Krzowski and P. Land (eds), *In Our Experience: Workshops at the Women's Therapy Centre*, The Women's Press, London, 1988.

Chapter 11
Identities

1. B. Martin, 'Sexual Practice and Changing Lesbian Identities', in M. Barrett and A. Phillips (eds), *Destabilizing Theory: Contemporary Feminist Debates*, Polity, Cambridge, 1992.
2. M. Foucault, *The History of Sexuality, Volume 1*, Penguin, Harmondsworth, 1981.
3. J. Padel, 'The Ego in Current Thinking', in G. Kohon (ed.), *The British School of Psychoanalysis: The Independent Tradition*, Free Association Books, London, 1986, p. 169, footnote.
4. J. Laplanche and J.-B. Pontalis, *The Language of Psychoanalysis*, Hogarth, London, 1973.
5. L. Grinberg, *The Goals of Psychoanalysis: Identification, Identity, and Supervision*, Karnac, London, 1990.
6. S. Freud, *Group Psychology and the Analysis of the Ego: VII, Identification, Standard Edition*, vol. 18, pp. 105–10.

7. J. Fletcher, 'Freud and his Uses: Psychoanalysis and Gay Theory', in S. Shepherd and M. Wallis (eds), *Coming on Strong: Gay Politics and Culture*, Unwin Hyman, London, 1989.

8. In *Group Psychology* Freud uses Dora's adoption of the same symptom as her father, a cough, as an example of desire regressing to identification. Earlier (1920), in a footnote to 'Psychogenesis of a Case of Female Homosexuality', he wrote: 'It is by no means rare for a love-relation to be broken off through a process of identification on the part of a lover with the loved object, a process akin to a kind of regression to narcissism.'

9. D. Fuss, 'Freud's Fallen Women: Identification, Desire, and "A Case of Homosexuality in a Woman" ', *Social Text*, forthcoming, 1993.

10. ibid.

11. Merleau-Ponty, 'The Child's Relation with Others', in *The Primacy of Perception*, NorthWestern University Press, 1964.

12. For an account of how different theories of language constitute different understandings of development, see J. Ryan, 'Early Language Development: Towards a Communicational Analysis', in M.P.M. Richards (ed.), *The Integration of a Child in a Social World*, Cambridge University Press, Cambridge, 1974.

13. Merleau-Ponty, 'The Child's Relations with Others', p. 113.

14. Michèle Barrett, 'Words and Things: Materialism and Method in Contemporary Feminist Analysis', in M. Barrett and A. Phillips (eds), *Destabilizing Theory*, provides a useful clarification of the range of epistemological issues at stake in post-modern conceptions of language.

15. J. Butler, *Gender Trouble: Feminism and the Subversion of Identity*, Routledge, London, 1990, p. xii.

16. J. Sklar, 'Gender Identity – Fifty Years on from Freud', *British Journal of Psychotherapy*, 5, 1989, 370–80.

17. ibid., p. 377.

18. J. Nestle, *A Restricted Country: Essays and Short Stories*, Sheba, London, 1987.

19. Butler, *Gender Trouble*; Martin, 'Sexual Practice'.

20. J. Roof, *The Lure of Knowledge: Lesbian Sexuality and Theory*, Columbia University Press, New York, 1991.

21. ibid., p. 246.

22. R. Greenson, 'On Homosexuality and Gender Identity', *International Journal of Psycho-Analysis*, 45, 1964, 217–19.

23. The way coming out has to be viewed with specific cultural

contexts is illustrated by a critique of white feminist assumptions. See Carmen, Gail, Shaila and, Pratiba, 'Becoming Visible: Black Lesbian Discussions', *Feminist Review*, 17, 1984, 53–74.

24. For example, C. Wolff, *Love Between Women*, Duckworth, London, 1971.

25. Martin, 'Sexual Practice'.

26. E. Wilson, 'I'll Climb the Stairway to Heaven: Lesbianism in the Seventies', in S. Cartledge and J. Ryan (eds), *Sex and Love: New Thoughts on Old Contradictions*, The Women's Press, London, 1983.

27. J. Brown, 'The Daughter is Mother of the Child: Cycles of Lesbian Sexuality', in Cartledge and Ryan (eds), *Sex and Love*.

28. Quoted in M. L. Ellis, 'Lesbians, Gay Men and Psychoanalytic Training', *Free Associations*, forthcoming, 1993.

Postscript

1. M. Foucault, *The Archeology of Knowledge*, Routledge, London, 1989, p. 49.

2. M. Merleau-Ponty, *The Phenomenology of Perception*, Routledge & Kegan Paul, London, 1962, pp. vii–ix.

3. F. Fanon, *Black Skin, White Masks*, Grove Press, New York, 1967.

4. J. Butler, 'The Lesbian Phallus and the Morphological Imaginary', *Differences: A Journal of Feminist Cultural Studies*, 4, 1992b, 141.

5. J. Benjamin, *The Bonds of Love*, Virago, London, 1990.

─── Bibliography ───

Adams, P., 'Of Female Bondage', in T. Brennan (ed.), *Between Feminism and Psychoanalysis*, Routledge, London, 1989

Balint, E., 'Technical Problems Found in the Analysis of Women by a Woman Analyst: a contribution to the question "What does a woman want?"', in G. Kohon (ed.), *The British School of Psychoanalysis: The Independent Tradition*, Free Association Books, London, 1986

Barrett, C. and Wittgenstein, L. (eds), *Lectures and Conversations on Aesthetics. Psychology and Religious Belief*, Basil Blackwell, Oxford, 1978

Barrett, M., 'Words and Things: Materialism and Method in Contemporary Feminist Analysis', in M. Barrett and A. Phillips (eds), *Destabilizing Theory: Contemporary Feminist Debates*, Polity Press Cambridge, 1992

Baruch, E. H. and Serrano, L. J. (eds), *Women Analyze Women*, New York University Press, New York and London, 1988

Benjamin, J., 'The Alienation of Desire: Women's Masochism and Ideal Love', in J. L. Alpert (ed.), *Psychoanalysis and Women: Contemporary Reappraisals*, Analytic Press, Hillsdale, NJ, 1986

Benjamin, J., *The Bonds of Love*, Virago, London, 1990

Benvenuto, B. and Kennedy, R., *The Works of Jacques Lacan*, Free Association Books, London, 1986

Bergin, A. E. and Garfield, S. L., *Handbook of Psychotherapy and Behaviour Change: An Empirical Analysis*, Wiley, New York, 1971

Bernheimer, C. and Kahane, C. (eds), *In Dora's Case*, Virago, London, 1985

Blackman, I., and Perry, K., 'Skirting the Issue: Lesbian Fashion for the 1990s', *Feminist Review*, 34, 1990, 67–78

Borch-Jacobsen, M., *Lacan, The Absolute Master*, Stanford University Press, Stanford, CA, 1991 (transl. D. Brick)

Boston Lesbian Psychologies Collective (eds), *Lesbian Psychologies: Explorations and Challenges*, University of Illinois Press, Urbana, 1987

Bowlby, R., 'Still Crazy after All These Years', in T. Brennan (ed.), *Between Feminism and Psychoanalysis*, Routledge, London, 1989

Brennan, T. (ed.), *Between Feminism and Psychoanalysis*, Routledge, London, 1989

Brown, J., 'The Daughter is Mother of the Child: Cycles of Lesbian Sexuality' in S. Cartledge and J. Ryan (eds), *Sex and Love: New Thoughts on Old Contradictions*, The Women's Press, London, 1983

Burch, B., 'Barriers to Intimacy: Conflicts over Power, Dependency and Nurturing in Lesbian Relationships', in *Lesbian Psychologies: Explorations and Challenges*, University of Illinois Press, Urbana, 1987

Butler, J., *Gender Trouble: Feminism and the Subversion of Identity*, Routledge, New York and London, 1990

Butler, J., 'The Body Politic of Julia Kristeva', in N. Fraser and S. L. Bartky (eds), *Revaluing French Feminism*, Indiana University Press, Bloomington, 1992a

Butler, J., 'The Lesbian Phallus and the Morphological Imaginary', *Differences: A Journal of Feminist Cultural Studies*, 4, 1992b, 133–171

Caprio, F. S., *Female Homosexuality: A Psychodynamic Study of Lesbianism*, Peter Owen, London, 1955

Carmen, Gail, Shaila, and Pratiba, 'Becoming Visible: Black Lesbian Discussions', *Feminist Review*, 17, 1984, 53–74

Casement, P., *On Learning from the Patient*, Tavistock, London, 1985

Chasseguet-Smirgel, J., *Creativity and Perversion*, Free Association Books, London, 1984

Chodorow, N., *The Reproduction of Mothering: Psychoanalysis and the Sociology of Gender*, University of California Press, Berkeley and Los Angeles, 1978

Clarke, W., 'The Dyke, the Feminist and the Devil', *Feminist Review*, 11, 1982, 30–39

Clavreul, J., 'The Perverse Couple' in Schneiderman, S. (ed.), *Returning to Freud: Clinical Psychoanalysis in the School of Lacan*, Yale University Press, New Haven, CT and London, 1980

Cooper, R. *et al.* (eds), *Thresholds between Philosophy and Psychoanalysis*, Free Association Books, London, 1989

Cunningham, R., 'When is a Pervert not a Pervert?', *British Journal of Psychotherapy*, 8, 1991, 48–70

Derrida, J., *Of Grammatology*, Johns Hopkins University Press, Baltimore, MD, 1976 (transl. G. C. Spivak)

Deutsch, H., 'Homosexuality in Women', *International Journal of Psycho-Analysis*, 14, 1933, 34–56

Deutsch, H., *The Psychology of Women*, Grune & Stratton, New York, 1944

Dinnerstein, D., *The Rocking of the Cradle and the Ruling of the World*, Souvenir Press, London, 1978

Dollimore, J., *Sexual Dissidence*, Clarendon, Oxford, 1991

Eichenbaum, L. and Orbach, S., *Outside In . . . Inside Out*, Penguin, Harmondsworth, 1982

Elise, D., 'Lesbian Couples: The Implications of Sex Differences in Separation–Individuation', *Psychotherapy*, 23, 1986, 305–10

Ellis, M. L., 'Lesbians, Gay Men and Psychoanalytic Training', *Free Associations*, forthcoming, 1994

Faderman, L., *Odd Girls and Twilight Lovers: A History of Lesbian Life in Twentieth-Century America*, Penguin, Harmondsworth, 1992

Fanon, F., *Black Skin, White Masks*, Grove Press, New York, 1967

Fletcher, J., 'Freud and his Uses: Psychoanalysis and Gay Theory', in S. Shepherd and M. Wallis (eds), *Coming on Strong: Gay Politics and Culture*, Unwin Hyman, London, 1989

Fordham, M., 'The Androgyne', in Samuels, A. (ed.), *Psychopathology: Contemporary Jungian Perspectives*, Karnac, London, 1989

Foucault, M., *The History of Sexuality, Volume 1*, Penguin, Harmondsworth, 1981

Foucault, M., *The Archeology of Knowledge*, Routledge, London, 1989

Freud, S. (1905), *Three Essays on the Theory of Sexuality*, in James Strachey (ed.), *The Standard Edition of the Complete Psychological Works of Sigmund Freud*, 24 vols, Hogarth, London, 1953–73, vol. 7, pp. 123–245

Freud, S. (1910), *Leonardo da Vinci and a Memory of his Childhood*; 'A Special Type of Choice of Object made by Men', *Standard Edition*, vol. 11, pp. 59–138, 163–75

Freud, S. (1914), 'On Narcissism: an Introduction', *Standard Edition*, vol. 14, pp. 67–102

Freud, S. (1920), 'Psychogenesis of a Case of Female Homosexuality', *Standard Edition*, vol. 18, pp. 145–72

Freud, S. (1921), Group Psychology and the Analysis of the Ego: VII,

Identification, Standard Edition, vol. 18,

Freud, S. (1931), 'Female Sexuality', *Standard Edition*, vol. 21, pp. 221–43

Freud, S. (1935), Letter published in *American Journal of Psychiatry*, 107, 1951, 786

Friedman, R.C., *Male Homosexuality: A Contemporary Psychoanalytic Perspective*, Yale University Press, New Haven, CT, 1988

Frosh, S., *The Politics of Psychoanalysis: An Introduction to Freudian and Post-Freudian Theory*, Macmillan, London, 1987

Fuss, D., 'Freud's Fallen Women: Identification, Desire, and "A Case of Homosexuality in a Woman" ', *Social Text*, forthcoming, 1993

Greenson, R., 'On Homosexuality and Gender Identity', *International Journal of Psycho-Analysis*, 45, 1964, 217–19

Grinberg, L., *The Goals of Psychoanalysis: Identification, Identity, and Supervision*, Karnac, London, 1990

Grosz, E., *Irigaray and the Divine*, Occasional Paper 9, Local Consumption, Sydney, Australia, 1986

Grosz, E., *Jacques Lacan: A Feminist Introduction*, Routledge, London, 1990a

Grosz, E., 'The Body of Signification', in J. Fletcher and A. Benjamin (eds), *Abjection, Melancholia and Love: The Work of Julia Kristeva*, Routledge, London, 1990b

Guntrip, H., *Schizoid Phenomena, Object Relations and the Self*, Hogarth, London, 1983

Hall, N., *The Moon and The Virgin*, The Women's Press, London, 1980

Hamer, D., 'Significant Others: Lesbians and Psychoanalytic Theory', *Feminist Review*, 31, 1990, 134–51

Heath, S., 'Joan Riviere and the Masquerade', in V. Burgin, J. Donald and C. Kaplan (eds), *Formations of Fantasy*, Methuen, London, 1986

Hollibaugh, A. and Moraga, C., 'What We're Rollin' Around in Bed With: Sexual Silences in Feminism', in A. Snitow, C. Stansell and S. Thompson (eds), *Desire: The Politics of Sexuality*, Virago, London, 1984

Hopke, R. H., *Jung, Jungians, and Homosexuality*, Shambala Publications, Boston, 1989

Horney, K., 'On the Genesis of the Castration Complex in Women', *International Journal of Psycho-Analysis*, 5, 1924, 50–65

Horney, K., 'The Flight from Womanhood', *International Journal of Psycho-Analysis*, 7, 1926, 324–39

Horney, K., 'The Overvaluation of Love', *Psychoanalytic Quarterly*, 3, 1934, 605–38

Irigaray, L., *Speculum of the Other Woman*, Cornell University Press,

New York, 1985a (transl. G.C. Gill)

Irigaray, L., 'When Our Lips Speak Together', in *This Sex Which Is Not One*, Cornell University Press, New York, 1985b

Irigaray, L., 'The Gesture in Psychoanalysis', in T. Brennan (ed.), *Between Feminism and Psychoanalysis* Routledge, London, 1989 (transl. E. Guild)

Irigaray, L., 'Women – Mothers, the Silent Substratum of the Social Order', 'The Bodily Encounter with the Mother', 'The Power of Discourse', 'The Poverty of Psychoanalysis', and 'The Limits of the Transference', in M. Whitford (ed.), *The Irigaray Reader*, Basil Blackwell, Oxford, 1991

Jacobus, M., 'Russian Tactics: Freud's "Case of Homosexuality in a Woman"', in M. Jacobus, *First Things: Literature, Psychoanalysis and Reproduction*, Routledge, London, forthcoming, 1994

Jones, E., 'The Early Development of Female Sexuality', *International Journal of Psycho-Analysis*, 8, 1927, 457–72

Jung, C.G., Foreword to J. Jacobi, *The Psychology of C.G. Jung*, Routledge & Kegan Paul, London, 1968

Jung, C.G., 'The Love Problem of a Student' and 'Psychological Aspects of the Mother Archetype', in *Aspects of the Feminine*, Routledge & Kegan Paul, London, 1982 (transl. R.F.C. Hull)

Jung, C.G., in R.H. Hopcke, *Jung, Jungians, and Homosexuality*, Shambhala Publications, Boston, MA and Shaftesbury, 1989

Khan, M., 'The Role of Infantile Sexuality in Early Object Relations in Female Homosexuality', in I. Rosen (ed.), *The Pathology and Treatment of Sexual Perversions*, Oxford University Press, Oxford, 1962

Khan, M. (ed.), *Alienation in Perversion*, Hogarth, London, 1979

Klein, M., 'Early Stages of the Oedipus Conflict' and 'The Oedipus Complex in the Light of Early Anxieties', in *Contributions to Psycho-Analysis 1921–1945*, Hogarth, London, 1984a

Klein, M., 'On the Criteria for the Termination of a Psycho-Analysis', 'The Origins of Transference', 'The Emotional Life of the Infant', 'Envy and Gratitude', 'The Development of Mental Functioning', and 'Our Adult World and Its Roots in Infancy', in *Envy and Gratitude and Other Works 1946–1963*, Hogarth, London, 1984b

Klein, M., *The Psycho-Analysis of Children*, Virago, London, 1989

Kovel, J., *The Age of Desire: Reflections of a Radical Psychoanalyst*, Pantheon, New York, 1982

Krestan, J., and Bepko, C., 'The Problem of Fusion in the Lesbian Relationship', *Family Process*, 19, 1980, 277–81

Kristeva, J., *The Powers of Horror*, Columbia University Press, New York, 1982

Kristeva, J., *Revolution in Poetic Language*, Columbia University Press, New York, 1984

Kristeva, J., 'Freud and Love: Treatment and Its Discontents', in T. Moi (ed.), *The Kristeva Reader*, Basil Blackwell, Oxford, 1986

Kulish, N. M., 'The Effect of the Sex of the Analyst on Transference', *Bulletin of the Menninger Clinic*, 48, 1984, 95–110

Kwawer, J. S., 'Transference and Countertransference in Homosexuality: Changing Psychoanalytic Views', *American Journal of Psychotherapy*, 34, 1980, 72–80

Lacan, J., *Ecrits: A Selection*, Tavistock, London, 1982, transl. Sheridan, A.

Lacan, J., 'Of the Subject of Certainty', in J. Lacan, *The Four Fundamental Concepts of Psycho-Analysis*, Penguin, Harmondsworth 1979

Lacan, J., 'Guiding Remarks for a Congress on Female Sexuality', and 'The Meaning of the Phallus', in J. Mitchell and J. Rose (eds), *Feminine Sexuality: Jacques Lacan and the Ecole Freudienne*, London, Macmillan, 1982

Lampl de Groot, J., 'The Evolution of the Oedipal Complex in Women', *International Journal of Psycho-Analysis*, 9, 1928, 332–45

Laplanche, J., and Pontalis, J.-B., *The Language of Psychoanalysis*, Hogarth, Press, London, 1973

Lester, E.P., 'The Female Analyst and the Eroticised Transference', *International Journal of Psycho-Analysis*, 66, 1985, 283–93

Lester, E.P., 'Gender and Identity Issues in the Analytic Process', *International Journal of Psycho-Analysis*, 71, 1990, 435–44

Lewes, K., *The Psychoanalytic Theory of Male Homosexuality*, Quartet, London, 1989

Limentani, A., 'Clinical Types of Homosexuality', in *Between Freud and Klein: The Psychoanalytic Quest For Knowledge and Truth*, Free Association Books, London, 1989

Lindenbaum, J., 'The Shattering of an Illusion: The Problem of Competition in Lesbian Relationships', *Feminist Studies*, 11, 1985, 85–103

McDougall, J., 'The Homosexual Dilemma: a clinical and theoretical study of female homosexuality', in I. Rosen (ed.), *Sexual Deviation*, Oxford University Press, Oxford, 1979

McDougall, J., *Plea for a Measure of Abnormality*, International Universities Press, New York, 1980

McDougall, J., 'Identifications, Neoneeds and Neosexualities', *International Journal of Psycho-Analysis*, 67, 1986a, 19–31

McDougall, J., 'Eve's Reflection: On the Homosexual Components of Female Sexuality', in H. C. Meyers (ed.), *Between Analyst and*

Patient, Analytic Press, Hillsdale, NJ, 1986b

McDougall, J., 'The Dead Father: on early psychic trauma and its relation to disturbance in sexual identity and in creative activity', *International Journal of Psycho-Analysis*, 70, 1989a, 205–19

McDougall, J., *Theatres of the Body*, Free Association Books, London, 1989b

McIntosh, M., 'The Homosexual Role', in K. Plummer (ed.) *The Making of the Modern Homosexual*, Hutchinson, London, 1981

Marcuse, H., *Eros and Civilisation: A Philosophical Enquiry into Freud*, Beacon Press, Boston, MA, 1955

Margolies, L., Becker, M. and Jackson-Brewer, K., 'Internalised Homophobia', in Boston Lesbian Psychologies Collective (eds), *Lesbian Psychologies: Explorations and Challenges*, University of Illinois Press, Urbana, 1987

Martin, B., 'Sexual Practice and Changing Lesbian Identities', in M. Barrett and A. Phillips (eds), *Destabilizing Theory: Contemporary Feminist Debates*, Polity, Cambridge, 1992

Meltzer, D., *Sexual States of Mind*, Clunie, Perthshire, Scotland, 1979a

Meltzer, D., *The Psycho-Analytical Process*, Clunie, Perthshire, Scotland, 1979b

Merck, M., 'The Train of Thought in Freud's "Case of Homosexuality in a Woman" ', *m/f*, 11/12, 1986, 35–46

Merck, M., *Perversions: Deviant Readings*, Virago, London, 1993

Merleau-Ponty, M., *The Phenomenology of Perception*, Routledge & Kegan Paul, London, 1962

Merleau-Ponty, M., *The Primacy of Perception*, NorthWestern University Press, 1964a

Merleau-Ponty, M., 'The Child's Relations with Others', in *The Primacy of Perception*, NorthWestern University Press, 1964b

Miller, J.-A., (ed.) *The Seminar of Jacques Lacan, Book I*, Cambridge University Press, Cambridge, 1988a

Miller, J.-A. (ed.), *The Seminar of Jacques Lacan, Book II*, Cambridge University Press, Cambridge, 1988b

Mitchell, J., *Psychoanalysis and Feminism*, Allen Lane, London, 1974

Mitchell, J., 'Introduction I', in J. Mitchell and J. Rose (eds), *Feminine Sexuality: Jacques Lacan and the Ecole Freudienne*, Macmillan, London and Basingstoke, 1982

Mitchell, J., 'Psychoanalysis: A Humanist Humanity or a Linguistic Science?', in J. Mitchell, *Women: The Longest Revolution, Essays in Feminism, Literature and Psychoanalysis*, Virago, London, 1984

Mitchell, S.A., 'The Psychoanalytic Treatment of Homosexuality: Some Technical Considerations', *International Review of Psycho-*

Analysis, 8, 1981, 63–80

Moi, T., 'Introduction', in T. Moi (ed.), *The Kristeva Reader*, Basil Blackwell, Oxford, 1986

Morganthaler, F. *Homosexuality, Heterosexuality, Perversion*, Analytic Press, Hillsdale, NJ, 1984

Nestle, J., *A Restricted Country: Essays and Short Stories*, Sheba, London, 1987

Oakley, C., 'Introducing an Incomplete Project', in R. Cooper *et. al.* (eds), *Thresholds between Philosophy and Psychoanalysis*, Free Association Books, London, 1989

O'Connor, N., 'The Anarche of Psychotherapy', in J. Fletcher and A. Benjamin (eds), *Abjection, Melancholia and Love: The Work of Julia Kristeva*, Routledge, London, 1990a

O'Connor, N., 'Is Melanie Klein the One Who Knows Who You Really Are?', *Women: A Cultural Review*, vol. 1, no. 2, Oxford University Press, Oxford, Summer 1990b, 180–88

Ogden, T. H., 'The Transitional Oedipal Development in Female Development', *International Journal of Psycho-Analysis*, 65, 1987, 485–98

Owen, U. (ed.), *Fathers: Reflections by Daughters*, Virago, London, 1983

Padel, J., 'The Ego in Current Thinking', in G. Kohon (ed.), *The British School of Psychoanalysis: The Independent Tradition*, Free Association Books, London, 1986

Perera, S. B., *Descent to the Goddess*, Inner City Books, Toronto, ON, 1981

Person, E. S., 'Women in Therapy: Therapist Gender as a Variable', *International Review of Psycho-Analysis*, 10, 1983, 193–204

Quinodoz, J.-M., 'Female Homosexual Patients in Psychoanalysis', *International Journal of Psycho-Analysis*, 70, 1989, 55–63

Rank, O., 'Perversion and Neurosis', *International Journal of Psycho-Analysis*, 4, 1923, 270–92

Reich, W., *The Sexual Revolution*, Farrar, Straus & Giroux, New York, 1935

Richards, B. (ed.), *Capitalism and Infancy: Essays on Psychoanalysis and Politics*, Free Association Books, London, 1984

Riviere, J., 'Womanliness as a Masquerade', *International Journal of Psycho-Analysis*, 10, 1929, 303–13

Roazen, P., *Helene Deutsch: A Psychoanalyst's Life*, Meridian, New York, 1985

Roof, J., *The Lure of Knowledge: Lesbian Sexuality and Theory*, Columbia University Press, New York, 1991

Rose, J., 'Hanna Segal Interview', *Women: A Cultural Review*, vol. 1, no. 2, Oxford University Press, Oxford, November 1990, 207–12

Rose, J., 'Introduction II', in J. Mitchell and J. Rose (eds), *Feminine Sexuality: Jacques Lacan and the Ecole Freudienne*, Macmillan, London and Basingstoke, 1982

Rosen, I., 'The General Psychoanalytical Theory of Perversion: A Critical and Clinical View', in I. Rosen (ed.), *Sexual Deviation*, Oxford University Press, Oxford, 1979

Roustang, F., *Dire Mastery*, Johns Hopkins University Press, Baltimore, MD, and London, 1982 (transl. N. Lukacher)

Ryan, J., 'Early Language Development: Towards a Communicational Analysis', in M.P.M. Richards (ed.), *The Integration of a Child in a Social World*, Cambridge University Press, Cambridge, 1974

Ryan, J., 'Psychoanalysis and Women Loving Women', in S. Cartledge and J. Ryan (eds), *Sex and Love: New Thoughts on Old Contradictions*, The Women's Press, London, 1983

Ryan, J. and Trevithick, P., 'Lesbian Workshop', in S. Krzowski and P. Land (eds), *In Our Experience: Workshops at the Women's Therapy Centre*, The Women's Press, London, 1988

Samuels, A., (ed.), *Psychopathology: Contemporary Jungian Perspectives*, Karnac, London, 1989

Sartre, J. P. (transl. Hazel E. Barnes), *Being and Nothingness*, Routledge, London and New York, 1989

Sayers, J., *Sexual Contradictions: Psychology, Psychoanalysis and Feminism*, Tavistock, London, 1986

Schafer, R., *The Analytic Attitude*, Hogarth, London, 1983

Schneiderman, S., *Returning to Freud: Clinical Psychoanalysis in the School of Lacan*, Yale University Press, New Haven, CT and London, 1980

Segal, H., *The Work of Hanna Segal*, Free Association Books, London, 1986

Siegal, E. V., *Female Homosexuality: Choice Without Volition*, Analytic Press, Hillsdale, NJ, USA, 1988

Siegal, E. V., 'The Search for the Vagina in Homosexual Women', in C. W. Socarides and V. D. Volkan (eds), *The Homosexualities and the Therapeutic Process*, International Universities Press, Madison, WI, 1991

Singer, J., *Androgyny*, Routledge & Kegan Paul, London, 1976

Sklar, J., 'Gender Identity – Fifty Years on from Freud', *British Journal of Psychotherapy*, 5, 1989, 370–80

Socarides, C. W., *The Overt Homosexual*, Grune & Stratton, New York, 1968

Socarides, C. W., 'The Psychoanalytic Theory of Homosexuality with Special Reference to Therapy' in I. Rosen (ed.), *Sexual Deviation*,

Oxford University Press, Oxford, 1979

Spivak, G. C., *The Post-Colonial Critic: Interviews, Strategies, Dialogues*, Routledge, London, 1990 (ed. S. Harasym)

Stoller, R., *Sex and Gender: On the Development of Masculinity and Femininity*, Hogarth, London, 1968

Stoller, R., *Perversion: The Erotic Form of Hatred*, Delta, New York, 1975

Stoller, R., *Observing the Erotic Imagination*, Yale University Press, New Haven, CT, 1985

Thompson, C., 'Cultural Pressures in the Psychology of Women', *Psychiatry*, 5, 1942, 331–9

Thompson, C., 'Changing Concepts of Homosexuality in Pyschoanalysis', *Psychiatry*, 10, 1947, 183–9

Thompson, C., 'Problems of Womanhood: Relations with her own Sex', in M. R. Green (ed.), *Interpersonal Psychoanalysis: Selected Papers of Clara Thompson*, Basic Books, New York, 1964

Waddell, M. and Williams, G., 'Reflections on Perverse States of Mind', *Free Associations*, 22, 1991, 203–13

Weeks, J., *Sex, Politics and Society*, Longman, London, 1981

Wehr, D. S., *Jung and Feminism: Liberating Archetypes*, Routledge & Kegan Paul, London, 1988

Welles, J. K., and Wrye, H. K., 'The Maternal Erotic Countertransference', *International Journal of Psycho-Analysis*, 72, 1991, 93–106

Whitford, M., *Luce Irigaray: Philosophy in the Feminine*, Routledge, London, 1991

Wilbur, C., 'Clinical Aspects of Female Homosexuality', in J. Marmor (ed.), *Sexual Inversion: The Multiple Roots of Homosexuality*, Basic Books, New York, 1965

Wilson, E., 'Psychoanalysis: Psychic Law and Order?', *Feminist Review*, 8, 1981, 63–78

Wilson, E., 'I'll Climb the Stairway to Heaven: Lesbianism in the Seventies', in S. Cartledge and J. Ryan (eds), *Sex and Love: New Thoughts on Old Contradictions*, The Women's Press, London, 1983

Wolff, C., *Love Between Women*, Duckworth, London, 1971

Wrye, H. K. and Welles, J. K., 'The Maternal Erotic Transference', *International Journal of Psychoanalysis*, 70, 1989, 673–84

Index

Also of interest from Virago

THE BONDS OF LOVE

Psychoanalysis, feminism and the problem of domination

Jessica Benjamin

'*The Bonds of Love* gives us Benjamin at her best, and psychoanalytic social theory at its best, as she demonstrates brilliantly the complex intertwining of familial, gender and social domination' – *Nancy Chodorow*

Why do people submit to authority and even derive pleasure from the power others have over them? What is the appeal of domination and submission, and why are they so prevalent in erotic life?

Jessica Benjamin makes use of feminist reinterpretations of psychoanalytic theory to consider anew the problem of domination, of individual development, gender difference and authority. Domination is revealed as a complex psychological process which ensnares both parties in bonds of complicity, and one which underlies our family life, social institutions and especially sexual relationships. In her questioning of gender polarities in which woman is object to the male subject she argues for a change which she describes as both 'modest and utopian' – in disentangling the bonds of love, we seek a mutual recognition of equal subjects which would lead to both personal and social transformation.

A WOMAN'S UNCONSCIOUS USE OF HER BODY

Dinora Pines

These illuminating and original papers by one of Britain's most eminent psychoanalysts are gathered together for the first time. Based on Dinora Pines' clinical experience, and her earlier work as a medical doctor and dermatologist, they give a fascinating account of key moments in women's lives and sexuality: the turbulent changes of adolescence; the conflicts of pregnancy; childbirth, abortion and infertility; the challenges of the menopause and old age.

Central to these papers is an examination of the ways in which the subconscious life of the mind expresses itself through a woman's body, and conversely, the manner in which the body's experiences impinge upon the mind. Included here are two papers about the Holocaust in which survivors themselves and children of survivors display unconscious and bodily communications of the horrors of the war and post-war years.

Dinora Pines has practised as a training analyst in London for many years and lectures worldwide.

Works by Melanie Klein

THE PSYCHOANALYSIS OF CHILDREN

The Psychoanalysis of Children, first published in 1932, is a classic in its subject and revolutionised child analysis. Here, Melanie Klein describes both the theory and practise of her methods which have made possible the extension of psychoanalysis to the field of early childhood.

LOVE, GUILT AND REPARATION
and other works 1921–1945

Love, Guilt and Reparation shows the growth of Melanie Klein's work and ideas between 1921 and 1945. Here we see her intense preoccupation with the impact of infant anxieties upon child development and the effect of these influences on, for example, criminality, and symbol formation. Also outlined are Klein's important theories about the psychogenesis of manic depressive states, and the early conceptualisations of her thinking about what she later came to call the depressive, and the paranoid-schizoid position.

ENVY AND GRATITUDE
and other works 1946–1963

Envy and Gratitude contains Melanie Klein's writings from 1946 until her death in 1960, including two papers published posthumously. Her major paper, 'Notes on Some Schizoid Mechanisms' introduces the developed concept of the paranoid-schizoid position; and other papers show the interplay of the paranoid-schizoid and depressive positions in infant and adult development. Also here is writing about the importance of play technique in revealing a child's unconscious, and her last major work, in which she introduces her important theory of primary envy.

NARRATIVE OF A CHILD ANALYSIS
The conduct of the psychoanalysis of children as seen in the treatment of a ten-year-old boy

In this, Melanie Klein's last book and a companion volume to *The Psychoanalysis of Children*, she gives a detailed account of the analysis of a ten-year-old boy, Richard. This fascinating and deeply instructive case study shows the fluctuations which characterise a psychoanalysis and reveal the dynamics of the steps which eventually lead to progress in treatment.